QUALITATIVE ANALYSIS AND ECONOMETRIC ESTIMATION OF CONTINUOUS TIME DYNAMIC MODELS

CONTRIBUTIONS
TO
ECONOMIC ANALYSIS

136

1931 N·H 1981
P C

NORTH-HOLLAND PUBLISHING COMPANY
AMSTERDAM · NEW YORK · OXFORD

QUALITATIVE ANALYSIS AND ECONOMETRIC ESTIMATION OF CONTINUOUS TIME DYNAMIC MODELS

GIANCARLO GANDOLFO
University of Rome

with contributions by
GIANCARLO MARTINENGO
and
PIETRO CARLO PADOAN
University of Rome

1931 N·H 1981
P C

NORTH-HOLLAND PUBLISHING COMPANY
AMSTERDAM • NEW YORK • OXFORD

ISBN 0444 86025 8

Publishers

NORTH-HOLLAND PUBLISHING COMPANY
AMSTERDAM • NEW YORK • OXFORD

Sole distributors for the U.S.A. and Canada:

ELSEVIER NORTH-HOLLAND INC.
52 VANDERBILT AVENUE
NEW YORK, N.Y. 10017

Library of Congress Cataloging In Publication Data

Gandolfo, Giancarlo.
Qualitative analysis and economètric estimation of continuous time dynamic models.

(Contributions to economic analysis ; 136)
Includes bibliographies and indexes.
1. Economics--Mathematical models. 2. Econometrics 3. Foreign exchange--Mathematical models. I. Martinengo, Giancarlo, joint author. II. Padoan, Pietro Carlo, joint author. III. Title. IV. Series.
HB141.G36 330'.028 80-17365
ISBN 0-444-86025-8

Printed in the Netherlands

Introduction to the series

This series consists of a number of hitherto unpublished studies, which are introduced by the editors in the belief that they represent fresh contributions to economic science.

The term "economic analysis" as used in the title of the series has been adopted because it covers both the activities of the theoretical economist and the research worker.

Although the analytical methods used by the various contributors are not the same, they are nevertheless conditioned by the common origin of their studies, namely theoretical problems encountered in practical research. Since for this reason, business cycle research and national accounting, research work on behalf of economic policy, and problems of planning are the main sources of the subjects dealt with, they necessarily determine the manner of approach adopted by the authors. Their methods tend to be "practical" in the sense of not being too far remote from application to actual economic conditions. In addition they are quantitative rather than qualitative.

It is the hope of the editors that the publication of these studies will help to stimulate the exchange of scientific information and to reinforce international cooperation in the field of economics.

The Editors

"... each of these three view points, that of statistics, economic theory, and mathematics, is a necessary, but not by itself a sufficient, condition for a real understanding of the quantitative relations in modern economic life. It is the *unification* of all three that is powerful. And it is this unification that constitutes econometrics."

R. Frisch, 1933, Editorial, *Econometrica* **1**, p. 2.

Contents

Preface

The choice of the kind of "time" (continuous or discrete) to be used in the construction of dynamic models is a moot question (see, for example, Gandolfo, 1980, passim). Let us recall that such a choice implies the use of different analytical tools (differential equations in the continuous case, difference equations in the discrete case), and that this is not neutral with respect to the results of the model, given the different behaviour of the solutions of these two types of functional equations and the different nature of the stability conditions.

In our opinion, mixed differential–difference equations are much more suitable than differential equations alone, or difference equations alone, for an adequate treatment of dynamic economic phenomena. However, the formal difficulty of mixed equations greatly limits their use in theoretical studies, and the impossibility of obtaining econometric estimates of their parameters excludes their use in applied research. Therefore a choice has to be made between the two basic formulations, that in terms of differential equations and that in terms of difference equations. But such a choice could hitherto be made only at the level of theoretical studies, and not at the level of applied research, because current econometric techniques for the estimation of complete models are based on discrete time; therefore, in order to estimate a model it was necessary to formulate it in discrete time or, if it had been conceived in continuous time, to approximate it with a discrete model (and approximations which have been used in the past are not acceptable once the problem is formulated rigorously). The consequence is a hiatus between theoretical modeling and econometric modeling, which is definitely not favourable to the advancement of scientific knowledge.

Fortunately, in the last few years a certain number of papers have appeared dealing with the problem of statistical inference in continuous time dynamic models, thus allowing a rigorous estimation of the parameters of systems of stochastic differential equations on the basis of samples of discrete observations such as are available in reality. The new methodology marks a great advance, because it allows the economist who has chosen a continuous model at the theoretical level, to estimate its parameters rigorously and independently of the observation interval. This means that the bias in favour of discrete models (imposed by current econometric methods and not by economic theory) disappears, thus leaving the researcher free to formulate his model as he thinks best and to estimate its parameters whether this formulation is discrete or continuous.

However, the papers which deal with the new methodology are mathematically quite sophisticated and make for very difficult reading, so that only the ultra-specialist can benefit. It is our opinion that the time is ripe for a systematic treatment of the new techniques in order to bring them within the grasp of the average econometrician and of the applied economist as well as of the economic theorist who wishes to test his theory empirically. This volume should help to fill the gap.

As a matter of fact, the new methodology has been instrumental in the estimation of a macrodynamic general disequilibrium model for the determination of the equilibrium exchange rate, a topic on which a research group directed by G. Gandolfo has been working for some years at the University of Rome. A series of lectures on the methodology was given by him to the members of the group in 1978, and to the econometric staff of ISPE (Istituto di Studi per la Programmazione Economica) as well as to other interested researchers from universities and research institutions in 1979. Mimeographed lecture notes were circulated and were commented on by participants and colleagues. Several points were discussed with Dr. Clifford Wymer. This material formed the basis for Part I of the present book, where the new methodology is treated; this Part also contains a chapter dealing with the specification and qualitative analysis of the models, which should prove useful to the economic theorist. Part II of the book deals with the model.

As regards Part I, it aims at a treatment which is comprehensible to the non-initiate: therefore all the proofs are worked out in great detail and no essential steps in the argument have been omitted. Moreover, some elementary digressions on topics, a knowledge of which is necessary in order to follow the main argument, have been inserted; it goes without saying that these digressions can be omitted by the reader who already knows the topics contained therein. Some more advanced proofs are given in appendices. Numerical examples are also provided. However, it is impossible to expound the new methodology below a certain minimum level, so that some knowledge of standard econometric theory (including its matricial treatment) as well as of differential equations (see, for example, Gandolfo, 1980, Parts II and III) is necessary.

As regards Part II, this contains the results of our work on the model for the determination of the equilibrium exchange rate, which is a simplified version of a larger model still in process of development (G. Martinengo and P. C. Padoan, two of the members of the research group referred to above, have contributed respectively ch. 4 and ch. 6). This topic is treated in such a way that it can be considered as an application of the methodology expounded in Part I. In other words, although Part II contains original research work, the material is presented along the same didactic lines used in Part I. The reader is led step by step through the construction, analysis and estimation of the model. This should prove an invaluable guide for anybody wanting to build, analyse and estimate his own models by means of the new technique.

Our principal (but non-incriminating) acknowledgment is to Dr. Clifford R. Wymer, who – in personal discussions and in correspondence – gave us the benefit of his great experience both as one of the originators of the new methodology and as the author of a complete set of computer programs to implement it, which he generously supplied. Some preliminary versions of the model were discussed with Flavio Casprini, Carlo Milana and Maria Luisa Petit (who, naturally, are absolved of any responsibility). Miss Anna Maria Olivari did a highly commendable job in typing several drafts from a difficult manuscript and in carrying out all the secretarial work.

The research was undertaken when the authors were all at the University of Rome (research support from the Ministry of Public Instruction and from the University of Rome is gratefully acknowledged); it was continued while G. Gandolfo was on temporary leave from the University to serve as Director General of ISPE, and was completed on his return to the University. None of these institutions is to be held responsible for the views expressed here.

University of Rome
December 1979

PART I

SPECIFICATION, QUALITATIVE ANALYSIS AND ECONOMETRIC ESTIMATION OF CONTINUOUS TIME DYNAMIC ECONOMIC MODELS

CHAPTER 1

Continuous and discrete models in economics

1.1. Introduction

The problem of the choice between continuous time dynamic models (formulated in terms of differential equations) and discrete time dynamic models (formulated in terms of difference equations) for the analysis of economic phenomena is rather complicated because it is necessary to distinguish a theoretical and an econometric aspect. From the theoretical point of view arguments in favour of either one or the other approach are not lacking (see, for example, Gandolfo, 1980, passim). From the econometric point of view until some time ago there was no possibility of choice, because the current econometric methods could only be used to estimate structural models formulated in discrete time. Therefore, even those economists who held the opinion that continuous time models were more suitable, had to translate them into discrete terms for their empirical testing, with approximations that often changed the nature of the original model. Fortunately in the last few years this situation has been changing, because a few researchers have developed econometric techniques and computer programs for the estimation of continuous time models[1] starting from samples of discrete

[1] The idea of formulating econometric models in continuous time was set forth in an essay contained in the volume that laid the foundation for modern econometric methodology (see Koopmans, 1950). In this essay Koopmans also illustrated some of the advantages of these models over those formulated in discrete time. These advantages led Marschak to state, in the general introduction to the afore mentioned volume, that "if proper mathematical treatment of stochastic models can be developed, such models [that is, those formulated in continuous time] promise to be a more accurate and more flexible tool for inference in economics than the discrete models used heretofore" (Marschak, 1950, p. 39; square brackets are ours). However – except in occasional works – these suggestions were not followed up and the topic has been taken up again and deepened only in the seventies.

observations, such as the ones which are available in the real world.[2] This topic will be dealt with here with the intention of giving a unified treatment both of the econometric aspect proper and of the preliminary aspect (which for the economic theorist is of equal importance) concerning the qualitative analysis of the models to be estimated.

Before going on we shall briefly expound the main arguments in favour of the use of continuous models,[3] which, for simplicity, we have grouped into seven categories.

(1) Although individual economic decisions are generally made at discrete time intervals, it is difficult to believe that they are coordinated in such a way as to be perfectly synchronized (that is, made at the same moment and with reference to the same time interval as postulated by period analysis) while, on the other hand, it is plausible to think that they overlap in time in some stochastic manner. As the variables that are usually considered and observed by the economist are the outcome of a great number of decisions taken by different operators at different points of time, it seems natural to treat economic phenomena as if they were continuous.

(2) Specification in continuous time is particularly useful for the formulation of market adjustment processes based on excess demand, a plausible discrete equivalent of which is often difficult to find. As an example (Wymer, 1976) let us consider the case where the interest rate changes as a function of the excess demand for real balances:

$$\mathrm{D}r = \alpha\left(\hat{m} - \frac{M}{p}\right),$$

or, in logarithmic terms,[4]

$$\mathrm{D}\log r = \alpha\left(\log\hat{m} - \log\frac{M}{p}\right) = \alpha\log\left(\frac{\hat{m}}{M/p}\right), \qquad (1)$$

[2] It is important to note that this invalidates one of the traditional arguments in favour of period analysis (see, e.g., Baumol, 1970, ch. VIII), that is the discrete nature of statistical data.

[3] See, for example, Aghevli and Khan (1977), Bergstrom (1967), Bergstrom and Wymer (1976), Foley (1975), Goodwin (1948), Khan (1977), Knight (1973, 1977), Knight and Wymer (1975, 1978), Koopmans (1950), May (1970), Turnovsky (1977), Reserve Bank of Australia (1977), Wymer (1973, 1975, 1976).

[4] The reason why the logarithmic formulation may be preferable will be clarified subsequently (see para. 2.1.3).

where D denotes the operator $\mathrm{d}/\mathrm{d}t$, $\hat{m}$ is the demand for real money balances (a function of income and of the interest rate, $\hat{m} = aYr^{\beta}$), and the other symbols have the usual meanings. For estimation purposes the following discrete approximation is usually adopted:

$$\begin{aligned}\Delta \log r_t &= \alpha[\log \hat{m}_t - \log(M/p)_{t-1}] \\ &= \alpha(\log Y_t + \beta \log r_t + \log a - \log M_{t-1} + \log p_{t-1}).\end{aligned} \tag{2}$$

However, eq. (2) is not a satisfactory representation of eq. (1), because the demand function contains a *flow* variable (income) which is measured over the observation interval, as well as "point" or "instantaneous" variables, such as the interest rate (which refers to the end of the current period) and real money balances (which are a stock variable and refer to the end of the previous period). It will be shown subsequently (see para. 3.3.2) that a better approximation to (1) is given by

$$\begin{aligned}\Delta \log r_t = \alpha\big[&\log Y_t + \tfrac{1}{2}\beta(\log r_t + \log r_{t-1}) + \log a \\ &- \tfrac{1}{2}(\log M_t + \log M_{t-1}) \\ &+ \tfrac{1}{2}(\log p_t + \log p_{t-1})\big],\end{aligned} \tag{3}$$

but it is also possible to derive and estimate the exact discrete equivalent model to the continuous model (see ch. 3, especially para. 3.3.1).

(3) What has been said under point (2) is connected with another advantage of continuous models. The estimator of these models is independent of the observation interval; furthermore, it takes explicitly into account the fact that a flow variable cannot be measured instantaneously, so that what we actually observe is the integral of such a variable over the observation period (this allows a correct treatment of stock-flow models). These properties do not hold for the discrete models usually employed, which therefore must be formulated explicitly in relation to the data which are available or which one wishes to use so that, for example, a model built to be estimated with quarterly data will be different from one built to be estimated with annual data.

(4) A further difficulty of discrete analysis is that usually there is no obvious time interval that can serve as a "natural" unit. Lacking

this, the assumption of a certain fixed period length may unwittingly be the cause of misleading conclusions: thus, it is necessary to check that no essential result of a discrete model depends on the actual time length of the period (the model should give the same results when such a period is, say, doubled or halved). But, if the results are unvarying with respect to the period length, they should remain valid when this length tends to zero (that is when one goes from discrete to continuous analysis). Some authors (e.g. May, 1970; Foley, 1975) attach a special importance to this property and argue that the test of the invariance of results with respect to the length of the period is fundamental to ascertain whether a discrete model is well defined and consistent. Moreover, the lack of clarification, in such models, of whether equilibrium obtains at the beginning or at the end of the period, may give rise to confusion between stock equilibria and flow equilibria (see also Drabicki and Takayama, 1979).

(5) As the partial adjustment function discussed under point (2) may have very high adjustment speeds and therefore very short mean time lags with respect to the observation period, it may happen that, when measuring the variables in discrete time, the desired value practically coincides with the observed value over the period, so that it is not possible to obtain an estimate of α. On the contrary, with the continuous formulation, it is always possible to obtain asymptotically unbiased estimates of α even for relatively long observation periods.

(6) The use of a continuous model may allow a more satisfactory treatment of distributed lag processes. In a discrete model the disturbances in successive observations are usually assumed to be independent, but this assumption can be maintained only if the size of the time unit inherent in the model is not too small relative to the observation period. The independence assumption thus entails a lower bound on the permissible size of the inherent time unit, and this precludes the correct treatment of a number of economic problems. The lags in the system are not always integral multiples of one time unit whose size is compatible with the independence assumption. Since it may happen that distributed time lags with a lower time limit of almost zero have to be considered, a continuous time specification is more correct.

(7) From the analytical point of view, differential equation systems are more easily handled than difference systems.

These arguments as a whole have great but not decisive weight. They – together with the undeniable presence in reality of discontinuous phenomena – should lead to the conclusion that an economic system could be represented better by a mixed differential –difference system. Unfortunately, as we said in the preface, these systems are usually intractable from the analytical point of view and no satisfactory estimation method has yet been developed. Therefore both continuous and discrete analysis must be considered as alternative approximations, neither of which can be regarded *a priori* as superior *in an absolute sense* to the other. Thus the development of estimation methods for continuous time models has had the effect of putting the two formulations in a situation of parity from the econometric point of view, as we said in the preface. However, some advantages of the new methodology, that the reader will be able to appreciate better further on,[5] might make a continuous formulation preferable.

Given the important position that adjustment equations have in disequilibrium dynamics, in the next section we shall recall some preliminary notions concerning these equations.[6]

1.2. A digression on distributed lags and partial adjustment equations

A distributed lag equation arises when the value that a variable y takes at time t is a function (for simplicity's sake assumed to be linear) of the present and past values of some other variable x, which for the moment we leave unspecified. Formally,

$$y_t = b_0 x_t + b_1 x_{t-1} + b_2 x_{t-2} + \cdots + b_n x_{t-n} + \cdots, \tag{4}$$

where the b's are known constants.

[5]Consider as an example points (2) and (3) above and the great advancement, for the examination of the dynamic behaviour and of the policy implications of the model, given by "sensitivity analysis" which we shall deal with in para. 2.2.4.

[6]The economic significance of adjustment equations will be examined in detail in section 2.1.

Many different reasons can give rise to distributed lag equations. Suppose that the changes in a variable x have their effect only gradually on y: some well known cases are those of the consumption function and of the investment function (see, e.g., Gandolfo, 1980, Part I, ch. 7, § 1). It is also frequently assumed that macroeconomic variables react more or less slowly to changes in policy instruments (money supply, government expenditure, etc.). In all these cases, distributed lag equations seem appropriate. Furthermore, as we shall see, a certain type of lag distribution is equivalent to the widely used *partial adjustment* equation, according to which, given a discrepancy between the desired and the actual value of a variable, the latter is adjusted towards the former only gradually, according to a coefficient of reaction.

Eq. (4) may contain a finite or infinite number of terms, but in any case the sum of the coefficients is assumed to be finite, that is

$$b_0 + b_1 + b_2 + \cdots = b, \tag{5}$$

where b is a finite constant. For, in the contrary case, a unit change in all past values of x would cause an infinite change in y. It is also usually assumed that the b_i are non-negative.

If we define a new set of coefficients w_i

$$w_i = b_i/b, \tag{6}$$

then eq. (4) can be rewritten as

$$y_t = b[w_0 x_t + w_1 x_{t-1} + w_2 x_{t-2} + \cdots + w_n x_{t-n} + \cdots],$$

$$\sum_{i=0}^{\infty} w_i = 1. \tag{4'}$$

From eq. (4′) it can be seen easily that if each value of x had been increased by one unit, the value of y_t would increase by b units (long term effect of a sustained[7] unit increment in x). Thus b is called the *long term distributed lag multiplier*; the coefficient b_0 is called *impact multiplier*, whereas the coefficients $b_i (i = 1, 2 \ldots)$ are called *delay* $-$ *i* multipliers.

[7]In the sense that all values of x increase by one unit and maintain their new value through time.

Let us now define the *mean time lag* (*mean lag* or *average lag* for brevity's sake) as the weighted arithmetic mean of the time lags,[8] where the weights are the coefficients w_i:

$$0 \cdot w_0 + 1 \cdot w_1 + 2 \cdot w_2 + \cdots + n \cdot w_n + \cdots = \sum_{i=0}^{\infty} i w_i, \tag{7}$$

or, identically,

$$\sum_{i=0}^{\infty} i b_i \Big/ \sum_{i=0}^{\infty} b_i = \sum_{i=0}^{\infty} i b_i \Big/ b. \tag{7'}$$

A particular case of lag distribution[9] is the geometric distributed lag equation developed by Koyck, where the coefficients b_0, b_1, $b_2, \ldots$ decrease in a given ratio k in an infinite geometric series:

$$b_i = k b_{i-1}, \qquad i = 1, 2, \ldots, \qquad 0 < k < 1. \tag{8}$$

Eq. (8) can be considered as a first-order difference equation, the solution of which is

$$b_i = b_0 k^i. \tag{8'}$$

The sum of the infinite geometric series of coefficients is

$$b = \sum_{i=0}^{\infty} b_i = b_0 \frac{1}{1-k}; \tag{8''}$$

substituting in (8′) we obtain

$$b_i = b(1-k)k^i, \tag{8'''}$$

and so the first coefficient, b_0, is fixed as $b(1-k)$ in order that the sum of the infinite geometric series of coefficients is b. Therefore eq. (4) can be written as

$$y_t = b(1-k)(x_t + k x_{t-1} + k^2 x_{t-2} + \cdots). \tag{9}$$

The useful feature of the Koyck scheme is that it can be reduced to a relationship involving y_t, x_t and y_{t-1} only. In fact, shifting all the time subscripts backwards by one unit and multiplying

[8] As the lags are amounts of time, their mean is an amount of time (this explains the denomination "mean *time* lag"). Furthermore, since the weights are assumed non-negative and their sum is one, eq. (7) can also be interpreted as the expected value of the set of numbers 0, 1, 2, ..., which occur with probabilities w_0, w_1, w_2, ...

[9] For a survey of the most frequently used lag distributions see, for example, Kenkel (1974, ch. 9).

throughout by k we have

$$ky_{t-1} = b(1-k)(kx_{t-1} + k^2x_{t-2} + \cdots). \tag{9'}$$

Subtraction of (9′) from (9) and elimination of the common terms yields

$$y_t - ky_{t-1} = b(1-k)x_t, \tag{9''}$$

whence

$$y_t = b(1-k)x_t + ky_{t-1}. \tag{9'''}$$

This equation can be manipulated still further: by subtracting y_{t-1} from both members we get

$$y_t - y_{t-1} = (1-k)(bx_t - y_{t-1}), \tag{10}$$

and if we further assume that the weights were normalized from the beginning in such a way that $b = \Sigma_{i=0}^{\infty} b_i = 1$, we obtain finally

$$y_t - y_{t-1} = (1-k)(x_t - y_{t-1}), \tag{10'}$$

which is the typical form of the *partial adjustment equation*, where x_t is the "desired" or "potential" value of y_t. Therefore, the generic partial adjustment equation

$$y_t - y_{t-1} = \alpha(\hat{y}_t - y_{t-1}), \qquad 0 < \alpha < 1, \tag{11}$$

is equivalent to a Koyck distributed lag equation.

The results obtained in discrete time can be extended to continuous time. A *continuously distributed lag* equation has the form

$$y(t) = \int_0^{\infty} [f(\tau)x(t-\tau)]\,\mathrm{d}\tau, \qquad \int_0^{\infty} f(\tau)\,\mathrm{d}\tau = 1,$$
$$\lim_{\tau\to\infty} f(\tau) = 0, \tag{12}$$

where $f(\tau)$ is the time-form of the weighting function; for simplicity we have assumed that the integral of the weights is one instead of an arbitrary positive constant.[10]

The continuous counterpart of the geometric lag distribution is the *exponential lag distribution*, where

$$y(t) = \int_0^{\infty} \alpha \mathrm{e}^{-\alpha\tau} x(t-\tau)\,\mathrm{d}\tau. \tag{13}$$

[10] In the contrary case we would write $y(t) = b\int_0^{\infty}[f(\tau)x(t-\tau)]\,\mathrm{d}\tau$, $\int_0^{\infty} f(\tau)\,\mathrm{d}\tau = 1/b$.

As the reader may check,

$$\int_0^{\infty} \alpha e^{-\alpha\tau} d\tau = [-e^{-\alpha\tau}]_0^{\infty} = -[e^{-\alpha\tau}]_0^{\infty} = -(0-1) = 1. \tag{14}$$

We now show that eq. (13) is equivalent to the *partial adjustment equation in continuous time*,

$$Dy(t) = \alpha[x(t) - y(t)], \tag{15}$$

where $x(t)$ can be interpreted as, e.g., the "desired" or "potential" value of y at time t, say $\hat{y}(t)$,[11] and α is the speed of adjustment. Let us perform a change of variable from τ to s in the integral (13), defining $s = t - \tau$ (whence $\tau = t - s$). According to the elementary rules of integral calculus[12] we have

$$y(t) = -\int_t^{-\infty} \alpha e^{-\alpha(t-s)} x(s)\, ds = \int_{-\infty}^{t} \alpha e^{-\alpha(t-s)} x(s)\, ds. \tag{16}$$

As t is a constant with respect to the integral, $\alpha e^{-\alpha t}$ can be considered as a multiplicative constant; therefore

$$y(t) = \alpha e^{-\alpha t} \int_{-\infty}^{t} e^{\alpha s} x(s)\, ds, \tag{16'}$$

whence

$$y(t) e^{\alpha t} = \alpha \int_{-\infty}^{t} e^{\alpha s} x(s)\, ds. \tag{16''}$$

Differentiating with respect to time, we have

$$\alpha y(t) e^{\alpha t} + [Dy(t)] e^{\alpha t} = \alpha \frac{d}{dt} \left\{ \int_{-\infty}^{t} e^{\alpha s} x(s)\, ds \right\}. \tag{16'''}$$

Performing the differentiation of the integral with respect to a

[11]An equation of type (15) can also arise in the case of *adaptive expectations*, where $y(t)$ is the expected value and $x(t)$ is the actual value.

[12]Remember that $\int_a^b \psi(\tau)\, d\tau = \int_c^d \psi[f(s)] f'(s)\, ds$, where $\tau = f(s)$, and $a = \psi(c), b = \psi(d)$. In our case, $s = t$ when $\tau = 0$ and $s = -\infty$ when $\tau = \infty$. Further remember that the property according to which the definite integral changes sign when the limits of integration are reversed also holds when one of the limits is infinite provided that the integral converges. See, e.g., Gillespie (1959), Courant (1961).

parameter which occurs in the upper limit,[13] we have

$$\frac{\mathrm{d}}{\mathrm{d}t}\left\{\int_{-\infty}^{t} \mathrm{e}^{\alpha s}x(s)\,\mathrm{d}s\right\} = \mathrm{e}^{\alpha t}x(t), \tag{17}$$

and so

$$\alpha y(t)\mathrm{e}^{\alpha t} + \mathrm{e}^{\alpha t}\mathrm{D}y(t) = \alpha\mathrm{e}^{\alpha t}x(t), \tag{17$'$}$$

whence, eliminating $\mathrm{e}^{\alpha t}$ and rearranging terms,

$$\mathrm{D}y(t) = \alpha[x(t) - y(t)], \tag{17$''$}$$

which coincides with eq. (15).

In continuous time the *mean lag* is defined as

$$\int_0^{\infty} \tau f(\tau)\,\mathrm{d}\tau, \tag{18}$$

that is, with an exponential weighting function

$$\alpha\int_0^{\infty} \tau\mathrm{e}^{-\alpha\tau}\mathrm{d}\tau. \tag{18$'$}$$

It can be checked easily that[14]

$$\begin{aligned}\int_0^{\infty} \tau\mathrm{e}^{-\alpha\tau}\mathrm{d}\tau &= \left[-\frac{\mathrm{e}^{-\alpha\tau}}{\alpha^2}(\alpha\tau+1)\right]_0^{\infty} = -\left[\frac{\mathrm{e}^{-\alpha\tau}}{\alpha^2}(\alpha\tau+1)\right]_0^{\infty} \\ &= -\frac{1}{\alpha^2}[\mathrm{e}^{-\alpha\tau}(\alpha\tau+1)]_0^{\infty} = -\frac{1}{\alpha^2}\left[\frac{\alpha\tau+1}{\mathrm{e}^{\alpha\tau}}\right]_0^{\infty} = \frac{1}{\alpha^2},\end{aligned} \tag{19}$$

and substituting in (18′), we have

$$\alpha\frac{1}{\alpha^2} = \frac{1}{\alpha}. \tag{18$''$}$$

Therefore when $\alpha \to +\infty$ the mean lag tends to zero, i.e. $y(t)$ tends to adjust immediately to $x(t)$.

[13] This is a particular case of the general formula for the differentiation of an integral with respect to a parameter which occurs in both limits as well as in the integrand. See Courant (1961, vol. II, p. 220). In our particular case, the derivative of the integral is equal to the derivative of the upper limit with respect to the parameter, multiplied by the integrand (in which the parameter has been substituted in the place of the variable of integration).

[14] $\int_0^{\infty}\tau\mathrm{e}^{-\alpha\tau}\,\mathrm{d}\tau = [(-\mathrm{e}^{-\alpha\tau}/\alpha^2)(\alpha\tau+1)]_0^{\infty} = (-1/\alpha^2)[\mathrm{e}^{-\alpha\tau}(\alpha\tau+1)]_0^{\infty} = (-1/\alpha^2)[(\alpha\tau+1)/\mathrm{e}^{\alpha\tau}]_0^{\infty}$. Application of l'Hôpital's rule shows that the expression in square brackets tends to zero as $\tau \to \infty$; for $\tau = 0$, it is equal to 1. Therefore the value of the definite integral under consideration is $-(1/\alpha^2)(0-1) = 1/\alpha^2$.

The mean lag $1/\alpha$ can also be interpreted as the time necessary for about 63% of the discrepancy between $y(t)$ and $\hat{y}(t)$ to be eliminated by changes in $y(t)$ following a change in $\hat{y}(t)$. Consider the expression for $y(t)$ given by eq. (16) and assume that ϑ units of time ago a change in x (that is in $\hat{y}$), say Δx, took place. Then the change in y is

$$\Delta y(t) = \int_{t-\vartheta}^{t} \alpha e^{-\alpha(t-s)} \Delta x \, ds, \tag{20}$$

that is, as Δx is a given constant

$$\Delta y(t) = \Delta x \int_{t-\vartheta}^{t} \alpha e^{-\alpha(t-s)} \, ds. \tag{20'}$$

A way of proving eq. (20) is as follows. Define a variable X which is equal to x for times farther away than ϑ units ago, and equal to $x + \Delta x$ for all times from $t - \vartheta$ up to t, that is

$$X = \begin{cases} x & \text{for } s \leq t - \vartheta, \\ x + \Delta x & \text{for } t - \vartheta \leq s \leq t, \end{cases}$$

and let Y be the new value of y following the change in x. Then[15]

$$\begin{aligned} Y(t) &= \int_{-\infty}^{t} \alpha e^{-\alpha(t-s)} x(s) \, ds \\ &= \int_{-\infty}^{t-\vartheta} \alpha e^{-\alpha(t-s)} x(s) \, ds \\ &\quad + \int_{t-\vartheta}^{t} \alpha e^{-\alpha(t-s)} [x(s) + \Delta x] \, ds, \end{aligned} \tag{20''}$$

and so

$$\begin{aligned} \Delta y(t) = Y(t) - y(t) &= Y(t) - \int_{-\infty}^{t} \alpha e^{-\alpha(t-s)} x(s) \, ds \\ &= Y(t) - \left[\int_{-\infty}^{t-\vartheta} \alpha e^{-\alpha(t-s)} X(s) \, ds \right. \\ &\quad \left. + \int_{t-\vartheta}^{t} \alpha e^{-\alpha(t-s)} x(s) \, ds \right]. \end{aligned} \tag{20'''}$$

[15]The function $X(s)$ is continuous in the interval $-\infty$ to t except for a finite discontinuity at $s = t - \vartheta$. It is well known that if a function has a finite number of discontinuities in the interval of integration, then it is integrable over that interval. See, e.g., Gillespie (1959, pp. 74–5), Courant (1961, vol. I, pp. 245 ff.).

Substituting $Y(t)$ from (20″) into (20‴) and simplifying we have eq. (20).

Consider now eq. (20′), and go back to the original variable τ,[16] obtaining

$$\begin{aligned}\Delta y &= \Delta x \int_0^{\vartheta} \alpha e^{-\alpha\tau}\, d\tau \\ &= \Delta x[-e^{-\alpha\tau}]_0^{\vartheta} \\ &= \Delta x(1 - e^{-\alpha\vartheta}),\end{aligned} \tag{21}$$

from which, letting the so far undetermined ϑ take on the value $1/\alpha$ and carrying out the computations, we obtain

$$\Delta y \simeq 0.632 \Delta x.$$

Therefore, as we stated above, $\vartheta = 1/\alpha$ is the time necessary for about 63% of the discrepancy between $y(t)$ and $x(t)$ to be eliminated by changes in $y(t)$ following a change in $x(t)$. Of course, this interpretation is particularly interesting when $x(t) = \hat{y}(t)$.

[16] The procedure is a change of variable from s to $\tau = t - s$.

CHAPTER 2

Specification and qualitative analysis of the models

2.1. Specification

The "philosophy of construction" of dynamic models for the treatment of continuous economic phenomena can be condensed to a number of characteristics whose examination is the object of the present section. The models under consideration can be either single- or multi-equation models; in the latter case they may represent either economy-wide macroeconomic models, or models concerning single aspects of the economy, or multi-sector models.

2.1.1. The *first characteristic* is that the equations are usually specified as dynamic equations. This means that the model is recursive (in the sense that it is expressed as a system of differential equations in which the derivative of each endogenous variable is in principle a function of the levels of all the variables) and so it has a "causal" interpretation.[1] This has some advantages from the econometric point of view, because the parameters of such models are identified and all the restrictions suggested by economic theory can be imposed directly on the model; furthermore, the effects of structural changes can be interpreted in terms of these parameters. But setting aside the econometric questions, which will be taken up

[1] On recursive models and on the notion of "causality" used here, see, for example, Bentzel and Hansen (1954), Strotz and Wold (1960), Malinvaud (1964). Actually, disequilibrium dynamic models (and, as we shall see further on in the text, specifying partial adjustment equations is a disequilibrium dynamics approach) are always recursive models if all operators are taken into account: see Bentzel and Hansen (1954). From the formal point of view it can be shown that systems of differential equations are recursive with respect to infinitesimal time intervals: see Wold (1959).

again in ch. 3, let us now examine the advantages of using dynamic equations such as eq. (15) of ch. 1 more deeply from the economic point of view.

To start with we observe that eq. (15) of ch. 1 includes both the case in which $x(t)$ is the "desired" or "potential" value of the variable which adjusts ($x(t)=\hat{y}(t)$: see section 1.2) – in which case we may speak of partial adjustment equations in the strict sense – and the case in which $x(t)$ is the desired value of some other variable. More generally, we may suppose that the variable adjusts in relation to the discrepancy between the desired and actual values of *other* variables: in this formulation are included, for example, all the cases of adjustment to excess demand when the variable which adjusts is not the actual quantity. Some clarification of this point may be useful. Adjustments to excess demand may be classified in two categories:

(a) the variable that adjusts to excess demand is a "price" variable (in a broad sense);
(b) the variable that adjusts to this excess is a "quantity" variable (in a broad sense).

Within the first category we might further distinguish between "tâtonnement" and "non-tâtonnement" processes, it being clear that models which purport to interpret reality must be based on non-tâtonnement processes; but we need not elaborate this point, well known in economic dynamics.

Some examples of category (a) adjustments are:

(a_1) the rate of interest varies according to excess demand for money, that is, according to the difference between the desired quantity of money (demand for money, which in turn is a function, e.g., of the rate of interest and of income) and the existing quantity of money (the supply of money, assumed to be exogenously controlled by the monetary authorities, or in some way rendered endogenous);
(a_2) the exchange rate varies according to excess demand for the foreign currency (where both demand for and supply of foreign exchange depend on the exchange rate and on other variables).

As we see, the difference between (a_1) and (a_2) is that in the former case the variable which adjusts is an argument of the demand function only, whereas in the latter case it is an argument of both demand and supply.

Some examples of category (b) adjustments are:

(b_1) national income (product) varies according to excess demand in the real market, that is, according to the difference between "desired" income (aggregate demand, which in turn is a function of actual income and of other variables) and actual income;

(b_2) the money supply is changed according to the difference between a "desired" quantity (e.g., the amount that "allows" a given target rate of interest[2]) and the actual quantity.

The difference between cases (b_1) and (b_2) is that in the former the variable which adjusts is an argument of the demand function whereas this does not happen in the latter.

Thus we can write in general

$$\mathrm{D}y(t) = f[x(t) - v(t)], \tag{1}$$

where f is a *sign-preserving* function, and $f[0] = 0$, $f'[0] > 0$. The variables $x(t)$ and $v(t)$ are to be defined; in the case in which $x(t) = \hat{y}(t)$ and $v(t) = y(t)$ we have a partial adjustment equation in the strict sense, whereas all the other cases of adjustment to excess demand can be obtained by suitable definitions: for example, if we let $x = x(y, \ldots)$ and $v = v(y, \ldots)$ we have case (a_2), and so on.

The logic underlying equations of type (1) can be based both on market mechanisms (an example is case (b_1)) and on reaction functions of the policy makers (or on the functions that represent such reaction in the model builder's opinion): an example is case (b_2). The market mechanisms may reflect adjustments to excess

[2] This implies that, given the demand for money as a function of the rate of interest and of income, the "desired" quantity of money is obtained by putting r = a given constant (target) in that function; therefore, the "desired" quantity becomes a function of income only. It goes without saying that the adjustment process under consideration is perfectly compatible with an adjustment process of type (a_1). An alternative to (b_2) might be that the money supply is changed according to the difference between the actual and desired values of the rate of interest.

demand or the existence of obstacles, frictions and delays of various kinds that prevent the operators from responding to change instantaneously, so that they cannot move onto their schedule immediately (this is the case of partial adjustment proper).

Eq. (1) is linearized, for example, in the form (see, however, para. 2.1.3)

$$\mathrm{D}y(t) = \alpha[x(t) - v(t)], \tag{2}$$

where the multiplicative constant α is $f'[0]$ and can be interpreted as a speed of adjustment or reaction coefficient. When (and only when) the equation is a partial adjustment equation in the strict sense, α can also be given the meaning examined in section 1.2. Let us note that it would also be possible to make the adjustment coefficient a function of other variables. This means that the original specification should not be (1) but a function in which these other variables appear as arguments, and since such a function should have the property of being zero when $x(t) = v(t)$ irrespective of the values of the other variables, the obvious form is the multiplicative one

$$\mathrm{D}y(t) = h(\dots)[x(t) - v(t)], \tag{3}$$

where $h(\dots)$ is a function of variables to be specified. Even under the usual simplifying assumption that h is a linear function, however, this adjustment equation would maintain a non-linear form.

In any case, the formulation of the model as a set of adjustment equations means admitting the possibility that the system is in a situation of disequilibrium, namely that the observed points do not necessarily lie on the behavioural schedules or (still more restrictively) on their intersection.

In other words, we are in a context of *disequilibrium dynamics*, which seems more appropriate to real life phenomena. Of course, if on the basis of *a priori* information there is a strong presumption that a certain market is practically always in equilibrium, the equation relative to it can be written as an equilibrium, instead of an adjustment, equation. In general, however, unless the *a priori* information is very sound, the formulation as an adjustment equation is preferable; if this is the case, econometric estimation will show, through a very high value of the adjustment coefficient, that the market under consideration is practically always in equilibrium.

Furthermore, adjustment models may – taking into account both economic theory and the institutional framework – yield useful information on the lags in policy measures (fiscal, monetary, etc.), and make it possible to determine the time profile of the effects of these measures. This could be of crucial importance to policy makers, and in any case allows a more fruitful discussion of the policy implications of the model.

It is outside the scope of the present book to discuss the relations between the disequilibrium modelling approach expounded here and the extensive literature on rational expectations; for an attempt at a synthesis see, for example, Clements and Jonson (1979).

2.1.2. The second characteristic is that the model in principle ought to have an equilibrium, usually a steady state equilibrium. It is important to note that this does *not* mean that the model is in this kind of equilibrium or that the equilibrium is necessarily stable: in other words, the adjustment processes are not *a priori* assumed to be such as to bring the model to its equilibrium. This seems an advance with respect to the usual assumption that the model must be stable. It is the econometric analysis that will ascertain whether the model is stable or not, thus inducing the model builder – if the answer is negative and *if* stability is believed an essential requisite[3] – to search for the cause of this instability and to modify the model. The characteristic under consideration is simply that an equilibrium should exist. This may appear an obvious requisite, because the concept of equilibrium, and therefore its existence, is central to the economist's traditional way of thinking – apart from the question of its stability. But a model could be built leaving aside the concept of equilibrium, that is, by simply specifying dynamic behaviour equations and then solving the system to obtain the actual path(s) of the model, giving no privileged position to any particular reference point or path (the "equilibrium" point or path, to be precise). This seems possible, but perhaps it would represent too radical a departure from the usual way of thinking in the profession, so that here we shall not pursue this matter further.

[3] We have stressed the "if", because it is known that in some models *instability* is an essential feature as, for example, in Hicks' trade cycle model (see Gandolfo, 1980, Part I, ch. 5, § 2 and Part I, ch. 7, § 1).

Once the notion of equilibrium is accepted, it seems logical that in a dynamic model intended to describe the economy for a sufficiently long period of time, the equilibrium to be considered is a steady state equilibrium.

To these economic justifications other formal justifications can be added. First of all, since the functions are usually non-linear, the model will have to be linearized, and the equilibrium is a convenient point where to perform such a linearization. Furthermore, the analysis of the steady state properties of the model not only gives information on the dynamic behaviour of the model, but helps as a check on the mathematical consistency of the model itself: "Implausible long-run behaviour could indicate a structural defect such as the omission of an important feedback. This could seriously affect the predictive powers of the model and its usefulness for either medium term forecasting or policy analysis. If a macroeconomic model... does not have a steady state the variables will be fluctuating in some way for all t and, except in special circumstances, these oscillations will be unstable" (Wymer, 1976, p. 12). Explosive oscillations, we may add, are neither desirable from the normative point of view nor realistic from the positive point of view.

It must however be pointed out that the presence of a steady state is not an indispensable characteristic, for it is possible to build and estimate models which lack it (see, for example, Wymer, 1973, 1975).

2.1.3. The *third characteristic*, of a purely formal nature, is that the adjustment equations are usually formulated expressing the variables in terms of (Naperian) logarithms. Taking up eq. (1) again, given the generic nature of the sign-preserving function, nothing prevents us from assuming that the functional operator f also contains the instruction "take the logarithm of the variables". If this is so, considering that $v(t)$ can often be identified with $y(t)$, for symmetry we should also take the logarithm of $y(t)$ on the l.h.s. member. Alternatively, we could assume that the adjustment process involves the proportional rate of change of the variable, $\mathrm{D}y(t)/y(t)$ instead of rate of change $\mathrm{D}y(t)$. In conclusion, when linearizing eq. (1), the following forms seem equally admissible:

$$\mathrm{D}\log y(t) = \alpha[\log x(t) - \log v(t)] = \alpha \log\left[\frac{x(t)}{v(t)}\right], \tag{1'}$$

$$\mathrm{D}y(t) = \alpha'[x(t) - v(t)]. \tag{2'}$$

The choice falls on form (1′) because, when we linearize the system[4] around the steady state to examine its local stability, we obtain a remainder which does not involve time explicitly, so that the conditions of the Poincaré–Liapunov–Perron theorem are automatically satisfied. But we shall go into this more fully in paragraph 2.2.3.

2.1.4. The *fourth characteristic* is that the models considered are small in size and amenable to a complete qualitative analysis (existence of the steady state, stability, comparative dynamics, sensitivity), whereas this is not usually possible with current econometric models, in which the analysis is normally of the quantitative type only (numerical simulations, etc.) with all its inherent limitations (validity for the single numerical case and not in general, etc.).

By "small in size" we mean a model of about 20 equations: models of this size can cover a broad range of economic relations and embody a sufficiently rich theoretical structure.

A limited number of equations, apart from the difficulties due to numerical problems, is also suggested by the fact that the mathematical difficulty of a complete qualitative analysis increases as the number of equations increases, up to the point of becoming intractable. Therefore, the benefits of manageability and of analytical tractability – particularly appreciated by the economic theorist and by the econometrician in the sense of Frisch's original definition (1933) – have to be weighed against the benefits of a more detailed description – particularly appreciated by those who believe that the benefits of an econometric model are an increasing function of its scale.[5]

[4] We mean the second linearization, that is the linearization of the functions x and v. These will be, in general, non-linear functions of the endogenous and exogenous variables (as an example, consider case (a_2) above, para. 2.1.1).

[5] In this case, the optimal scale is determined where the marginal benefit of added scale equals the marginal cost of added scale. See Intriligator (1978, p. 459).

In conclusion, the model can be written as a first-order differential system in normal form, of the type

$$\mathrm{D}\log \boldsymbol{Y}(t) = \boldsymbol{H}[\log \boldsymbol{Y}(t), \boldsymbol{Z}(t), \boldsymbol{\vartheta}] + \boldsymbol{u}(t), \tag{4}$$

where $\boldsymbol{Y}(t)$ is the vector of the endogenous variables, $\boldsymbol{Z}(t)$ the vector of the exogenous variables, $\boldsymbol{\vartheta}$ a vector of parameters consisting of a subvector $\boldsymbol{\alpha}$ of adjustment coefficients and a subvector $\boldsymbol{\beta}$ of other behavioural parameters (propensions, elasticities, partial equilibrium ratios,[6] etc.), $\boldsymbol{H}$ a vector of linear or non-linear differentiable functions, and $\boldsymbol{u}(t)$ a vector of disturbances with classic properties (white noise). The symbol D denotes, as before, the differential operator $\mathrm{d}/\mathrm{d}t$. In what follows, for simplicity's sake we shall omit $\boldsymbol{u}(t)$, as it is relevant only for econometric analysis, which will be taken up in ch. 3.

Let us note, finally, that, in principle, the differential system could be in non-normal form or of an order higher than the first. In these cases it can be reduced to a first order system in normal form by means of suitable manipulations and under certain conditions (see, for example, Gandolfo, 1980, Part II, ch. 8, § 8.4 and Part III, ch. 2, § 3).

2.2. Qualitative analysis

By qualitative analysis we mean the analysis of the general properties of the model, abstracted from the single numerical case. In fact, one of the advantages of the models under consideration is the extent to which methods in use in mathematical economics (search for the steady state, comparative dynamics, stability) can be applied to them, thus allowing a complete analysis from the theoretical point of view. Furthermore, a new technique recently introduced allows the study of the sensitivity of the latent roots of the system with respect to the parameters. Therefore the qualitative analysis

[6] "Partial equilibrium" ratios in the sense that they would ensure, *ceteris paribus*, equilibrium in a given equation. Consider for example the equation $\mathrm{D}\log C = \alpha(\log \hat{C} - \log C)$, where $\hat{C} = \beta Y$ is desired consumption corresponding to any given level of income. The coefficient β is the desired ratio of consumption to income, and βY is the partial equilibrium level of consumption: if the actual ratio of consumption to income is equal to β, there is no tendency, *ceteris paribus*, for consumption to change.

articulates at several stages, which we shall examine separately: (i) search for the steady state; (ii) comparative dynamics; (iii) stability; (iv) sensitivity. Naturally, the first two stages come into play only if the model has to possess a steady state.

2.2.1. *Search for the steady state*

The reasons for the search for a steady state have already been illustrated in para 2.1.2. This search is carried out by assuming that all the exogenous variables grow at a constant proportional rate, namely

$$Z_i(t) = Z_i^* e^{\lambda_i t}, \qquad \forall i. \tag{5}$$

The rates of growth λ_i may be equal or different; positive, negative or zero,[7] and relations may exist between them as well as between the initial values Z_i^*. These relations derive from economic theory and are present in the specification of the model.

A steady state is given by a particular solution of system (4) having the form

$$Y_i(t) = Y_i^* e^{\rho_i t}, \qquad \forall i, \tag{6}$$

where the values of Y_i^*, and of ρ_i are to be determined. Thus the search for the steady state is an application of the method of undetermined coefficients (see Gandolfo, 1980, passim): eqs. (6) and, of course, eqs. (5) are substituted in system (4) and the values of Y_i^* and of ρ_i are determined so that the system is identically satisfied. In other words, after these substitutions, the condition for (6) to be a solution is that the resulting system be identically satisfied, and this will give rise to a set of equations in the unknowns Y_i^* and ρ_i.[8] The solution, provided that it exists, will express these unknowns in terms of the knowns; usually we shall obtain

$$\rho_i = g_i(\boldsymbol{\lambda}, \boldsymbol{\beta}), \tag{7}$$

$$Y_i^* = G_i(\boldsymbol{Z}^*, \boldsymbol{\lambda}, \boldsymbol{\vartheta}). \tag{8}$$

[7]The last case, of course, is equivalent to assuming that the corresponding exogenous variable is a constant.

[8]The ρ_i are usually obtained by solving the equations derived form equating to zero the coefficients of the terms containing t whereas the Y_i^* are obtained by solving the equations derived from equating to zero all the other terms not containing t.

The functions g_i are not very complicated: in a closed economy model the ρ_i will usually be simple functions of the exogenous growth rates λ and of the long-run propensities and elasticities (namely, some components only of the vector $\boldsymbol{\beta}$ will be involved); in an open economy model the ρ_i will usually be simple linear functions of the exogenous growth rates only. On the contrary, the functions G_i are often very complicated.

In any case, if we postulate that the model possesses a steady state, at least one[9] solution which is consistent with economic theory must exist for the ρ_i and for the Y_i^*. It is important to note that the procedure for finding the solution may help in the determination of the structure of the model in the sense that, in order to obtain this solution, it may be necessary to impose restrictions on certain parameters and/or to change the form of some of the functions. In particular, the solution for the ρ_i usually ensures that certain homogeneity conditions[10] hold, and the solution for the Y_i^* may suggest additional constraints on elasticities or other parameters.

2.2.2. *Comparative dynamics*

Comparative dynamics is concerned with the effects of changes in parameters, etc., on the whole motion over time of a dynamic model, and can be used to analyze the effects of shifts in a particular exogenous element or internal parameter on the steady state equilibrium growth path.[11] Formally, this amounts to computing the partial derivatives of ρ_i and of Y_i^*; these derivatives are obtained by partially differentiating the functions (7) and (8) with respect to the exogenous element or internal parameter whose shift

[9]As the system is non-linear, the solution may not be unique.

[10]That is to say, certain functions are homogeneous of a certain degree, as postulated by economic theory. However, we could reverse the causation and state that it is the presence of the homogeneity conditions which makes possible the existence of a steady state.

[11]For a general treatment of comparative dynamics see Gandolfo (1980, Part III, ch. 1, § 6). It must be noted that comparative dynamics, as such, does not say anything about the transition from one equilibrium growth path to another; the study of this transition belongs to stability analysis.

we are examining. The results express the long-term effects of the shift (provided that the steady state is stable); the impact effects can be seen directly from the model and the medium-term effects can be tracked heuristically.

Equations (7) and (8) also allow the effects of setting one or more parameters to zero to be ascertained. For example, one might wish to know the effects of the assumption that policy makers do not take into consideration certain targets that the model builder has included in the model: this amounts to setting to zero the elements of $\boldsymbol{\theta}$ corresponding to the presence of the targets in the postulated reaction functions of the policy makers.

2.2.3. *Stability*

The relevance of stability analysis, both for its own sake and for the purpose of comparative dynamics, is well known. Since system (4) is in general non-linear, the study of *global* stability requires the use of Liapunov's second method (Gandolfo, 1980, Part III, ch. 2). This, however, is outside the scope of our study, and we shall examine *local* stability only.

The usual procedure is to linearize, that is, to expand in a Taylor series about the equilibrium state[12] and to neglect all higher-order terms. As system (4) contains (known) functions of time (also called "forcing functions"), it is non-autonomous, and particular care is required in checking the conditions under which it is legitimate to consider only the first-order terms in the Taylor series expansion. These conditions are given by the Poincaré–Liapunov–Perron theorem,[13] which states that if the linearized system near equilibrium (obtained by the procedure just described) is uniformly asymptotically stable and is a uniformly good approximation to the original

[12]As we shall see, in the econometric applications it may be convenient to linearize around the sample means. From the theoretical point of view, however, it is the linearization around the equilibrium which is relevant.

[13]Attributed to Liapunov and Poincaré (for example by Bellman, 1953, p. 93, and by Sansone and Conti, 1964, ch. IX, § 3.1), and to Perron (for example by Coddington and Levinson, 1955, p. 314). A joint attribution seems preferable because it seems that all the three authors have proved the theorem under consideration.

system near the equilibrium state, then the equilibrium state of the original system is locally uniformly asymptotically stable (Kalman and Bertram, 1960, pp. 383–4). In general, the null solution $\boldsymbol{x}(t) = \mathbf{0}$ of a differential system of the type

$$\mathrm{D}\boldsymbol{x}(t) = \boldsymbol{A}\boldsymbol{x}(t) + \boldsymbol{f}(\boldsymbol{x}, t), \tag{9}$$

where $\boldsymbol{A}$ is a matrix of constants, is asymptotically stable if $\|\boldsymbol{f}(\boldsymbol{x}, t)\| / \|\boldsymbol{x}(t)\|$ tends to zero uniformly in t as $\|\boldsymbol{x}\|$ tends to zero and all the characteristic roots of $\boldsymbol{A}$ have negative real parts.

Let us first show how system (9) arises in the course of the procedure for the analysis of the local stability of a generic non-linear system: we shall next apply the theorem, and then examine some problems deriving from the nature of system (4).

Consider the generic non-linear, non-autonomous differential system

$$\mathrm{D}\boldsymbol{X}(t) = \boldsymbol{F}[\boldsymbol{X}(t), t], \tag{10}$$

and let $\boldsymbol{X}^{\mathrm{e}}(t)$ be some particular solution of (10). To study the properties of the solutions of system (10) in the neighbourhood of the solution $\boldsymbol{X}^{\mathrm{e}}(t)$, we make the substitution $x_i(t) = X_i(t) - X_i^{\mathrm{e}}(t)$, where the subscript i denotes the ith element of the appropriate vector, that is

$$\boldsymbol{x}(t) = \boldsymbol{X}(t) - \boldsymbol{X}^{\mathrm{e}}(t), \tag{11}$$

and call $\boldsymbol{x}(t) = \mathbf{0}$, or $\boldsymbol{X}(t) = \boldsymbol{X}^{\mathrm{e}}(t)$ the unperturbed motion or null solution (Krasovskiĭ, 1963, p. 1). Since the variables $X_i(t)$ satisfy system (10), the new variables $x_i(t)$ satisfy the differential system

$$\mathrm{D}\boldsymbol{x}(t) = \boldsymbol{\varphi}[\boldsymbol{x}(t), t], \tag{12}$$

where

$$\boldsymbol{\varphi}[\boldsymbol{x}(t), t] \equiv \boldsymbol{F}[\boldsymbol{x}(t) + \boldsymbol{X}^{\mathrm{e}}(t), t] - \boldsymbol{F}[\boldsymbol{X}^{\mathrm{e}}(t), t]. \tag{13}$$

The validity of eqs. (12) – called the equations of perturbed motion – can be checked by direct substitution, remembering that $\boldsymbol{X}^{\mathrm{e}}(t)$ is a particular solution of system (10), and so satisfies it by definition. The next step to examine the local stability of system (10) is to expand the right hand side of system (12) in a Taylor series about the null solution. Thus we obtain a system of type (9), where $\boldsymbol{A}$ is the Jacobian matrix of the φ_i evaluated at $\boldsymbol{x}(t) = \mathbf{0}$, and $\boldsymbol{f}(\boldsymbol{x}, t)$

represents all higher-order terms in the Taylor series expansion, which will be functions of time if the original system is non-autonomous. Now, the linearized system

$$\mathrm{D}\boldsymbol{x}(t) = \boldsymbol{A}\boldsymbol{x}(t), \tag{14}$$

is called a *uniformly good approximation* to the original system if $\|\boldsymbol{f}(\boldsymbol{x}, t)\|/\|\boldsymbol{x}\|$ tends to zero uniformly in t as $\boldsymbol{x}$ tends to zero.[14] When this is true, it is enough to consider the linearized system (14) in order to check the local stability of the original system; the former, as we know, will be uniformly asymptotically stable if, and only if, all the characteristic roots of the matrix $\boldsymbol{A}$ have negative real parts.

It is important to point out that, when the original system is autonomous, the $\boldsymbol{f}$ in its Taylor series expansion does not depend explicitly on time, so that the linearized system is always a uniformly good approximation: this is due to the fact that, when $\boldsymbol{f}$ does not contain t explicitly, the problem of *uniform* convergence does not arise, and it is certain that $\|\boldsymbol{f}(\boldsymbol{x})\|/\|\boldsymbol{x}\|$ tends to zero as $\|\boldsymbol{x}\|$ tends to zero because $\|\boldsymbol{f}(\boldsymbol{x})\|$ represents all higher-order terms, which are of a lower order of smallness than $\|\boldsymbol{x}\|$ as $\|\boldsymbol{x}\|$ tends to zero. It goes without saying that in this case the analysis of local stability is greatly simplified, as it is not necessary to check the uniform convergence we have been worrying about, and the legitimacy of the usual procedure described at the beginning of this paragraph is warranted.

Let us now turn to the analysis of the local stability of system (4). Letting $\log \boldsymbol{Y}(t) = \boldsymbol{X}(t)$ and subsuming the parameters and the

[14]Let us recall the notion of uniform convergence. Let $\boldsymbol{\omega}(\boldsymbol{x}, t)$ be a continuous vector-valued function and consider any real $\varepsilon > 0$ and any real $\mu > 0$. We say that $\boldsymbol{\omega}(\boldsymbol{x}, t)$ converges to zero in t if, given a t_0 it is possible to find a real number $\delta = \delta(\varepsilon, t_0) > 0$ and a real number $T = T(\mu) > 0$ such that $\|\boldsymbol{x}_0\| \leq \delta$ implies

$$\|\boldsymbol{\omega}(\boldsymbol{x}, t)\| \leq \varepsilon \qquad \text{for all } t \geq t_0 \qquad \text{(convergence)},$$

and

$$\|\boldsymbol{\omega}(\boldsymbol{x}, t)\| \leq \mu \qquad \text{for all } t \geq t_0 + T \quad \text{(asymptotic convergence)}.$$

If δ is independent of t_0 (namely if the value of δ depends only on ε) the convergence is called uniform. In other words, after giving arbitrarily small positive values to ε and μ, the sufficiently small neighbourhood of the starting point depends only on ε and not on the initial time. See Kalman and Bertram, 1960, pp. 375 ff.

functional form of the Z_i into the functional form of this system, it becomes of type (10). Then, considering the deviations from the steady state solution, we have

$$\boldsymbol{x}(t) = \boldsymbol{X}(t) - \boldsymbol{X}^{\mathrm{e}}(t) = \log \frac{\boldsymbol{Y}(t)}{\boldsymbol{Y}^{\mathrm{e}}}, \tag{15}$$

where $\boldsymbol{Y}^{\mathrm{e}}$ is the vector whose elements are the functions (6), naturally after the determination of (7) and (8). Now, a convenient property of systems of type (4) is that in many cases the transformation (15) reduces them to autonomous systems, that is system (12) becomes of the type

$$\mathrm{D}\boldsymbol{x}(t) = \boldsymbol{\varphi}[\boldsymbol{x}(t)], \tag{16}$$

and so in the linearization procedure the question of uniform convergence does not arise. In other words, the logarithms of the ratios of the variables to their steady state paths usually satisfy a non-linear system of differential equations which does not involve t explicitly. In principle, the procedure to be followed is not difficult. Consider system (4) in deterministic form,

$$\mathrm{D}\log \boldsymbol{Y}(t) = \boldsymbol{H}[\log \boldsymbol{Y}(t), \boldsymbol{Z}(t), \boldsymbol{\vartheta}]. \tag{4'}$$

This system is satisfied by definition by the steady state solution, so that we have

$$\mathrm{D}\log \boldsymbol{Y}^{\mathrm{e}}(t) = \boldsymbol{H}[\log \boldsymbol{Y}^{\mathrm{e}}(t), \boldsymbol{Z}(t), \boldsymbol{\vartheta}], \tag{4''}$$

where the elements of the steady state vector $\boldsymbol{Y}^{\mathrm{e}}(t)$ are given by (5), naturally taking into account (7) and (8). Subtraction of (4″) from (4′) gives

$$\mathrm{D}\log \frac{\boldsymbol{Y}(t)}{\boldsymbol{Y}^{\mathrm{e}}(t)} = \boldsymbol{H}[\log \boldsymbol{Y}(t), \boldsymbol{Z}(t), \boldsymbol{\vartheta}] - \boldsymbol{H}[\log \boldsymbol{Y}^{\mathrm{e}}(t), \boldsymbol{Z}(t), \boldsymbol{\vartheta}]. \tag{4'''}$$

Suitable (but often lengthy and tedious) manipulations of the right hand side of (4‴) usually allow the elimination of $\boldsymbol{Z}(t)$ and the writing of the system in the form (16), where $\boldsymbol{x}(t)$ is as defined in (15). A simple example is given in para 2.3.2.

In the case in which the original model has been built in such a way as not to possess a steady state, the situation is simpler. In such a case, in fact, the exogenous variables are not assumed to be functions of time, and so system (4) is autonomous; therefore – as we already said in relation to (14) – the question of uniform convergence does not arise from the beginning.

2.2.4. *Sensitivity*

2.2.4.1. *General results*

As we saw in the previous paragraph, stability depends on the characteristic roots of the matrix $\boldsymbol{A}$. As the characteristic roots of a matrix are functions of the elements of the matrix, and since these elements are functions of the parameters of the model, it is possible to examine the effects of changes in the parameters on the characteristic roots by computing the partial derivatives of such roots with respect to the parameters. This is what we mean by *sensitivity analysis* in dynamical systems.[15] This analysis is particularly useful for the examination of the dynamic behaviour and of the policy implications of the model. For example, the effects on the dynamic behaviour of the model of introducing or excluding a feedback can be determined, and the nature of the cycles, if any are present (e.g. whether a cycle is an inventory cycle) can be ascertained by examining the partial derivatives of the relevant characteristic roots with respect to the parameters concerned. If policy functions are present in the model, it is possible to ascertain the effect of a change in any one of the parameters in these functions on the dynamic properties of the model in a general way, without having to use numerical simulations. This could help with a) the assignment of instruments

[15] To be precise, in the mathematical literature this expression is used in a wider sense (state variable sensitivity, eigensystem sensitivity, etc.: see Laughton, 1964). The definition given in the text follows Wymer (1968, 1976), who was the first to stress the importance of this analysis and to bring Laughton's original work to the attention of econometricians. It is also possible to compute the partial derivatives of the characteristic vectors with respect to the parameters. This, however, is less interesting to our purposes; anyone interested in this is referred to the works of Laughton and Wymer just cited.

to targets,[16] if it turns out that some parameters crucially affect the stability of the model, and b) the computation of the change that one or more policy parameters must undergo in order that certain characteristic roots, and therefore the dynamic behavior of the model, are modified in a given direction (for example, to eliminate or reduce instability or an undesired cyclical component). Suppose that $\lambda_i > 0$ for a given i and let ϑ_l be a policy parameter; to reduce instability we must change ϑ_l in such a way as to decrease λ_i (possibly to make it negative). Indicating by $\mathrm{d}\lambda_i < 0$ the desired change in λ_i, starting from the (partial) differential $\mathrm{d}\lambda_i = (\partial\lambda_i/\partial\vartheta_l)\,\mathrm{d}\vartheta_l$ we obtain to a first approximation[17] $\mathrm{d}\vartheta_l = (\partial\lambda_i/\partial\vartheta_l)^{-1}\,\mathrm{d}\lambda_i$. Of course it will be necessary to check that other characteristic roots are not affected to an undesirable extent, that is we shall have to compute all the partial differentials $\mathrm{d}\lambda_j = (\partial\lambda_j/\partial\vartheta_l)\,\mathrm{d}\vartheta_l = (\partial\lambda_j/\partial\vartheta_l)(\partial\lambda_i/\partial\vartheta_l)^{-1}\,\mathrm{d}\lambda_i$, $j \neq i$, and check that the real parts of $\lambda_j + \mathrm{d}\lambda_j$ do not become positive given $\mathrm{Re}(\lambda_j) < 0$, and so on.

It is well known that – assuming distinct characteristic roots[18] – the following diagonalization relationship holds:

$$\boldsymbol{\Lambda} = \boldsymbol{H}^{-1}\boldsymbol{A}\boldsymbol{H}, \tag{17}$$

where $\boldsymbol{\Lambda}$ is the diagonal matrix of characteristic roots λ_i and $\boldsymbol{H}$ is the matrix of characteristic vectors.

As we shall prove presently the matrix of the partial derivatives of the ith characteristic root with respect to the elements a_{jk} of $\boldsymbol{A}$

[16]For a general treatment of the "assignment problem" see Gandolfo (1980, Part I, ch. 9, § 6). In the context under examination, the problem is slightly different. Suppose, for example, that $\lambda_i > 0$ is a positive characteristic root and that $\partial\lambda_i/\partial\vartheta_l < 0$, where ϑ_l is a parameter in a policy function. Now, to achieve stability an increase in ϑ_l is required, but suppose that ϑ_l cannot be increased (e.g. for institutional or other reasons): this could signal the fact that the policy assignment underlying the way in which ϑ_l was included in the policy function is incorrect and needs revision.

[17]The partial derivatives $\partial\lambda_i/\partial\vartheta_l$ are usually fairly invariant; therefore, the change in the characteristic roots are generally consistent with these derivatives even for large changes in the parameters, and vice-versa.

[18]This does not involve an appreciable loss of generality. In fact, since the characteristic roots of a matrix are continuous functions of its elements, if the matrix $\boldsymbol{A}$ has multiple roots, a slight alteration to any coefficient produces a neighbour system with distinct roots that for all practical purposes is the same as the original system.

(these partial derivatives are also called *sensitivity coefficients*) is given by

$$\frac{\partial \lambda_i}{\partial \boldsymbol{A}} = \left[\frac{\partial \lambda_i}{\partial a_{jk}} \right] = \boldsymbol{h}_i^* \boldsymbol{h}_i^{\mathrm{T}}, \qquad i = 1, 2, \ldots, m, \tag{18}$$

where $\boldsymbol{h}_i^*$ is the column vector obtained by transposing the ith row of $\boldsymbol{H}^{-1}$ and $\boldsymbol{h}_i^{\mathrm{T}}$ is the row vector obtained by transposing the ith column of $\boldsymbol{H}$ (the superscript T denotes transposition). Of course, there will be as many matrices as characteristic roots.

Now, since the elements a_{jk} are differentiable functions of the parameters, $a_{jk} = a_{jk}(\vartheta_1, \vartheta_2, \ldots, \vartheta_p)$, denoting by ϑ_l the lth parameter ($l = 1, 2, \ldots, p$), we have

$$\frac{\partial \lambda_i}{\partial \vartheta_l} = \sum_j \sum_k \frac{\partial \lambda_i}{\partial a_{jk}} \frac{\partial a_{jk}}{\partial \vartheta_l}, \qquad i = 1, 2, \ldots, n; \quad l = 1, 2, \ldots, p, \tag{19}$$

where, for each i, the partial derivatives $\partial \lambda_i / \partial a_{jk}$ are the elements of the matrix (18). In general these derivatives seem to be fairly invariant with respect to the point where they have been computed, and this means that – even if the application of eqs. (19) requires the computation of the characteristic roots and vectors – the results that we obtain partake of the nature of qualitative results[19]. Let us note that several terms in the double summation (19) will usually be zero, because not all the parameters will appear as arguments in all the elements a_{jk}.

The proof of the basic result (18) is rather difficult and lengthy; the reader who is not interested in this can skip the next paragraph and turn to section 2.3 without loss with regard to the main argument.

2.2.4.2. *Proof of the basic formula for the sensitivity matrix*

Let $\boldsymbol{A}$ be a square matrix, whose characteristic equation is $|\boldsymbol{A} - \lambda \boldsymbol{I}| = 0$, and let us consider a finite change δa_{kl} in the element a_{kl}, *ceteris paribus*. The procedure that we shall follow is to compute the

[19]See below, end of para. 2.3.1.

consequent change $\delta\lambda_j$ in the jth characteristic root λ_j, and to apply the definition of partial derivative as the limit of the (partial) difference quotient $\delta\lambda_j/\delta a_{kl}$ as δa_{kl} tends to zero.[20]

Denoting by $\boldsymbol{E}_{kl}$ a square matrix (of the same order as $\boldsymbol{A}$), all of whose entries are zero except for the element in position (k, l), which is equal to 1, the new matrix is $[\boldsymbol{A} + \delta a_{kl}\boldsymbol{E}_{kl}]$ and its characteristic equation is $|\boldsymbol{A} + \delta a_{kl}\boldsymbol{E}_{kl} - \lambda \boldsymbol{I}| = 0$. Since this matrix differs from the previous one only by the component δa_{kl}, it can easily be seen that, by expanding the characteristic determinant according to elements of the line containing the element (k, l) (kth row or lth column), the new characteristic determinant is equal to the previous one plus the product of δa_{kl} by the cofactor of element (k, l) in the previous matrix. Formally,

$$|\boldsymbol{A} + \delta a_{kl}\boldsymbol{E}_{kl} - \lambda \boldsymbol{I}| = |\boldsymbol{A} - \lambda \boldsymbol{I}| + \delta a_{kl}\Delta_{kl}(\lambda), \tag{20}$$

where $\Delta_{kl}(\lambda)$, a function of λ, denotes the cofactor of element (k, l) in the matrix $[\boldsymbol{A} - \lambda \boldsymbol{I}]$.

As the characteristic equation is a polynomial of degree n in λ which may be written, according to a well known theorem in algebra, as the product of the differences between λ and each characteristic root, we have[21]

$$\prod_i (\lambda'_i - \lambda) = \prod_i (\lambda_i - \lambda) + \delta a_{kl}\Delta_{kl}(\lambda), \tag{21}$$

where λ'_i are the characteristic roots of $[\boldsymbol{A} + \delta a_{kl}\boldsymbol{E}_{kl}]$ and λ_i are the roots of $\boldsymbol{A}$.

Consider now a generic root λ_j, and let $\lambda = \lambda_j$ in (21). Then the first term on the r.h.s. becomes zero; the l.h.s., defining $\lambda'_j - \lambda_j = \delta\lambda_j$, becomes $\delta\lambda_j \Pi_{i \neq j}(\lambda'_i - \lambda_j)$ and so

$$\frac{\delta\lambda_j}{\delta a_{kl}} = \frac{\Delta_{kl}(\lambda_j)}{\prod_{i \neq j} (\lambda'_i - \lambda_j)}. \tag{22}$$

[20] Ours is an elaboration of Laughton's (1964, pp. 580–2) original proof. For the notions of matrix algebra that will be used in this paragraph, see, e.g., Frazer, Duncan, and Collar (1938); Gantmacher (1959, Vol. I).

[21] Let us assume distinct roots (see footnote (18)). As the coefficient of λ^n in the characteristic polynomial is $(-1)^n$, the form is $(-1)^n \Pi_i(\lambda - \lambda_i)$. As $(\lambda - \lambda_i) = -(\lambda_i - \lambda)$, $i = 1, 2, \ldots, n$, we have $\Pi_i(\lambda - \lambda_i) = (-1)^n \Pi_i(\lambda_i - \lambda)$ and so $(-1)^n \Pi_i(\lambda - \lambda_i) = (-1)^{2n} \Pi_i(\lambda_i - \lambda) = \Pi_i(\lambda_i - \lambda)$.

In the limit, as δa_{kl} tends to zero, λ_i' tends to λ_i and so, as

$$\partial\lambda_j/\partial a_{kl} = \lim_{\delta a_{kl}\to 0} \delta\lambda_j/\delta a_{kl},$$

we have

$$\frac{\partial\lambda_j}{\partial a_{kl}} = \frac{\Delta_{kl}(\lambda_j)}{\prod_{i\neq j}(\lambda_i - \lambda_j)}. \tag{23}$$

Let us now obtain an alternative expression for the denominator in (23). By differentiating the identity $|A - \lambda I| = \prod_i(\lambda_i - \lambda)$ with respect to λ, we obtain

$$\left(\frac{\mathrm{d}}{\mathrm{d}\lambda}|A - \lambda I|\right)_{\lambda=\lambda_j} = \left(\frac{\mathrm{d}}{\mathrm{d}\lambda}\prod_i(\lambda_i - \lambda)\right)_{\lambda=\lambda_j}. \tag{23$'$}$$

Use of the rule for differentiating a product yields

$$\frac{\mathrm{d}}{\mathrm{d}\lambda}\prod_i(\lambda_i - \lambda) = -\sum_h \prod_{i\neq h}(\lambda_i - \lambda). \tag{23$''$}$$

It is clear that for $\lambda = \lambda_j$ all the products become zero except for the one in which $h = j$ (in fact, in it, the term $(\lambda_j - \lambda_j)$—which derives from having set $\lambda = \lambda_j$ and $i = j$—does not appear). Thus we get

$$\left(\frac{\mathrm{d}}{\mathrm{d}\lambda}|A - \lambda I|\right)_{\lambda=\lambda_j} = -\prod_{i\neq j}(\lambda_i - \lambda_j). \tag{24}$$

For simplicity of notation let us denote the expression $(\mathrm{d}/\mathrm{d}\lambda)|A - \lambda I|$ by $\Delta^{(1)}(\lambda)$. It follows that an alternative expression for the partial derivative (23) is

$$\frac{\partial\lambda_j}{\partial a_{kl}} = -\frac{\Delta_{kl}(\lambda_j)}{\Delta^{(1)}(\lambda_j)}. \tag{25}$$

Recalling the definition of adjoint matrix, the matrix whose elements are the cofactors $\Delta_{kl}(\lambda)$, $k, l = 1, 2, \ldots, n$ is the *transpose* of the adjoint of the matrix $[A - \lambda_j I]$, and so the matrix whose elements are the partial derivatives $\partial\lambda_j/\partial a_{kl}$, $k, l = 1, 2, \ldots, n$, is

$$\left[\frac{\partial\lambda_j}{\partial a_{kl}}\right] = -\frac{\{\mathrm{adj}[A - \lambda_j I]\}^{\mathrm{T}}}{\Delta^{(1)}(\lambda_j)}. \tag{26}$$

Equation (26) is a first expression for the matrix we are interested in. However, the form (18) is more useful for practical purposes also because the characteristic vectors are a standard output in current computer programs. Therefore the next step is to show how to transform (26) into (18). Let us begin by observing that, as we have assumed distinct characteristic roots, the matrix $[\boldsymbol{A} - \lambda_j \boldsymbol{I}]$ is simply degenerate and the adjoint $\{\text{adj}\,[\boldsymbol{A} - \lambda_j \boldsymbol{I}]\}$ is a matrix of unit rank expressible as the product of two vectors (Frazer *et al.*, 1938, p. 61) and, to be precise, of a column vector proportional to any non-zero column of the matrix $\{\text{adj}\,[\boldsymbol{A} - \lambda_j \boldsymbol{I}]\}$ and of a row vector proportional to any non-zero row of the same matrix,[22] that is

$$\{\text{adj}[\boldsymbol{A} - \lambda_j \boldsymbol{I}]\} = \underset{(n\times 1)}{\boldsymbol{W}_j} \; \underset{(1\times n)}{\boldsymbol{U}_j} \; . \tag{27}$$

Furthermore, as by definition the product of a matrix by its adjoint is a diagonal matrix all of whose diagonal entries are equal to the determinant of the matrix, that is

$$[\boldsymbol{A} - \lambda \boldsymbol{I}]\{\text{adj}[\boldsymbol{A} - \lambda \boldsymbol{I}]\} = |\boldsymbol{A} - \lambda \boldsymbol{I}|\boldsymbol{I}, \tag{28}$$

it follows that

$$\begin{aligned}\frac{\mathrm{d}}{\mathrm{d}\lambda}([\boldsymbol{A} - \lambda \boldsymbol{I}]\{\text{adj}[\boldsymbol{A} - \lambda \boldsymbol{I}]\}) &= \left(\frac{\mathrm{d}}{\mathrm{d}\lambda}|\boldsymbol{A} - \lambda \boldsymbol{I}|\right)\boldsymbol{I} \\ &= \Delta^{(1)}(\lambda)\boldsymbol{I}.\end{aligned} \tag{28$'$}$$

By carrying out the differentiation of the first member in (28′), according to the product rule, we obtain

$$\begin{aligned}&\{\text{adj}[\boldsymbol{A} - \lambda \boldsymbol{I}]\}\frac{\mathrm{d}}{\mathrm{d}\lambda}[\boldsymbol{A} - \lambda \boldsymbol{I}] \\ &\quad + [\boldsymbol{A} - \lambda \boldsymbol{I}]\frac{\mathrm{d}}{\mathrm{d}\lambda}\{\text{adj}[\boldsymbol{A} - \lambda \boldsymbol{I}]\} = \Delta^{(1)}(\lambda)\boldsymbol{I}.\end{aligned} \tag{29}$$

If we premultiply by $\{\text{adj}\,[\boldsymbol{A} - \lambda \boldsymbol{I}]\}$ and recall that $(\mathrm{d}/\mathrm{d}\lambda)[\boldsymbol{A} - \lambda \boldsymbol{I}] = -\boldsymbol{I}$, we get

$$\begin{aligned}&- \{\text{adj}[\boldsymbol{A} - \lambda \boldsymbol{I}]\}^2 \\ &\quad + \{\text{adj}[\boldsymbol{A} - \lambda \boldsymbol{I}]\}[\boldsymbol{A} - \lambda \boldsymbol{I}]\frac{\mathrm{d}}{\mathrm{d}\lambda}\{\text{adj}[\boldsymbol{A} - \lambda \boldsymbol{I}]\} \\ &\quad = \{\text{adj}[\boldsymbol{A} - \lambda \boldsymbol{I}]\}\Delta^{(1)}(\lambda).\end{aligned} \tag{29$'$}$$

[22] Frazer *et al.*, (1938, p. 20). Actually, a matrix of rank 1 has one linearly independent column and one linearly independent row. See also *op. cit.*, p. 65.

If we let $\lambda = \lambda_j$ and remember that $\{\text{adj}[\boldsymbol{A} - \lambda \boldsymbol{I}]\}[\boldsymbol{A} - \lambda \boldsymbol{I}] = |\boldsymbol{A} - \lambda \boldsymbol{I}|\boldsymbol{I}$ which is zero for $\lambda = \lambda_j$ (by definition of characteristic equation and of characteristic root), we have

$$-\{\text{adj}[\boldsymbol{A} - \lambda_j \boldsymbol{I}]\}^2 = \{\text{adj}[\boldsymbol{A} - \lambda_j \boldsymbol{I}]\}\Delta^{(1)}(\lambda_j), \tag{30}$$

whence, using (27) and changing sign

$$\underset{(n\times 1)}{(\boldsymbol{W}_j} \ \underset{(1\times n)}{\boldsymbol{U}_j)} \ \underset{(n\times 1)}{(\boldsymbol{W}_j} \ \underset{(1\times n)}{\boldsymbol{U}_j)} = -\Delta^{(1)}(\lambda_j)\{\text{adj}[\boldsymbol{A} - \lambda_j \boldsymbol{I}]\}. \tag{31}$$

Now, $(\boldsymbol{W}_j\boldsymbol{U}_j)(\boldsymbol{W}_j\boldsymbol{U}_j) = \boldsymbol{W}_j(\boldsymbol{U}_j\boldsymbol{W}_j)\boldsymbol{U}_j = (\boldsymbol{U}_j\boldsymbol{W}_j)\boldsymbol{W}_j\boldsymbol{U}_j$ because $\boldsymbol{U}_j\boldsymbol{W}_j$ is a scalar; and since $\boldsymbol{W}_j\boldsymbol{U}_j = \{\text{adj}\,\boldsymbol{A} - \lambda \boldsymbol{I}\}$, eq. (31) becomes

$$\boldsymbol{U}_j\boldsymbol{W}_j\{\text{adj}[\boldsymbol{A} - \lambda_j \boldsymbol{I}]\} = -\Delta^{(1)}(\lambda_j)\{\text{adj}[\boldsymbol{A} - \lambda_j \boldsymbol{I}]\}, \tag{32}$$

and so

$$-\Delta^{(1)}(\lambda_j) = \boldsymbol{U}_j\boldsymbol{W}_j. \tag{33}$$

Thus we can write, using (27) and (33)

$$\frac{\{\text{adj}[\boldsymbol{A} - \lambda_j \boldsymbol{I}]\}}{-\Delta^{(1)}(\lambda_j)} = \frac{\boldsymbol{W}_j\boldsymbol{U}_j}{\boldsymbol{U}_j\boldsymbol{W}_j} = \boldsymbol{W}_j\frac{\boldsymbol{U}_j}{\boldsymbol{U}_j\boldsymbol{W}_j}. \tag{34}$$

Let us now consider the relationship[23]

$$\boldsymbol{U}\boldsymbol{W} = -\boldsymbol{D}, \tag{35}$$

where $\boldsymbol{U}$ is the matrix whose jth row is $\boldsymbol{U}_j$, $\boldsymbol{W}$ is the matrix whose

[23]A proof of eq. (35) is the following. We first prove that

$$\{\text{adj}[\boldsymbol{A} - \lambda_p \boldsymbol{I}]\}\{\text{adj}[\boldsymbol{A} - \lambda_q \boldsymbol{I}]\} = \boldsymbol{0}, \quad p \neq q. \tag{a}$$

To this purpose, consider the characteristic equation $|\boldsymbol{A} - \lambda \boldsymbol{I}| = (-1)^n \Pi_i(\lambda - \lambda_i) = 0$.

According to the Cayley–Hamilton theorem, every matrix satisfies its characteristic equation, and so

$$(-1)^n \prod_j [\boldsymbol{A} - \lambda_j \boldsymbol{I}] = \boldsymbol{0}, \tag{b}$$

where the order of the j's is arbitrary, as it is arbitrary in the characteristic equation. This means that any $[\boldsymbol{A} - \lambda_j \boldsymbol{I}]$ can be put in the first place in (b). Let us also recall that

$$\{\text{adj}[\boldsymbol{A} - \lambda_r \boldsymbol{I}]\}[\boldsymbol{A} - \lambda_r \boldsymbol{I}] = |\boldsymbol{A} - \lambda_r \boldsymbol{I}|\boldsymbol{I} = \boldsymbol{0}, \tag{c}$$

because $|\boldsymbol{A} - \lambda_r \boldsymbol{I}| = 0$ by definition of characteristic root. Eq. (b) can be rewritten as

$$\left\{(-1)^n \prod_{j\neq r} [\boldsymbol{A} - \lambda_j \boldsymbol{I}]\right\}[\boldsymbol{A} - \lambda_r \boldsymbol{I}] = \boldsymbol{0}. \tag{d}$$

jth column is $\boldsymbol{W}_j$, and $\boldsymbol{D}$ is the diagonal matrix whose (j,j) entry is $\Delta^{(1)}(\lambda_j)$. If we premultiply both members by $-\boldsymbol{D}^{-1}$ we have

$$-\boldsymbol{D}^{-1}\boldsymbol{U}\boldsymbol{W} = \boldsymbol{I}, \tag{36}$$

and so, given the definition of inverse matrix, it must be

$$-\boldsymbol{D}^{-1}\boldsymbol{U} = \boldsymbol{W}^{-1}. \tag{37}$$

The (j,j) entry of $-\boldsymbol{D}^{-1}$ is $-1/\Delta^{(1)}(\lambda_j)$, and so the jth row of $-\boldsymbol{D}^{-1}\boldsymbol{U}$ is $\boldsymbol{U}_j/\boldsymbol{U}_j\boldsymbol{W}_j$. Given (37), such a row is the jth row of $\boldsymbol{W}^{-1}$.

Let us now note that the characteristic vector $\boldsymbol{h}_j$ associated with the characteristic root λ_j can be taken proportional to the cofactors of any line of $[\boldsymbol{A} - \lambda_j\boldsymbol{I}]$ and so proportional to the elements of any non-zero line of $\{\text{adj}[\boldsymbol{A} - \lambda_j\boldsymbol{I}]\}$ so that, considering any non-zero column of the latter matrix we get, apart from scalar multiples, $\boldsymbol{h}_j = \boldsymbol{W}_j$ and so

$$\boldsymbol{W} = \boldsymbol{H}, \tag{38}$$

From (c) and (d) it follows that

$$\{\text{adj}[\boldsymbol{A} - \lambda_r\boldsymbol{I}]\} = \left\{(-1)^n \prod_{j\neq r} [\boldsymbol{A} - \lambda_j\boldsymbol{I}]\right\}. \tag{e}$$

Thus, by letting $r = p$ and then $r = q$ in (e), we have

$$\{\text{adj}[\boldsymbol{A} - \lambda_p\boldsymbol{I}]\}\{\text{adj}[\boldsymbol{A} - \lambda_q\boldsymbol{I}]\} = (-1)^{2n} \prod_{j\neq p} [\boldsymbol{A} - \lambda_j\boldsymbol{I}] \prod_{j\neq q} [\boldsymbol{A} - \lambda_j\boldsymbol{I}]$$

$$= \prod_{j} [\boldsymbol{A} - \lambda_j\boldsymbol{I}] \prod_{\substack{j\neq p\\ j\neq q}} [\boldsymbol{A} - \lambda_j\boldsymbol{I}] = \boldsymbol{0}, \tag{f}$$

where the index $j = p$ has been shifted from the second to the first $\prod$, and where the equality to $\boldsymbol{0}$ derives from (b). This proves (a).

Using (27) we can rewrite (a) as

$$\boldsymbol{W}_p\boldsymbol{U}_p\boldsymbol{W}_q\boldsymbol{U}_q = \boldsymbol{0}. \tag{a'}$$

Now, $(\boldsymbol{W}_p\boldsymbol{U}_p)(\boldsymbol{W}_q\boldsymbol{U}_q) = \boldsymbol{W}_p(\boldsymbol{U}_p\boldsymbol{W}_q)\boldsymbol{U}_q = (\boldsymbol{U}_p\boldsymbol{W}_q)\boldsymbol{W}_p\boldsymbol{U}_q$. This expression is a zero matrix either if the scalar $\boldsymbol{U}_p\boldsymbol{W}_q$ is zero or if $\boldsymbol{W}_p\boldsymbol{U}_q$ is a zero matrix. In the second case it is necessary that at least one of the vectors $\boldsymbol{W}_p$ and $\boldsymbol{U}_q$ is a zero vector: in fact, suppose that an arbitrary component w_k of $\boldsymbol{W}_p$ and u_l of $\boldsymbol{U}_q$ are different from zero; then element (k,l) in the matrix $\boldsymbol{W}_p\boldsymbol{U}_q$, which is $w_k u_l$, will be non-zero, and $\boldsymbol{W}_p\boldsymbol{U}_q$ cannot be a zero matrix. But $\boldsymbol{W}_p$ and $\boldsymbol{U}_q$ are non-zero by definition. Therefore it must be

$$\boldsymbol{U}_p\boldsymbol{W}_q = 0.$$

Since $\boldsymbol{U}_p\boldsymbol{W}_q$ is element (p,q) in the matrix $\boldsymbol{U}\boldsymbol{W}$, and $p \neq q$, it follows that such a matrix has all zero entries outside the main diagonal and this, together with (33), proves (35).

where $\boldsymbol{H}$ is the matrix of characteristic vectors already defined. Given (38) and (37), eq. (34) can be written as

$$\frac{\{\mathrm{adj}[\boldsymbol{A}-\lambda_j \boldsymbol{I}]\}}{-\Delta^{(1)}(\lambda_j)} = \boldsymbol{h}_j \boldsymbol{h}_j^{-1}, \tag{39}$$

where $\boldsymbol{h}_j^{-1}$ is the jth row of $\boldsymbol{H}^{-1}$. By transposing and denoting $(\boldsymbol{h}_j^{-1})^{\mathrm{T}}$ by $\boldsymbol{h}_j^*$, we have

$$\frac{\{\mathrm{adj}[\boldsymbol{A}-\lambda_j \boldsymbol{I}]\}^{\mathrm{T}}}{-\Delta^{(1)}(\lambda_j)} = \boldsymbol{h}_j^* \boldsymbol{h}_j^{\mathrm{T}}. \tag{40}$$

From (40) and (26) we obtain finally

$$\left[\frac{\partial \lambda_j}{\partial a_{kl}}\right] = \boldsymbol{h}_j^* \boldsymbol{h}_j^{\mathrm{T}}. \tag{41}$$

As the sets of indices j, k, l, coincide with the sets of indices i, j, k, eq. (41) is the same as eq. (18). This completes the proof.

2.3. Some examples

The only purpose of the exposition of the models that follow is to illustrate the methodology explained in the previous paragraphs. Therefore we shall not discuss the validity or economic plausibility of these models.

2.3.1. *Wymer (1976)*

2.3.1.1. *General treatment*

We shall elaborate here the example given by Wymer (1976, pp. 15ff.). Let us consider the system

$$\begin{aligned}
\mathrm{D}\log p &= -\alpha_1 \log\left(\frac{p a Y r^{-\beta}}{M}\right), \qquad \alpha_1 > 0,\\
\mathrm{D}^2 \log M &= \alpha_2 \log\left(\frac{p_f}{p}\right) - \alpha_3(\mathrm{D}\log p - \pi), \quad \alpha_2 > 0, \quad \alpha_3 > 0.
\end{aligned} \tag{42}$$

The first equation specifies the rate of change of the domestic price level as a function of the excess demand for real money balances.[24] M is the nominal volume of money and so M/p is the real volume of money; the demand for real money balances is a function of real income and of the rate of interest such that when r is constant the velocity of circulation is constant and when Y is constant the demand with respect to r is decreasing, convex and asymptotic to the axes. The minus sign is due to the fact that a positive (negative) excess demand exerts a downward (upward) pressure on prices. Thus the first equation is an example of adjustment to excess demand.

The second equation is a policy reaction function, where the change in the rate of change in the money stock depends positively on the ratio of foreign to home prices (the exchange rate is assumed to be fixed and equal to 1) and negatively on the difference between the actual ($\mathrm{D}\log p$) and desired (π) domestic inflation rates. The first term on the r.h.s. of this equation can be considered as connected with the balance of payments (for simplicity identified with the current balance): if, for example, foreign prices are higher than home prices, then a surplus in the balance of payments occurs and the "rules of the game" require that the policy makers favour a monetary expansion. The second term means that the policy makers react to an excessive inflation rate by curbing the rate of monetary expansion.

System (42) is not of the first order but it can be transformed easily into such a system by defining a new variable $m = \mathrm{D}\log M$, so that we have

$$\begin{aligned}
\mathrm{D}\log p &= -\alpha_1 \log\left(\frac{paYr^{-\beta}}{M}\right), \\
\mathrm{D}m &= \alpha_2 \log\left(\frac{p_f}{p}\right) - \alpha_3(\mathrm{D}\log p - \pi), \qquad (42') \\
\mathrm{D}\log M &= m.
\end{aligned}$$

[24] Note that from the mathematical point of view the expressions $aYr^{-\beta}/M/p$ and $paYr^{-\beta}/M$ are equivalent. From the economic point of view the first is the demand for real money balances/real volume of money ratio and the second is the demand for nominal money balances/nominal volume of money ratio.

Let us now assume that the growth paths of the exogenous variables are

$$Y(t) = Y^* e^{\mu t}, \qquad p_f(t) = p_f^* e^{\lambda t}, \qquad r(t) = r^*,$$

and let us apply the method of undetermined coefficients to find the steady state, by trying a particular solution of the type

$$p(t) = p^* e^{\rho_1 t},$$

$$M(t) = M^* e^{\rho_2 t}.$$

Since $\mathrm{D}\log p = \rho_1$, $\mathrm{D}\log M = \rho_2$, $\mathrm{D}m = 0$, substitution in (42′) yields

$$\rho_1 = -\alpha_1 \log \frac{p^* e^{\rho_1 t} a Y^* e^{\mu t} r^{*-\beta}}{M^* e^{\rho_2 t}},$$

$$0 = \alpha_2 \log\left(\frac{p_f^* e^{\lambda t}}{p^* e^{\rho_1 t}}\right) - \alpha_3(\rho_1 - \pi),$$

$$\rho_2 = m,$$

whence (omitting the third equation which does not help us here)

$$\rho_1 = -\alpha_1[\log p^* + \rho_1 t + \log a + \log Y^* + \mu t - \beta \log r^* - \log M^* - \rho_2 t],$$

$$0 = \alpha_2[\log p_f^* + \lambda t - \log p^* - \rho_1 t] - \alpha_3 \rho_1 + \alpha_3 \pi.$$

Let us collect the terms containing t

$$\rho_1 = -\alpha_1[(\rho_1 + \mu - \rho_2)t + \log p^* + \log a + \log Y^* - \beta \log r^* - \log M^*],$$

$$0 = \alpha_2[(\lambda - \rho_1)t + \log p_f^* - \log p^*] - \alpha_3 \rho_1 + \alpha_3 \pi.$$

If we rearrange terms we obtain

$$\alpha_1(\rho_1 + \mu - \rho_2)t + [(\alpha_1 \log p^* - \alpha_1 \log M^*) + \rho_1 + \alpha_1(\log a + \log Y^* - \beta \log r^*)] = 0,$$

$$\alpha_2(\lambda - \rho_1)t + [\alpha_2 \log p_f^* - \alpha_2 \log p^* - \alpha_3 \rho_1 + \alpha_3 \pi] = 0.$$

For these expressions to be identically satisfied the coefficients of t and the expressions in square brackets must be zero. Therefore, equating to zero the coefficients of t

$$\rho_1 + \mu - \rho_2 = 0,$$
$$\lambda - \rho_1 = 0,$$

whence $\rho_1 = \lambda$ and so $\rho_2 = \mu + \lambda$. If we equate to zero the expressions in square brackets, substitute the value of ρ_1 just found, and rearrange terms we have

$$\begin{aligned} -\alpha_1 \log p^* + \alpha_1 \log M^* &= \lambda + \alpha_1(\log a + \log Y^* - \beta \log r^*), \\ \alpha_2 \log p^* &= \alpha_2 \log p_f^* - \alpha_3\lambda + \alpha_3\pi. \end{aligned} \tag{43}$$

From the second equation we obtain immediately

$$\log p^* = \log p_f^* - \alpha_3(\lambda - \pi)/\alpha_2,$$

that is, taking antilogarithms

$$p^* = p_f^* \exp[-\alpha_3(\lambda - \pi)/\alpha_2]. \tag{44}$$

If we substitute (44) in the first equation of (43), divide through by α_1 and rearrange terms we have

$$\begin{aligned} \log M^* = \log p_f^* - \alpha_3(\lambda - \pi)/\alpha_2 + \lambda/\alpha_1 \\ + \log a + \log Y^* - \beta \log r^*, \end{aligned}$$

whence

$$M^* = a p_f^* Y^* r^{*-\beta} \exp\left[\frac{\lambda}{\alpha_1} - \alpha_3\frac{\lambda - \pi}{\alpha_2}\right]. \tag{45}$$

Therefore the steady state solution is

$$p(t) = p^* e^{\lambda t}, \qquad M(t) = M^* e^{(\mu + \lambda)t}, \tag{46}$$

where p^* and M^* are given by (44) and (45).

Note that, as stated in footnote 8, the ρ_i have been obtained by equating to zero the coefficients of the terms containing t, whereas the initial levels of the steady states have been obtained by equating to zero all the other terms (in which the previously found values of the ρ_i have been substituted).

As the steady state growth rates are very simple linear functions of the exogenous growth rates, the *comparative dynamics* analysis is quite easy: it is immediately obvious that $\partial\rho_1/\partial\mu = 0$, $\partial\rho_1/\partial\lambda = 1$, $\partial\rho_2/\partial\mu = 1$, $\partial\rho_2/\partial\lambda = 1$. Thus an increase in the steady state growth rate of income increases the steady state growth rate of the volume of money only, whereas an increase in the growth rate of foreign prices, increases the steady-state growth rate of both endogenous variables.

To complete the comparative dynamics analysis, the partial derivatives of p^* and M^* with respect to the parameters should be computed. As an example, consider

$$\partial p^*/\partial \alpha_3 = [-(\lambda - \pi)/\alpha_2]\, p^*,$$
$$\partial M^*/\partial \alpha_3 = [-(\lambda - \pi)/\alpha_2]\, M^*.$$

It follows that an increase in the policy parameter which expresses the authorities' reaction to a divergence between the desired and the actual rate of inflation raises (lowers) the position of the steady state growth paths of domestic prices and of the volume of money according to whether the growth rate of income is greater (smaller) than the desired rate of inflation.

Let us now come to stability analysis. System (42′) can be written, by substituting from the first into the second equation

$$\begin{aligned} \mathrm{D}\log p &= -\alpha_1 \log p + \alpha_1 \log M \\ &\quad + [\alpha_1 \beta \log r - \alpha_1 \log Y - \alpha_1 \log a], \\ \mathrm{D}m &= (\alpha_1\alpha_3 - \alpha_2)\log p - \alpha_1\alpha_3 \log M + [\alpha_1\alpha_3 \log Y \\ &\quad - \alpha_1\alpha_3\beta \log r + \alpha_2 \log p_f + \alpha_1\alpha_3 \log a + \alpha_3\pi], \\ \mathrm{D}\log M &= m, \end{aligned} \tag{47}$$

that is, in matrix form

$$\mathrm{D}\boldsymbol{X}(t) = \boldsymbol{A}\boldsymbol{X}(t) + \boldsymbol{B}\boldsymbol{Z}(t), \tag{47′}$$

where

$$\boldsymbol{X}(t) = \begin{bmatrix} \log p \\ m \\ \log M \end{bmatrix}, \qquad \boldsymbol{Z}(t) = \begin{bmatrix} \log Y \\ \log r \\ \log p_f \\ 1 \end{bmatrix},$$

$$\boldsymbol{A} = \begin{bmatrix} -\alpha_1 & 0 & \alpha_1 \\ \alpha_1\alpha_3 - \alpha_2 & 0 & -\alpha_1\alpha_3 \\ 0 & 1 & 0 \end{bmatrix},$$

$$\boldsymbol{B} = \begin{bmatrix} -\alpha_1 & \alpha_1\beta & 0 & -\alpha_1 \log a \\ \alpha_1\alpha_3 & -\alpha_1\alpha_3\beta & \alpha_2 & \alpha_1\alpha_3 \log a + \alpha_3\pi \\ 0 & 0 & 0 & 0 \end{bmatrix}.$$

System (47) is already linear and with constant coefficients, so that no linearization procedure is required. A particular solution to this non-homogeneous system is given by (46); the stability will depend on the roots of the characteristic equation of the matrix $\boldsymbol{A}$, which turns out to be

$$\begin{vmatrix} -\alpha_1 - \lambda & 0 & \alpha_1 \\ \alpha_1\alpha_3 - \alpha_2 & -\lambda & -\alpha_1\alpha_3 \\ 0 & 1 & -\lambda \end{vmatrix} = -\lambda^3 - \alpha_1\lambda^2 - \alpha_1\alpha_3\lambda - \alpha_1\alpha_2 = 0,$$

that is

$$\lambda^3 + \alpha_1\lambda^2 + \alpha_1\alpha_3\lambda + \alpha_1\alpha_2 = 0. \tag{48}$$

As the coefficients are all positive, all that remains is to check the condition (Gandolfo, 1980, Part II, ch. 6)

$$\alpha_1^2\alpha_3 - \alpha_1\alpha_2 > 0,$$

that is

$$\alpha_1\alpha_3 - \alpha_2 > 0. \tag{49}$$

This condition means that the product of the speed with which prices react to excess demand for real balances and the reaction coefficient of the authorities to the discrepancy between the desired and actual inflation rates should be greater than the coefficient which measures the effect of the balance of payments on the change in the rate of growth of the money stock. As α_3 (and possibly α_2) is a policy parameter, in principle it is always possible to make (49) verified by setting $\alpha_3 > \alpha_2/\alpha_1$. In the contrary case, explosive oscillations will occur.

Let us now assume the following numerical values: $\alpha_1 = 0.5$, $\alpha_2 = 0.9$, $\alpha_3 = 1.6$ and carry out the *sensitivity analysis*. The detailed passages are shown in para. 2.3.1.2. Here we shall simply examine the results. The characteristic equation turns out to be $-\lambda^3 - 0.5\lambda^2 - 0.8\lambda - 0.45 = 0$, and the characteristic roots are

$$\lambda_1 \simeq -0.546,$$

$$\lambda_2, \lambda_3 \simeq 0.023 \pm 0.908i.$$

Therefore, explosive oscillations will take place.

The partial derivatives of the characteristic roots with respect to the parameters are

$$\frac{\partial\lambda_1}{\partial\alpha_1} \simeq -0.28, \qquad \frac{\partial\lambda_1}{\partial\alpha_2} \simeq 0.44, \qquad \frac{\partial\lambda_1}{\partial\alpha_3} \simeq 0.24,$$

$$\frac{\partial\lambda_{2,3}}{\partial\alpha_1} \simeq -0.36 \pm 0.68\mathrm{i}, \qquad \frac{\partial\lambda_{2,3}}{\partial\alpha_2} \simeq 0.22 \pm 0.14\mathrm{i},$$

$$\frac{\partial\lambda_{2,3}}{\partial\alpha_3} \simeq -0.12 \pm 0.20\mathrm{i}.$$

These results confirm the stabilizing effect of including the inflation term in the policy reaction function. An increase in α_3, in fact, reduces the real part of the complex roots, that is the amplitude of the cycles.[25] On the contrary, a decrease in α_3 has destabilizing effects: in the limit, setting α_3 to zero, the characteristic equation becomes

$$-\lambda^3 - 0.5\lambda^2 - 0.45 = 0,$$

whose characteristic roots are

$$\lambda_1 \simeq -0.974, \qquad \lambda_2, \lambda_3 \simeq 0.237 \pm 0.637\mathrm{i},$$

so that when the policy reaction function lacks the inflation term, the oscillatory behaviour of the model becomes more unstable. Note that despite the large change in α_3 the change in the characteristic roots is consistent with the partial derivatives concerned: for example, $\mathrm{d}\lambda_1 \simeq -0.429$, whereas by using the partial derivative of λ_1 with respect to α_3, we have

$$\mathrm{d}\lambda_1 = (\partial\lambda_1/\partial\alpha_3)\,\mathrm{d}\alpha_3 \simeq 0.24 \times (-1.6) \simeq -0.384.$$

This confirms what we said in general with reference to eq. (19), that the partial derivatives of the characteristic roots with respect to the parameters are fairly invariant, so that the results that we obtain are quite close to qualitative results.

[25]An increase in α_3 increases λ_1, and this is an unfavourable effect. However, it is possible to increase α_3 without making λ_1 positive: eq. (48), in fact, cannot have positive real roots. Therefore, a slower convergence of the monotonic term is more than compensated by a reduction in the amplitude of the oscillatory terms. It can easily be checked, by using condition (49), that the critical value of α_3 is 1.8: namely, for $\alpha_3 \lesseqqgtr 1.8$ the complex roots will have a positive, zero, negative real part respectively.

2.3.1.2. A numerical example

In this paragraph we shall derive the numerical results stated at the end of the previous paragraph. This can serve as an illustration of the general formulae proved in paragraph 2.2.4.2 and can be skipped by those readers who are not interested in numerical computations without loss for the main argument.

With the given numerical values of the parameters the matrix $\boldsymbol{A}$ becomes

$$\boldsymbol{A} = \begin{bmatrix} -0.5 & 0 & 0.5 \\ -0.1 & 0 & -0.8 \\ 0 & 1 & 0 \end{bmatrix} \quad \text{and so}$$

$$[\boldsymbol{A} - \lambda \boldsymbol{I}] = \begin{bmatrix} -0.5-\lambda & 0 & 0.5 \\ -0.1 & -\lambda & -0.8 \\ 0 & 1 & -\lambda \end{bmatrix}.$$

Therefore

$$|\boldsymbol{A} - \lambda \boldsymbol{I}| = -\lambda^3 - 0.5\lambda^2 - 0.8\lambda - 0.45 = 0,$$

whose solution yields

$$\lambda_1 = -0.54555278,$$

$$\lambda_2, \lambda_3 = 0.02277639 \pm 0.907927685\mathrm{i}.$$

As the complex roots have a positive real part, an unstable cycle will occur, with period equal to $2\pi/0.907927685 \cong 6.92$ units of time (years, assuming that the unit is one year). That the model is unstable can also be seen from the fact that condition (49) is not verified.

Let us now come to sensitivity analysis. For convenience we put the derivatives $\partial a_{jk}/\partial \alpha_l$ together in matrices, which turn out to be

$$\left[\frac{\partial a_{jk}}{\partial \alpha_1}\right] = \begin{bmatrix} -1 & 0 & 1 \\ \alpha_3(1.6) & 0 & -\alpha_3(-1.6) \\ 0 & 0 & 0 \end{bmatrix},$$

$$\left[\frac{\partial a_{jk}}{\partial \alpha_2}\right] = \begin{bmatrix} 0 & 0 & 0 \\ -1 & 0 & 0 \\ 0 & 0 & 0 \end{bmatrix},$$

$$\left[\frac{\partial a_{jk}}{\partial \alpha_3}\right] = \begin{bmatrix} 0 & 0 & 0 \\ \alpha_1(0.5) & 0 & -\alpha_1(-0.5) \\ 0 & 0 & 0 \end{bmatrix},$$

where the numerical values resulting from the assumptions are denoted in parentheses where necessary.

We must now compute the matrices $[\partial\lambda_i/\partial a_{jk}]$. Let us begin with λ_1. We have

$$[\boldsymbol{A} - \lambda_1 \boldsymbol{I}] = \begin{bmatrix} 0.04555278 & 0 & 0.5 \\ -0.1 & 0.54555278 & -0.8 \\ 0 & 1 & 0.54555278 \end{bmatrix}.$$

In the case of manual computations it is easier to apply (26) rather than (18): in fact, if we are not concerned with the characteristic vectors, their computation can be omitted and (26) is less laborious than (18). However, to illustrate the procedure fully, we shall also apply (18). We have

$$\Delta^{(1)}(\lambda_1) = \left[\frac{\mathrm{d}}{\mathrm{d}\lambda}(-\lambda^3 - 0.5\lambda^2 - 0.8\lambda - 0.45)\right]_{\lambda=\lambda_1}$$

$$= [-3\lambda^2 - \lambda - 0.8]_{\lambda=\lambda_1} = -1.147330727.$$

Alternatively

$$\Delta^{(1)}(\lambda_1) = -(\lambda_2 - \lambda_1)(\lambda_3 - \lambda_1)$$

$$= -(0.568329 + 0.907928\mathrm{i})(0.568329 - 0.907928\mathrm{i})$$

$$= -1.14733.$$

Furthermore,

$$\{\mathrm{adj}[\boldsymbol{A} - \lambda_1 \boldsymbol{I}]\}$$

$$= \begin{bmatrix} 1.097628 & 0.5 & -0.27277639 \\ 0.054553 & 0.0248514 & -0.013559 \\ -0.1 & -0.04555278 & 0.0248514 \end{bmatrix}.$$

Incidentally note that, as stated in (27), this matrix can be expressed as the product, e.g., of the column vector $\boldsymbol{W}_j$ equal to the first column and of the row vector $\boldsymbol{U}_j$ proportional (according to the coefficient 1/1.097628) to the first row, that is

$$\{\mathrm{adj}[\boldsymbol{A} - \lambda_1 \boldsymbol{I}]\}$$

$$= \begin{bmatrix} 1.097628 \\ 0.054553 \\ -0.1 \end{bmatrix} \begin{bmatrix} 1 & \dfrac{0.5}{1.097628} & \dfrac{-0.27277639}{1.097628} \end{bmatrix}.$$

Therefore

$$\{\text{adj}[\boldsymbol{A} - \lambda_1 \boldsymbol{I}]\}^{\mathrm{T}}$$

$$= \begin{bmatrix} 1.097628 & 0.054553 & -0.1 \\ 0.5 & 0.0248514 & -0.04555278 \\ -0.27277639 & -0.013559 & 0.0248514 \end{bmatrix},$$

and so, applying (26),

$$\left[\frac{\partial \lambda_1}{\partial a_{kl}}\right] = -\frac{\{\text{adj}[\boldsymbol{A} - \lambda_1 \boldsymbol{I}]\}^{\mathrm{T}}}{\Delta^{(1)}(\lambda_1)}$$

$$= \begin{bmatrix} 0.956680 & 0.047548 & -0.087159 \\ 0.435794 & 0.021660 & -0.0397033 \\ -0.237749 & -0.011818 & 0.0216602 \end{bmatrix}.$$

Let us now pass to the application of (18). This requires the computation of the characteristic vectors associated with each root, and so we must write, in addition to $[\boldsymbol{A} - \lambda_1 \boldsymbol{I}]$, also the expression for $[\boldsymbol{A} - \lambda_{2,3} \boldsymbol{I}]$, which is

$$[\boldsymbol{A} - \lambda_{2,3} \boldsymbol{I}]$$

$$= \begin{bmatrix} -0.52277639 \mp 0.907927685\mathrm{i} & 0 & -0.5 \\ -0.1 & -0.02277639 \mp 0.907927685\mathrm{i} & -0.8 \\ 0 & 1 & -0.02277639 \mp 0.907927685\mathrm{i} \end{bmatrix},$$

where the $\mp$ sign before the imaginary part corresponds to λ_2 and λ_3 respectively.

The components of the characteristic vector associated with the ith characteristic root are equal or proportional to the cofactors of any line of the matrix $[\boldsymbol{A} - \lambda_i \boldsymbol{I}]$; taking for example the first row (which is the same as taking the first column of $\{\text{adj}[\boldsymbol{A} - \lambda_i \boldsymbol{I}]\}$, as in the general proof) we have, for $i = 1$,

$$\boldsymbol{h}_1 = \begin{bmatrix} 1.097628 \\ 0.054553 \\ -0.1 \end{bmatrix}.$$

In a similar way we obtain $\boldsymbol{h}_2$ and $\boldsymbol{h}_3$.[26] Therefore we have the following matrix of characteristic vectors:

$$\boldsymbol{H} = \begin{bmatrix} 1.097628 & \begin{matrix}-0.023814\\ +0.041359\mathrm{i}\end{matrix} & \begin{matrix}-0.023814\\ -0.041359\mathrm{i}\end{matrix} \\ 0.054553 & \begin{matrix}-0.0022776\\ -0.0907928\mathrm{i}\end{matrix} & \begin{matrix}-0.0022776\\ +0.0907928\mathrm{i}\end{matrix} \\ -0.1 & -0.1 & -0.1 \end{bmatrix}.$$

Let us now compute the inverse of $\boldsymbol{H}$, $\boldsymbol{H}^{-1} = \{\operatorname{adj} \boldsymbol{H}\}/|\boldsymbol{H}|$. Now $|\boldsymbol{H}|$, the determinant of $\boldsymbol{H}$, turns out to be a pure imaginary number:

$$|\boldsymbol{H}| = 0.0208338822\mathrm{i}.$$

Furthermore

$$\operatorname{adj}\boldsymbol{H} = \begin{bmatrix} \begin{vmatrix} -0.0022776-0.0907928\mathrm{i} & -0.0022776+0.0907928\mathrm{i} \\ -0.1 & -0.1 \end{vmatrix} & -\begin{vmatrix} -0.023814+0.041359\mathrm{i} & -0.023814-0.041359\mathrm{i} \\ -0.1 & -0.1 \end{vmatrix} & \begin{vmatrix} -0.023814+0.041359\mathrm{i} & -0.023814-0.041359\mathrm{i} \\ -0.0022776-0.0907928\mathrm{i} & -0.0022776+0.0907928\mathrm{i} \end{vmatrix} \\ -\begin{vmatrix} 0.0545553 & -0.0022776+0.007928\mathrm{i} \\ -0.1 & -0.1 \end{vmatrix} & \begin{vmatrix} 1.097628 & -0.023814-0.041359\mathrm{i} \\ -0.1 & -0.1 \end{vmatrix} & -\begin{vmatrix} 1.097623 & -0.023814-0.041359\mathrm{i} \\ 0.0545553 & -0.0022776+0.0907928\mathrm{i} \end{vmatrix} \\ \begin{vmatrix} 0.0545553 & -0.0022776-0.0907928\mathrm{i} \\ -0.1 & -0.1 \end{vmatrix} & -\begin{vmatrix} 1.097628 & -0.023814+0.041359\mathrm{i} \\ -0.1 & -0.1 \end{vmatrix} & \begin{vmatrix} 1.097628 & -0.023814+0.041359\mathrm{i} \\ 0.0545553 & -0.0022776-0.0907928\mathrm{i} \end{vmatrix} \end{bmatrix}$$

$$= \begin{bmatrix} 0.0185856\mathrm{i} & 0.0082718\mathrm{i} & -0.004512678\mathrm{i} \\ 0.00568329-0.00907928\mathrm{i} & -0.1121442-0.0041359\mathrm{i} & 0.0012007776-0.1019130721\mathrm{i} \\ -0.00568329-0.00907928\mathrm{i} & 0.1121442-0.041359\mathrm{i} & -0.001200776-0.1019130721\mathrm{i} \end{bmatrix},$$

[26] The following rules for manipulating complex numbers come into play (see, for example, Phillips, 1961, pp. 2–3):
Addition and subtraction: $(a + b\mathrm{i}) \pm (\alpha + \beta\mathrm{i}) = (a \pm \alpha) + (b \pm \beta)\mathrm{i}$,
Multiplication: $(a + b\mathrm{i})(\alpha + \beta\mathrm{i}) = (a\alpha - b\beta) + (a\beta + \alpha b)\mathrm{i}$,
Division: $(a + b\mathrm{i})/(\alpha + \beta\mathrm{i}) = (a\alpha + b\beta)/(\alpha^2 + \beta^2) + [(\alpha b - a\beta)/(\alpha^2 + \beta^2)]\mathrm{i}$,
where of course a, b, α, β are real numbers with their sign. Addition and subtraction are evident; for the multiplication it is enough to recall that $\mathrm{i}\cdot\mathrm{i} = \mathrm{i}^2 = -1$. The division is slightly more complicated. Let $x + y\mathrm{i}$ be the unknown result, that is $(a + b\mathrm{i})/(\alpha + \beta\mathrm{i}) = x + y\mathrm{i}$. If we multiply throughout by $(\alpha + \beta\mathrm{i})$ we have $a + b\mathrm{i} = (\alpha + \beta\mathrm{i})(x + y\mathrm{i}) = (\alpha x - \beta y) + (\alpha y + \beta x)\mathrm{i}$. It follows that

$$\alpha x - \beta y = a,$$
$$\beta x + \beta y = b,$$

whence, by solving for the unknowns x and y, we obtain the formula stated above.

and so

$$H^{-1}=\begin{bmatrix} 0.871588 & 0.397036 & -0.216603 \\ -0.435794 & -0.198518 & -4.891699 \\ -0.272791\mathrm{i} & +5.382780\mathrm{i} & -0.057636\mathrm{i} \\ -0.435794 & -0.198518 & -4.891699 \\ +0.272791\mathrm{i} & -5.382780\mathrm{i} & +0.057636\mathrm{i} \end{bmatrix}.$$

Let us now apply (18). Take the first row of H^{-1} and transpose it, then multiply the resulting column vector by the row vector obtained by transposing the first column of H, that is

$$\left[\frac{\partial \lambda_1}{\partial a_{jk}}\right]=\begin{bmatrix} 0.871588 \\ 0.397036 \\ -0.216603 \end{bmatrix}[1.097628 \quad 0.0545553 \quad -0.1]$$

$$=\begin{bmatrix} 0.956679 & 0.047550 & -0.0871588 \\ 0.435798 & 0.021660 & -0.0397036 \\ -0.237750 & -0.011817 & 0.0216603 \end{bmatrix}.$$

This matrix, apart from differences on the sixth decimal due to rounding, coincides with the one previously found by applying (26). To compute the partial derivatives with respect to the parameters we use (19), obtaining

$$\frac{\partial \lambda_1}{\partial \alpha_1}=0.956679\times(-1)+(-0.0871588)\times 1+0.435798\times 1.6$$

$$+(-0.0397036)\times(-1.6)=-0.283035\simeq -0.28.$$

Similarly

$$\frac{\partial \lambda_1}{\partial \alpha_2}=-0.435798\simeq -0.44, \qquad \frac{\partial \lambda_1}{\partial \alpha_3}=0.237751\simeq 0.24.$$

Let us now consider the complex conjugate roots. We first compute

$$\left[\frac{\partial \lambda_{2,3}}{\partial a_{jk}}\right]=\begin{bmatrix} -0.435794 \mp 0.272791\mathrm{i} \\ -0.198518 \pm 5.382780\mathrm{i} \\ -4.891699 \mp 0.057636\mathrm{i} \end{bmatrix}$$

$$\times[-0.023814 \pm 0.041359\mathrm{i} \quad -0.0022776 \mp 0.0907928\mathrm{i} \quad -0.1],$$

where the first of the two signs before the imaginary part refers to λ_2 and the second to λ_3. If we note that in the matrices which contain the $\partial a_{jk}/\partial \alpha_l$ only the elements (1, 1); (1, 3); (2, 1); (2, 3) are different from zero, it is enough to compute the elements of $[\partial \lambda_{2,3}/\partial a_{jk}]$ in these positions. Therefore

$$\left[\frac{\partial \lambda_{2,3}}{\partial a_{jk}}\right] = \begin{bmatrix} 0.021660 \mp 0.011528\mathrm{i} & \dots & 0.0435794 \pm 0.0272791\mathrm{i} \\ -0.217899 \mp 0.136396\mathrm{i} & \dots & 0.0198518 \mp 0.538278\mathrm{i} \\ \dots & \dots & \dots \end{bmatrix},$$

and so, by using (19), we have finally

$$\frac{\partial \lambda_{2,3}}{\partial \alpha_1} = -0.358482 \pm 0.681818\mathrm{i} \simeq -0.36 \pm 0.68\mathrm{i},$$

$$\frac{\partial \lambda_{2,3}}{\partial \alpha_2} = 0.217899 \pm 0.136396\mathrm{i} \simeq 0.22 \pm 0.14\mathrm{i},$$

$$\frac{\partial \lambda_{2,3}}{\partial \alpha_3} = -0.118875 \pm 0.200941\mathrm{i} \simeq -0.12 \pm 0.20\mathrm{i}.$$

This completes the derivation of the partial derivatives stated at the end of the previous paragraph.

2.3.2. *Bergstrom* (1967)

The previous example gives an incomplete illustration of the procedure because it is linear in the logarithms and so no linearization about the steady state is necessary. To illustrate this, it is convenient to consider the "prototype" model by Bergstrom (1967, ch. 5). Two considerations suggested this choice: first, it is simple enough to allow a clear illustration of the procedure; second, it is a "prototype" model in the sense that it constitutes the basis for subsequent theoretical and empirical work on continuous time models by Bergstrom himself and by other authors (see, for example, Knight and Wymer, 1975; Bergstrom and Wymer, 1976; Bergstrom, 1978; Knight and Wymer, 1978).

The basic equations of the model are

$$C = (1 - s)Y, \qquad 0 < s < 1, \tag{50}$$

the consumption function in real terms, where s is the propensity to save and a relation of proportionality is assumed.

$$\mathrm{D}\log K = \gamma \log\left\{\frac{pY - wL}{(1+c)rpK}\right\}, \qquad \gamma > 0, \quad c > 0, \tag{51}$$

investment function in real terms, assumed to be an increasing function of the rate of profit and a decreasing function of the rate of interest. The rate of profit is measured as the ratio of profits in real terms to the capital stock, $(1/p)(pY - wL)/K$. The coefficient c can be interpreted as a risk premium. Thus $(1 + c)r$ is the critical value of the rate of profit that induces entrepreneurs not to change the stock of capital; if the rate of profit is greater (smaller) than this value, entrepreneurs will increase (decrease) the capital stock. The coefficient γ is a velocity of adjustment.

$$\mathrm{D}Y = \lambda(C + \mathrm{D}K - Y), \qquad \lambda > 0, \tag{52}$$

is the adjustment equation of income to excess demand.

$$L = B\mathrm{e}^{-\rho t} Y^b K^{1-b}, \qquad \rho > 0, \quad B > 0, \quad b > 1, \tag{53}$$

is a production function of the Cobb–Douglas type, where L (level of employment) has been expressed in term of the other variables. Starting from the function $Y = A\mathrm{e}^{ht}L^{\alpha}K^{1-\alpha}$, $0 < \alpha < 1$, we have $L = A^{-1/\alpha}\mathrm{e}^{-(h/\alpha)t}Y^{1/\alpha}K^{(\alpha-1)/\alpha}$ whence, if we define $B \equiv A^{-1/\alpha}$, $\rho \equiv h/\alpha$, $b \equiv 1/\alpha$, we have eq. (53). Note that, as $0 < \alpha < 1$, b is greater than one. Eq. (53) can also be considered as an employment function, which determines the level of employment as a function of output and of the stock of capital.

$$p = (1 + \pi)w\frac{\partial L}{\partial Y} = \frac{b(1+\pi)wL}{Y}, \qquad \pi > 0, \tag{54}$$

is the price determination equation. The price of output is determined by the short-run marginal cost (that is, given the capital stock: this cost then consists of labour cost only, $w(\partial L/\partial Y)$) to which a markup π, which depends on the degree of imperfection of the economy, is applied. From eq. (53) we have

$$\frac{\partial L}{\partial Y} = bB\mathrm{e}^{-\rho t}Y^{b-1}K^{1-b} = b\frac{L}{Y},$$

whence the last member of (54); this may also be interpreted as indicating that price is determined by applying a markup $[b(1 + \pi)$

$-\ 1]$ to the cost of labour per unit of output, wL.

$$\mathrm{D}\log w = \beta \log\left\{\frac{L}{L_s}\right\} + a, \qquad \beta > 0, \quad a > 0, \tag{55}$$

is the wage adjustment equation, where the proportional rate of change in the wage rate is an increasing function of the employment ratio (L is employment and L_s is the labour force). The underlying assumption is that, if the employment ratio exceeds a certain critical level, competition among entrepreneurs for labour will raise the wage rate, whereas, if the proportion of the labour force employed is less than this level, competition among workers for jobs will cause a decrease in the wage rate (Phillips curve). This leads to a relation of the type $\mathrm{D}\log w = \mathrm{f}(L/L_s - n)$ where n is the critical value; assuming a log-linear function we have $\mathrm{D}\log w = \beta[\log(L/L_s) - \log n]$ whence, setting $-\beta \log n = a$, we get eq. (55). As $n < 1$, a is positive.

$$\frac{M_d}{p} = AY^u r^{-v}, \qquad u > 0, \quad v > 0, \tag{56}$$

is the real demand for money, an increasing function of real output and a decreasing function of the rate of interest.

$$M_d = M_s; \tag{57}$$

this equation implicitly assumes that the interest rate adjusts instantaneously so that the demand for money always equals the supply. Alternatively, and more realistically, one could assume an adjustment equation of the type $\mathrm{D}\log r = h\log(M_d/M_s)$, but for simplicity we assume that (57) holds.

$$L_s = L_0 e^{lt}, \qquad L_0 > 0, \quad l > 0, \tag{58}$$

$$M_s = M_0 e^{mt}, \qquad M_0 > 0, \quad m > 0. \tag{59}$$

The supply of labour increases at the constant proportional rate l, and the money supply increases at the constant proportional rate m (neutral monetary policy). We shall now reduce the model to a system of three differential equations. From (54) we obtain

$$wL = \frac{pY}{b(1+\pi)}, \tag{54'}$$

and so, if we substitute in (51),

$$\mathrm{D}\log K = \gamma \log\left\{ \frac{pY - pY/b(1+\pi)}{(1+c)rpK} \right\}$$

$$= \gamma \log\left\{ \frac{[b(1+\pi) - 1]Y}{b(1+\pi)(1+c)rK} \right\}, \tag{51'}$$

whence

$$\mathrm{D}\log K = \gamma(\log Y - \log K - \log r)$$

$$+ \gamma \log\left\{ \frac{b(1+\pi) - 1}{b(1+\pi)(1+c)} \right\}. \tag{60}$$

Consider now eqs. (56), (57) and (59). Substitute M_s from (59) into (56) given (57) and take the logarithms, solving for $\log r$:

$$\log r = \frac{u}{v} \log Y + \frac{1}{v} \log p - \frac{mt}{v} + \frac{1}{v} \log\left\{ \frac{A}{M_0} \right\}. \tag{61}$$

Substitution of (61) into (60) yields

$$\mathrm{D}\log K = \gamma\left(1 - \frac{u}{v}\right)\log Y - \gamma \log K - \frac{\gamma}{v} \log p + \frac{\gamma mt}{v}$$

$$+ \gamma\left[\log\left\{ \frac{b(1+\pi) - 1}{b(1+\pi)(1+c)} \right\} - \frac{1}{v} \log\left\{ \frac{A}{M_0} \right\} \right]. \tag{62}$$

From eq. (54) we obtain

$$\log p = \log b(1+\pi) + \log w + \log(L/Y),$$

and, since (53) yields $L/Y = B\mathrm{e}^{-\rho t} Y^{b-1} K^{1-b}$, we get

$$\log p = \log b(1+\pi) + \log w + \log B - \rho t$$

$$+ (b-1)\log Y + (1-b)\log K.$$

Substituting this expression into (62) and collecting terms we have

$$\mathrm{D}\log K = \frac{\gamma}{v}(v - u + 1 - b)\log Y - \frac{\gamma}{v}(1 + v - b)\log K$$

$$- \frac{\gamma}{v} \log w + \frac{\gamma}{v}(m + \rho)t$$

$$+ \frac{\gamma}{v}\left[v \log\left\{ \frac{b(1+\pi) - 1}{b(1+\pi)(1+c)} \right\} \right.$$

$$\left. + \log\left\{ \frac{M_0}{b(1+\pi)AB} \right\} \right]. \tag{63}$$

Substituting the expression for L_s given by (58) and the expression for L given by (53) into (55) we obtain

$$\mathrm{D}\log w = \beta b \log Y - \beta(b-1)\log K - \beta(\rho + l)t + a + \beta \log\left\{\frac{B}{L_0}\right\}. \tag{64}$$

Substitution of (50) into (52) and division by Y yields

$$\mathrm{D}\log Y = \lambda\left\{\frac{K}{Y}\mathrm{D}\log K - s\right\}. \tag{65}$$

Eqs. (63), (64), (65) constitute the fundamental dynamic system of the model. This system is of the first order, but it is not in normal form; the latter, however, can easily be obtained by substituting (63) in (65), as we shall do later.

Let us now search for the steady state solution by the method of undetermined coefficients. Therefore, we shall try a particular solution of the type

$$w = w^* \mathrm{e}^{\eta_1 t}, \qquad K = K^* \mathrm{e}^{\eta_2 t}, \qquad Y = Y^* \mathrm{e}^{\eta_3 t},$$

where the η_i, $i = 1, 2, 3$, and w^*, K^*, Y^* are constants to be determined. Substitution in the fundamental dynamic system yields the equations

$$\begin{aligned}\eta_2 = {} & \frac{\gamma}{v}(v - u + 1 - b)(\log Y^* + \eta_3 t) \\ & - \frac{\gamma}{v}(1 + v - b)(\log K^* + \eta_2 t) - \frac{\gamma}{v}(\log w^* + \eta_1 t) \\ & + \frac{\gamma}{v}(m + \rho)t + \frac{\gamma}{v}\left[v \log\left\{\frac{b(1+\pi) - 1}{b(1+\pi)(1+c)}\right\}\right. \\ & \left. + \log\left\{\frac{M_0}{b(1+\pi)AB}\right\}\right],\end{aligned} \tag{66}$$

$$\begin{aligned}\eta_1 = {} & \beta b(\log Y^* + \eta_3 t) - \beta(b-1)(\log K^* + \eta_2 t) - \beta(\rho + l)t \\ & + a + \beta \log\left\{\frac{B}{L_0}\right\},\end{aligned}$$

$$\eta_3 = \lambda\left\{\frac{K^*}{Y^*}\mathrm{e}^{(\eta_2 - \eta_3)t}\eta_2 - s\right\},$$

all of which must be identically satisfied. The last equation implies

$\eta_2 = \eta_3$: in the opposite case, in fact, the presence of the exponential function, which takes on different values for different t, makes impossible to satisfy the equation identically with constant values of η_2 and η_3. By setting then $\eta_2 = \eta_3$ in the first two equations and by collecting the terms containing t we have

$$\frac{\gamma}{v}[(1 + v - b)\eta_3 + \eta_1 - (m + \rho) - (v - u + 1 - b)\eta_3]t$$
$$+\left[\eta_3 - \frac{\gamma}{v}(v - u + 1 - b)\log Y^* + \frac{\gamma}{v}(1 + v - b)\log K^* + \frac{\gamma}{v}\log w^*\right]$$
$$- \frac{\gamma}{v}\left[v\log\left\{\frac{b(1 + \pi) - 1}{b(1 + \pi)(1 + c)}\right\} + \log\left\{\frac{M_0}{b(1 + \pi)AB}\right\}\right] = 0, \tag{67}$$

$$[\beta(b - 1)\eta_3 - \beta b\eta_3 + \beta(\rho + l)]t + \left[\eta_1 - \beta b\log Y^* + \beta(b - 1)\log K^* - a - \beta\log\left\{\frac{B}{L_0}\right\}\right] = 0.$$

For these equations to be identically satisfied, in each of them the coefficients of t must be zero and also the sums of all the terms not containing t must be zero. Thus, by equating the coefficients of t to zero, we have

$$u\eta_3 + \eta_1 = m + \rho, \qquad \beta\eta_3 = \beta(\rho + l),$$

whence

$$\eta_3 = \rho + l; \qquad \eta_1 = m + \rho - u(\rho + l) = (1 - u)(\rho + l) + m - l, \tag{68}$$

and so $\eta_2 = \rho + l$ too. Substituting η_1, η_2 and η_3 in the last equation of (66) we obtain the following relation between K^* and Y^*:

$$\frac{K^*}{Y^*} = \frac{\rho + l + \lambda s}{\lambda(\rho + l)},$$

whence

$$\log K^* - \log Y^* = \log\left\{\frac{\rho + l + \lambda s}{\lambda(\rho + l)}\right\},$$

and so

$$\log Y^* = \log K^* - \log\left\{\frac{\rho + l + \lambda s}{\lambda(\rho + l)}\right\}. \tag{69}$$

Now by equating the expressions not containing t in (67) to zero, we have, after substitution of (68) and (69) in them,

$$(\rho + l) - \frac{\gamma}{v}(v - u + 1 - b)\left[\log K^* - \log\left\{\frac{\rho + l + \lambda s}{(\rho + l)}\right\}\right]$$
$$+ \frac{\gamma}{v}(1 + v - b)\log K^* + \frac{\gamma}{v}\log w^*$$
$$= \frac{\gamma}{v}\left[v\log\left\{\frac{b(1 + \pi) - 1}{b(1 + \pi)(1 + c)}\right\} + \log\left\{\frac{M_0}{b(1 + \pi)AB}\right\}\right],$$
$$(1 - u)(\rho + l) + m - l - \beta b\log K^* + \beta b\log\left\{\frac{\rho + l + \lambda s}{\lambda(\rho + l)}\right\}$$
$$+ \beta(b - 1)\log K^* = a + \beta\log\left\{\frac{B}{L_0}\right\},$$

whence, rearranging terms

$$\begin{aligned}\log w^* + u\log K^* = &-\frac{v}{\gamma}(\rho + l)\\ &- (v - u + 1 - b)\log\left\{\frac{\rho + l + \lambda s}{\lambda(\rho + l)}\right\}\\ &+\left[v\log\left\{\frac{b(1 + \pi) - 1}{b(1 + \pi)(1 + c)}\right\}\right.\\ &\left.+\log\left\{\frac{M_0}{b(1 + \pi)AB}\right\}\right],\\ \log K^* = \log\left\{\frac{L_0}{B}\right\} &+ b\log\left\{\frac{\rho + l + \lambda s}{\lambda(\rho + l)}\right\}\\ &- \frac{1}{\beta}\{a + l - m - (1 - u)(\rho + l)\}.\end{aligned} \tag{70}$$

The second equation in (70) gives K^* directly, and so Y^* is determined by using (69); by substituting in the first equation of (70) and by rearranging terms we have finally

$$\log w^* = \log\left\{\frac{M_0}{b(1+\pi)AB}\right\} - u\log\left\{\frac{L_0}{B}\right\}$$
$$+ v\log\left\{\frac{b(1+\pi)-1}{b(1+\pi)(1+c)}\right\}$$
$$- \{v-(1-u)(b-1)\}\log\left\{\frac{\rho+l+\lambda s}{\lambda(\rho+l)}\right\}$$
$$+ \frac{u}{\beta}\{a+l-m-(1-u)(\rho+l)\} - \frac{v}{\gamma}(\rho+l). \tag{71}$$

This completes the finding of the steady state growth paths of the endogenous variables w, K, Y, that we shall now consider from the economic point of view.

The steady state growth rate of K and Y is $\rho + l$ (as in the simple neoclassical growth model), and their levels are the greater, the greater the propensity to save (in fact, $\partial K^*/\partial s > 0$, $\partial Y^*/\partial s > 0$). A new result is that these levels are greater, the greater is the rate of growth of the money supply ($\partial K^*/\partial m > 0$, $\partial Y^*/\partial m > 0$). This follows from the fact that when K and Y are on their steady state path, the proportion of the labour force employed is an increasing function of m. In fact, by substituting the steady state value of w in (55) and by solving for $\log(L/L_s)$ we have

$$\log\left\{\frac{L}{L_s}\right\} = -\frac{1}{\beta}\{a+l-m-(1-u)(\rho+l)\}. \tag{72}$$

Furthermore, given (58), from eq. (72) we obtain the steady state growth path of L

$$L = L^*e^{lt}, \tag{73}$$

where

$$\log L^* = \log L_0 - \frac{1}{\beta}\{a+l-m-(1-u)(\rho+l)\}.$$

Note that the equilibrium growth rate of L must be the same as that of L_s for (72) to be satisfied; this equation then serves to determine L^*. As employment cannot exceed the labour force, $L(t) \leq L_s(t)$, we must assume $L^* \leq L_0$, and this implies the assumption

$$a + l - m - (1 - u)(\rho + l) \geq 0.$$

As we have seen above, the steady state growth rate of the wage rate is $(1 - u)(\rho + l) + m - l$ and, if we take account of (68) and of (73), the equilibrium growth rate of the price level is

$$\begin{aligned} \mathrm{D}\log p &= \mathrm{D}\log w + \mathrm{D}\log L - \mathrm{D}\log Y \\ &= (1 - u)(\rho + l) + m - l + l - (\rho + l) \\ &= m - u(\rho + l). \end{aligned} \tag{74}$$

In the particular case in which $u = 1$ (unit income elasticity of the demand for money) the rate of increase in the price level is given by the rate of increase in the money supply minus the sum of the rate of increase in the labour force and of the rate of increase in labour productivity due to technical progress.

By substituting the steady state paths of Y and K in (60), we find that in the steady state the rate of interest is a constant given by

$$\log r^* = \log\left[\frac{\lambda(\rho + l)\{b(1 + \pi) - 1\}}{b(\rho + l + \lambda s)(1 + \pi)(1 + c)}\right] - \frac{\rho + l}{\gamma}. \tag{75}$$

As $\partial r^*/\partial b > 0$ and $\partial r^*/\partial s < 0$, it follows that the more "important" is capital in the productive process and the lower is the propensity to save, the higher is the equilibrium rate of interest. Furthermore, eq. (75) shows that r^* is independent of the money supply and of the parameters in the liquidity preference function (A, u, v): "the explanation of this result is that, when all variables are on their equilibrium growth paths, the wage rate is so adjusted to the money supply and the liquidity preference parameters as to neutralise their influence on the interest rate and the real variables in the system" (Bergstrom, 1967, p. 58).

Eqs. (61) and (75) "clarify the relation between the Keynesian and classical theories of interest. According to the classical theory the interest rate is determined by the real phenomena affecting saving and the demand for capital, whereas, according to the Keynesian theory monetary phenomena play a predominant role in determining the interest rate. In the model under discussion the Keynesian theory, which can be represented by (61), applies to the actual interest rate at any point of time, while the classical theory, which can be represented by (75), applies to the equilibrium interest rate only" (Bergstrom, 1967, p. 58: the numeration of the equations has been changed to follow our numbering).

Having completed the analysis of the steady state and of the comparative dynamics results, we turn to stability analysis. Let us recall that, as explained in paragraph 2.2.3, the first step is to express the system in terms of logarithmic deviations from the steady state. To this purpose, consider system (63)–(65), and define the following new variables:

$$\begin{aligned} x_1 &= \left\{\log \frac{w}{w^* e^{\{(1-u)(\rho+l)+m-l\}t}}\right\}, \\ x_2 &= \log\left\{\frac{K}{K^* e^{(\rho+l)t}}\right\}, \\ x_3 &= \log\left\{\frac{Y}{Y^* e^{(\rho+l)t}}\right\}. \end{aligned} \tag{76}$$

As eq. (64) is satisfied by the steady state values by definition, we have

$$\begin{aligned} \mathrm{D}\log(w^* e^{\eta_1 t}) = \beta b \log Y^* e^{(\rho+l)t} - \beta(b-1)\log K^* e^{(\rho+l)t} \\ - \beta(\rho+l)t + a + \beta\log\left\{\frac{B}{L_0}\right\}, \end{aligned} \tag{77}$$

where η_1 is defined in (68). Subtracting eq. (77) from eq. (64) and using definitions (76) we have

$$\mathrm{D}x_1 = -\beta(b-1)x_2 + \beta b x_3. \tag{78}$$

Similarly from (63) we obtain

$$\mathrm{D}x_2 = -\frac{\gamma}{v}x_1 - \frac{\gamma}{v}(1+v-b)x_2 + \frac{\gamma}{v}(1+v-u-b)x_3. \tag{79}$$

The manipulation of (65) is slightly more laborious. In the steady state we have

$$\mathrm{D}\log Y^* e^{(\rho+l)t} = \lambda\left\{\frac{K^* e^{(\rho+l)t}}{Y^* e^{(\rho+l)t}}\mathrm{D}\log K^* e^{(\rho+l)t} - s\right\}.$$

From (69) we get

$$K^*/Y^* = \frac{\rho + l + \lambda s}{\lambda(\rho + l)}.$$

Furthermore,

$$\mathrm{D}\log K^* \mathrm{e}^{(\rho+l)t} = \rho + l.$$

Therefore

$$\mathrm{D}x_3 = \lambda \frac{K}{Y} \mathrm{D}\log K - (\rho + l + \lambda s).$$

Addition and subtraction of

$$\lambda \frac{K}{Y} \mathrm{D}\log K^* \mathrm{e}^{(\rho+l)t} \equiv \lambda \frac{K}{Y}(\rho + l),$$

yields

$$\mathrm{D}x_3 = \lambda \frac{K}{Y} \mathrm{D}x_2 + \lambda \frac{K}{Y}(\rho + l) - (\rho + l + \lambda s).$$

By multiplying and dividing the first two terms on the r.h.s. by K^*/Y^* we get

$$\mathrm{D}x_3 = \lambda \frac{K^*}{Y^*} \frac{K/K^*}{Y/Y^*} \mathrm{D}x_2 + \lambda \frac{K^*}{Y^*} \frac{K/K^*}{Y/Y^*}(\rho + l) - (\rho + l + \lambda s). \tag{65'}$$

If we substitute

$$\frac{K^*}{Y^*} = \frac{\rho + l + \lambda s}{\lambda(\rho + l)}$$

in (65′), and since

$$\mathrm{e}^{x_2} = K/K^* \mathrm{e}^{(\rho+l)t}, \qquad \mathrm{e}^{x_3} = Y/Y^* \mathrm{e}^{(\rho+l)t},$$

whence

$$\mathrm{e}^{x_2}/\mathrm{e}^{x_3} = \mathrm{e}^{x_2 - x_3} = \frac{K/K^*}{Y/Y^*},$$

then, after simplifying and collecting terms, we have

$$\mathrm{D}x_3 = \left\{ \frac{\rho + l + \lambda s}{\rho + l} \right\} \mathrm{e}^{x_2 - x_3} \mathrm{D}x_2 + (\rho + l + \lambda s)(\mathrm{e}^{x_2 - x_3} - 1). \tag{80}$$

Equations (78), (79), (80) constitute the system of equations of perturbed motion to be analyzed. This system is autonomous and therefore no problem arises in the application of the Poincaré–Liapunov–Perron theorem (see para. 2.2.3). As (80) is not in normal form, it can be converted into such a form simply by substituting from (79). Thus we have

$$\mathrm{D}x_3 = \left\{\frac{\rho + l + \lambda s}{\rho + l}\right\}\left\{-\frac{\gamma}{v}x_1 - \frac{\gamma}{v}(1 + v - b)x_2 + \frac{\gamma}{v}(1 + v - u - b)x_3\right\}\mathrm{e}^{x_2 - x_3} + (\rho + l + \lambda s)(\mathrm{e}^{x_2 - x_3} - 1). \tag{80'}$$

Eqs. (78) and (79) are already linear; therefore the linearization concerns eq. (80′) only. Since

$$\left(\frac{\partial \mathrm{e}^{x_2 - x_3}}{\partial x_2}\right)_0 = \mathrm{e}^{x_2^0 - x_3^0}, \qquad \left(\frac{\partial \mathrm{e}^{x_2 - x_3}}{\partial x_3}\right)_0 = \mathrm{e}^{x_2^0 - x_3^0},$$

we have

$$\mathrm{e}^{x_2 - x_3} \simeq \mathrm{e}^{x_2^0 - x_3^0} + \mathrm{e}^{x_2^0 - x_3^0}(x_2 - x_2^0) - \mathrm{e}^{x_2^0 - x_3^0}(x_3 - x_3^0).$$

As the linearization is performed about the steady state, that is where $K = K^*\mathrm{e}^{(\rho + l)t}$, etc., it follows from (76) that $x_1^0 = x_2^0 = x_3^0 = \log 1 = 0$. Therefore

$$\mathrm{e}^{x_2 - x_3} \simeq (1 + x_2 - x_3).$$

We must now linearize the expressions

$$x_1\mathrm{e}^{x_2 - x_3},\ x_2\mathrm{e}^{x_2 - x_3},\ x_3\mathrm{e}^{x_2 - x_3}.$$

We have

$$\begin{aligned} x_1\mathrm{e}^{x_2 - x_3} &\simeq x_1^0\mathrm{e}^{x_2^0 - x_3^0} + \mathrm{e}^{x_2^0 - x_3^0}(x_1 - x^0) + x_1^0\mathrm{e}^{x_2^0 - x_3^0}(x_2 - x_2^0) \\ &\quad - x_1^0\mathrm{e}^{x_2^0 - x_3^0}(x_3 - x_3^0) \\ &= x_1, \\ x_2\mathrm{e}^{x_2 - x_3} &\simeq x_2^0\mathrm{e}^{x_2^0 - x_3^0} + \left(\mathrm{e}^{x_2^0 - x_3^0} + x_2^0\mathrm{e}^{x_2^0 - x_3^0}\right)(x_2 - x_2^0) \\ &\quad + \left(-x_2^0\mathrm{e}^{x_2^0 - x_3^0}\right)(x_3 - x_3^0) \\ &= x_2, \\ x_3\mathrm{e}^{x_2 - x_3} &\simeq x_3^0\mathrm{e}^{x_2^0 - x_3^0} + x_3^0\mathrm{e}^{x_2^0 - x_3^0}(x_2 - x_2^0) \\ &\quad + \left(\mathrm{e}^{x_2^0 - x_3^0} - x_3^0\mathrm{e}^{x_2^0 - x_3^0}\right)(x_3 - x_3^0) \\ &= x_3. \end{aligned}$$

By substituting all these results in (80′) and rearranging terms we have finally

$$\mathrm{D}x_3 = -\frac{\gamma(\rho + l + \lambda s)}{v(\rho + l)}x_1 + (\rho + l + \lambda s)\left\{1 - \frac{\gamma(1 + v - b)}{v(\rho + l)}\right\}x_2 + (\rho + l + \lambda s)\left\{\frac{\gamma(1 + v - u - b)}{v(\rho + l)} - 1\right\}x_3. \tag{80''}$$

The characteristic equation of the differential system (78), (79), (80″) is

$$\begin{vmatrix} -\mu & -\beta(b-1) & \beta b \\ -\dfrac{\gamma}{v} & -\dfrac{\gamma}{v}(1 + v - b) - \mu & \dfrac{\gamma}{v}(1 + v - u - b) \\ -\dfrac{\gamma(\rho + l + \lambda s)}{v(\rho + l)} & (\rho + l + \lambda s)\left\{1 - \dfrac{\gamma(1 + v - b)}{v(\rho + l)}\right\} & (\rho + l + \lambda s)\left\{\dfrac{\gamma(1 + v - u - b)}{v(\rho + l)} - 1\right\} - \mu \end{vmatrix} = 0, \tag{81}$$

whence:

$$-\mu^3 + \left[-\frac{\gamma}{v}(1 + v - b) + (\rho + l + \lambda s)\left\{\frac{\gamma(1 + v - u - b)}{v(\rho + l)} - 1\right\}\right] \times \mu^2 - \left[-\frac{\gamma}{v}\beta(b - 1) + \frac{\gamma(\rho + l + \lambda s)}{v(\rho + l)}\beta b - \frac{\gamma}{v}(1 + v - b)(\rho + l + \lambda s)\left\{\frac{\gamma(1 + v - u - b)}{v(\rho + l)} - 1\right\}\right.$$

$$- \frac{\gamma}{v}(1 + v - u - b)(\rho + l + \lambda s)\left\{1 - \frac{\gamma(1 + v - b)}{v(\rho + l)}\right\}\Bigg]\mu$$

$$+ \Bigg[-\beta(b - 1)\frac{\gamma}{v}(\rho + l + \lambda s)\left\{\frac{\gamma(1 + v - u - b)}{v(\rho + l)} - 1\right\}$$

$$+ \beta(b - 1)\frac{\gamma^2}{v^2}(1 + v - u - b)\frac{(\rho + l + \lambda s)}{(\rho + l)}$$

$$- \beta b\frac{\gamma}{v}(\rho + l + \lambda s)\left\{1 - \frac{\gamma(1 + v - b)}{v(\rho + l)}\right\}$$

$$- \beta b\frac{\gamma^2(\rho + l + \lambda s)}{v^2(\rho + l)}(1 + v - b)\Bigg] = 0,$$

$$\mu^3 + \Bigg[\frac{\gamma}{v}(1 + v - b) - (\rho + l + \lambda s)\frac{\gamma(1 + v - u - b)}{(\rho + l)}$$

$$+ (\rho + l + \lambda s)\Bigg]\mu^2$$

$$+ \Bigg[-\frac{\gamma}{v}\beta b + \frac{\gamma}{v}\beta + \frac{\gamma(\rho + l) + \gamma\lambda s}{v(\rho + l)}$$

$$\times \beta b - \frac{\gamma^2}{v^2}(1 + v - b)(\rho + l + \lambda s)\frac{(1 + v - u - b)}{(\rho + l)}$$

$$+ \frac{\gamma}{v}(1 + v - b)(\rho + l + \lambda s)$$

$$- \frac{\gamma}{v}(1 + v - u - b)(\rho + l + \lambda s)$$

$$+ (1 + v - u - b)(\rho + l + \lambda s)\frac{\gamma^2(1 + v - b)}{v^2(\rho + l)}\Bigg]\mu$$

$$- \Bigg[-\beta(b - 1)\frac{\gamma^2}{v^2}(\rho + l + \lambda s)\frac{(1 + v - u - b)}{(\rho + l)}$$

$$+ \beta b\frac{\gamma}{v}(\rho + l + \lambda s) - \beta\frac{\gamma}{v}(\rho + l + \lambda s)$$

$$+ \beta(b - 1)\frac{\gamma^2}{v^2}(1 + v - u - b)\frac{(\rho + l + \lambda s)}{(\rho + l)}$$

$$- \beta b \frac{\gamma}{v}(\rho + l + \lambda s)$$

$$+ \beta b \frac{\gamma}{v}(\rho + l + \lambda s)\frac{\gamma(1 + v - b)}{v(\rho + l)}$$

$$\left. - \beta b \frac{\gamma^2(\rho + l + \lambda s)}{v^2(\rho + l)}(1 + v - b)\right] = 0,$$

$$\mu^3 + \left[\frac{\gamma}{v}(1 + v - b) - (\rho + l)\frac{\gamma(1 + v - u - b)}{v(\rho + l)}\right.$$

$$\left. - \lambda s \frac{\gamma(1 + v - u - b)}{v(\rho + l)} + (\rho + l + \lambda s)\right]\mu^2$$

$$+ \left[-\frac{\gamma}{v}\beta b + \frac{\gamma}{v}\beta + \frac{\gamma}{v}\beta b + \frac{\gamma \lambda s}{v(\rho + l)}\beta b + \frac{\gamma u}{v}(\rho + l + \lambda s)\right]\mu$$

$$+ \frac{\gamma\beta}{v}(\rho + l + \lambda s) = 0,$$

and finally,

$$\mu^3 + \left[(\rho + l + \lambda s) + \frac{\gamma u}{v} + \frac{\gamma \lambda s(b + u - v - 1)}{v(\rho + l)}\right]\mu^2$$

$$+ \left[\frac{\gamma u}{v}(\rho + l + \lambda s) + \frac{\gamma\beta}{v}\left(1 + \frac{\lambda s b}{\rho + l}\right)\right]\mu$$

$$+ \frac{\gamma\beta}{v}(\rho + l + \lambda s) = 0. \tag{82}$$

Necessary and sufficient stability conditions (Gandolfo, 1980, Part II, ch. 6) are that the coefficients of (82) be positive and that the product of the coefficient of μ^2 by the coefficient of μ be greater than the constant term.

Now, if $b + u - v > 1$, all these conditions will be satisfied: in fact, all the coefficients are positive and, as regards the last condition, the multiplication of the first term in the coefficient of μ^2 by the last term in the coefficient of μ gives an expression which is greater than the constant term; all the other terms of the product are also positive. Therefore a *sufficient* stability condition is

$$b + u - v > 1, \tag{83}$$

from which we deduce that a high income elasticity of the demand for money – that is, a high value of u – has a stabilizing influence, whereas a high interest elasticity of the same demand – that is, a high value of v – has a destabilizing influence. For an intuitive description of these results see Bergstrom (1967, pp. 58–60).

CHAPTER 3

Econometric estimation

3.1. Introduction

The models under consideration do not raise problems of identification,[1] as we saw in section 2.1. On the contrary, they are usually heavily overidentified, with the same parameters or functions of parameters appearing in several equations, and with cross-equation restrictions on the parameters. Therefore, full information methods of estimation will be necessary to take adequate account of all these restrictions, in order to obtain efficient estimates notwithstanding the smallness of the samples. Among these methods, full-information maximum likelihood (FIML) is preferable to the other major full-information technique (three-stage least squares), because it has the advantage of using in the estimation procedure a wide range of *a priori* information, pertaining not only to each equation individually but also to several equations simultaneously, such as non-linear within and across equation restrictions on the parameters. Furthermore, a lot is known about the properties of FIML estimators. It goes without saying that the model will have to be specified with great care, in view of the well known sensitivity of full information methods to specification errors; on the other hand, this sensitivity may be an advantage, because it helps the model builder to detect these errors, which might remain undetected when using other estimation methods.

[1]For the identification problem in general, see Fisher (1966). In the case under consideration – that is, a system of differential equations – the condition is that the system cannot be reduced to an equivalent system where any equation is of a lower order, so that the model is invariant under a linear transformation of time and the parameters of the differential equations may be identified (Koopmans, 1950; Wymer, 1975; see also Phillips, 1973).

As regards the estimation procedure proper, the ideal, of course, would be to be able to estimate the original non-linear differential system directly. One approach might be the following: (i) assume initial values of the parameters (perhaps obtained by the estimation of a linear approximation, about which see below); (ii) solve the original system of non-linear differential equations numerically; (iii) evaluate the determinant of the residual variance matrix calculated by using the differences between the actual and solution values of the endogenous variables;[2] (iv) minimize this determinant by an iterative procedure.

However, the properties of the estimates so obtained are unknown and need to be investigated, and there are several other theoretical problems discussed by Wymer (1979). Furthermore, this procedure would be so enormously time consuming that it is not feasible on the present generation of computers, and probably will not be on the next.

A second approach has been suggested by Bailey, Hall and Phillips (1979). It involves the following steps: (i) integrate the original non-linear model over the observation interval; (ii) perform a non-linear discrete approximation to these integrals; (iii) estimate the resulting system of equations, which is a non-linear in variables and parameters simultaneous equations model.

This procedure, although feasible on the current generation of computers, is very expensive, especially if the original differential system contains cross-equation restrictions on the parameters, so that a non-linear full information estimator is required.[3] Furthermore, when there are exogenous variables in the model it is not

[2]Steps (ii) and (iii) could be implemented either by "starting off" the solution to the differential system from the first observation taken as initial value of the variables and letting this solution go on through time up to the point in time where the last observation lies, or by re-initializing the solution at each successive discrete observation and letting it go on just up to the point in time where the next observation lies. The second procedure seems preferable (and is comparable, *mutatis mutandis*, to the procedure described below for estimation of the linearized exact discrete model), but of course it is more complicated and expensive than the first.

[3]If no such restrictions are involved, a much less expensive non-linear limited information estimator may be used as suggested by Bailey *et al.* (*op. cit.*). However, as we said at the beginning of this section, cross-equation restrictions are usually present, the more they are, the more we want to exploit the restrictions suggested or imposed by economic theory.

possible to estimate directly the *exact* analogue to the non-linear continuous model. The question then arises as to whether better estimates of the "true" parameters are obtained using an *exact* discrete analogue to the linearized form of the original non-linear differential model or using an *approximate* non-linear discrete analogue to the same model. A lot of theoretical and empirical (Monte Carlo) work needs to be done.

While referring the reader to Wymer (1979) and to Bailey, Hall, and Phillips (1979) for a fuller discussion of the problems no more than touched upon here, we think that the problems and costs involved in the direct estimation of non-linear differential systems are such that, for the time being, the use of linearized models will still be required for the estimation of the parameters of these systems. It is important to point out, however, that the use of a linear approximation for the estimation of the parameters does *not* mean that we cannot use the original non-linear differential system for analysis and forecasting (see section 3.4).

Let us now consider the linearization procedure (some useful formulae for the linearization are given in Appendix I). The first problem is where to perform the linearization.

If the model has a steady state and if the sample period is sufficiently long for substantial changes in the variables to have occurred, *linearization about the steady state* may be more appropriate. It should be noted, however, that when the steady state is complicated and when the model is subject to modifications, this linearization is very time consuming because the steady state (and then the linearization) must be computed again after each modification.

On the other hand, when the sample period is not too long and the changes in the variables are not substantial, or when the steady state is very complicated, it may be convenient to *linearize about sample means*. Even if we are dealing with a case in which the linearization about the steady state seems more appropriate, the linearization about sample means may be used for the preliminary screening of the model: once a satisfactory specification has been determined, the linearization about the steady state will be used to obtain the final estimates.

It should be pointed out that whichever linearization is employed, the parameters being estimated are always those of the original non-linear model. Therefore, if the model has a steady state, to study its properties (stability, etc.) we must substitute the estimates obtained by the linear approximation in the original non-linear model and analyse it using the techniques described in ch. 2, especially in section 2.2. Of course, if the linearization about the steady state has been used to estimate the parameters, the results can be used directly to analyse the dynamic behaviour of the model (see, for example, Knight and Wymer, 1975, p. 166). On the contrary, if the linearization about sample means has been used, then the estimated values of the parameters must be substituted in the original non-linear model (by using the formulae given in paragraph 2.2.1 in order to obtain estimates for the steady state paths, then performing a comparative dynamics analysis) and in the approximation about the steady state to study the stability and sensitivity (paragraphs 2.2.3 and 2.2.4).

It goes without saying that no problem of choice arises when the model has been constructed in such a way as not to possess a steady state.

In any case, whichever linearization is adopted, we have to deal with a system of the type

$$\mathrm{D}\boldsymbol{x}(t) = \boldsymbol{A}\boldsymbol{x}(t) + \boldsymbol{B}\boldsymbol{z}(t) + \boldsymbol{u}(t), \tag{1}$$

where the transformations to pass from $\boldsymbol{Y}$ to $\boldsymbol{x}$ and from $\boldsymbol{Z}$ to $\boldsymbol{z}$ depend on the non-linearities of the original system – see ch. 2, eq. (4) – and on the point about which the linearization is performed. Of course the matrices $\boldsymbol{A}$ and $\boldsymbol{B}$ will be different in the two cases (linearization about the steady state and linearization about sample means). In the case of linearization about the steady state the elements of these matrices will usually be *complicated functions* of the parameters, of the exogenous rates of growth and perhaps of the initial values of the exogenous variables [in effect some of the elements will contain the G_i defined in ch. 2, eqs. (8)]. In the case of linearization about sample means the elements of the matrices under consideration will usually be *simple functions* of the parameters and of the means of the variables. This is an undoubted practical advantage of the latter linearization over the former.

We turn now to the estimation of model (1). The basic idea is to represent the differential equation system by a stochastically equivalent system of difference equations such that this "exact"[4] discrete analogue is satisfied by any set of equispaced observations generated by the differential system; it will therefore be possible to estimate the parameters of the model from a sample of discrete observations.[5]

3.2. A digression on stochastic processes

Before going on, it might be useful to recall some basic definitions concerning continuous stochastic processes.[6]

Consider a stochastic process such that for each t a continuous random variable $X(t)$ is defined, as well as its probability density function $f(X,t)$ with the usual property

$$\int_{l_1}^{l_2} f(X,t)\,\mathrm{d}X = 1,$$

where l_1 and l_2 are the extremes of the range of X (usually taken to be $-\infty$ and $+\infty$ respectively). Of course in any instant t only one value of X will occur and will actually be observed. In the definitions that follow all the integrals are definite integrals evaluated in the interval l_1, l_2:

mean

$$\mu(t) = \mathrm{E}[X(t)] = \int X(t)\,\mathrm{d}F(X,t),$$

variance

$$\sigma^2(t) = \mathrm{E}\{[X(t) - \mu(t)]^2\} = \int [X(t) - \mu(t)]^2\,\mathrm{d}F(X,t),$$

[4] "Exact" in the sense that it is stochastically equivalent, and not an approximation, to the differential system (1).

[5] This clarifies what was stated in section 1.1, category (3), namely that the estimator is independent of the observation interval.

[6] For a fuller treatment of the topics just touched upon in this section see, e.g., Bartlett (1956), Cramér and Leadbetter (1967), Kendall and Stuart (1976), Wilks (1962), Yaglom (1962).

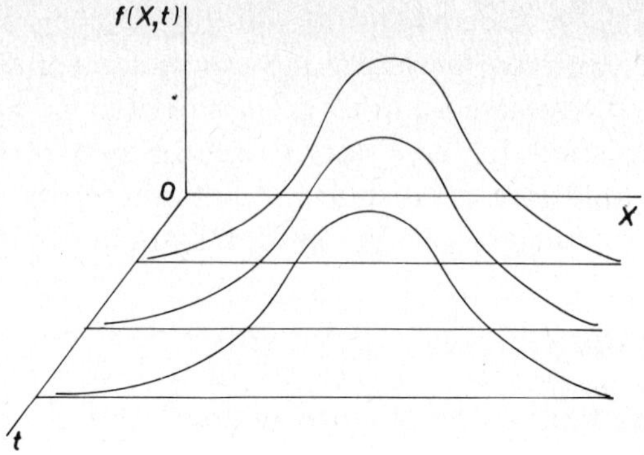

Fig. 1

autocovariance

$$\sigma(t,s) = \mathrm{E}\{[X(t)-\mu(t)][X(s)-\mu(s)]\}$$
$$= \int\int \{[X(t)-\mu(t)][X(s)-\mu(s)]\}\,\mathrm{d}F(X_t, X_s;\, t,s),$$

where $F(X,t)$ is the distribution function of $X(t)$ and $F(X_t, X_s;\, t,s)$ is the joint distribution function of $X(t)$ and $X(s)$; s denotes another point in time different from t, but has of course the same domain as t;

autocorrelation

$$\rho(t,s) = \frac{\sigma(t,s)}{\sqrt{\sigma^2(t)\sigma^2(s)}}, \qquad \text{where} \quad |\rho(t,s)| \leq 1.$$

A stochastic process is said to be *stationary in the stronger sense* if its distribution function is the same for each t, that is $F(X,t) = F(X)$. When only certain characteristics of this function are invariant under translations of the t axis, the process is said to be *stationary in the weaker sense*; more precisely, the weaker form of stationarity is defined in relation to the moments of the process, which will be called *stationary to the rth order* if all the moments up to the rth are invariant. As many of the properties of stationary processes depend only on the structure of the process as specified by its first and second moments, stationarity in the weaker sense is usually identified with *stationarity to the second order*, that is when the mean and variance are constants independent of time, and the autocovariance between values of the process at two time points depends only on the distance between these time points and not on time itself. Formally,

$$\mu(t) = \mu, \qquad \sigma^2(t) = \sigma^2, \qquad \sigma(t,s) = \sigma_h,$$

where h is the difference between t and s.

The mean μ can be set to zero without any loss of generality; note also that the autocovariance (and so the autocorrelation) are even functions of h, because $\sigma(t, t+h) = \sigma_h = \sigma(t, t-h) = \sigma_{-h}$.

From now on, for brevity, we shall use the expression "stationary process" to mean "stochastic process stationary to the second order".

Let us now introduce some particular cases of stationary processes.

A stochastic process whose autocovariance (and hence autocorrelation) is zero for any two different time points – that is for any $h \neq 0$ – is called *white noise*.

When the correlation between the increments of the process in any two disjoint time intervals is zero, that is when

$$\mathrm{E}\{[X(t_1) - X(t_2)][X(t_3) - X(t_4)]\} = 0,$$
$$\forall t_1 > t_2 \geq t_3 > t_4,$$

the process is said to be with *uncorrelated increments* (or *orthogonal*).

A stochastic process is said to be *homogeneous* when the probability of passing from one state at time t to another state at time $s = t + h$ depends only on the distance h and not on t and s themselves.

We have so far considered unidimensional stochastic processes; the definitions can be extended to multidimensional processes. In the latter case, instead of considering the single random variable X, we shall consider a vector $\boldsymbol{X}$ of random variables, taking care to define the vectors suitably (row vectors or column vectors) in the various operations. For example, the definition of homogeneity becomes

$$\mathrm{E}\{[\boldsymbol{X}(t+h) - \boldsymbol{X}(t)][\boldsymbol{X}(t+h) - \boldsymbol{X}(t)]^{\mathrm{T}}\} = \boldsymbol{\Omega}|h|,$$

where $\boldsymbol{\Omega}$ is a matrix of constants and $\boldsymbol{X}$ is a column vector.

As in the next chapter we shall have to deal with stochastic integrals and derivatives, these operations must be defined: to this purpose it is necessary to deal briefly with the concept of *stochastic convergence*.

Let us therefore introduce the following definitions relative to a sequence of random variables $X_1, X_2, \ldots, X_n$.

Convergence in probability (i.p.). The sequence of stochastic variables $X_1, X_2, \ldots, X_n$ converges in probability to the stochastic limit X as $n \to \infty$ (or, more synthetically, X_n converges in probability to X) if for any positive ε,

$$\lim_{n\to\infty} \mathrm{P}\{|X_n - X| > \varepsilon\} = 0, \tag{2}$$

that is if, for any positive ε and η there is a $N_0 = N_0(\varepsilon, \eta)$ such that

$$\mathrm{P}\{|X_n - X_m| > \varepsilon\} < \eta,$$

for all $n, m \geq N_0$. A more compact form for writing the convergence i.p. is

$$\mathrm{p}\lim X_n = X.$$

Convergence "in the mean" or "in mean square" (m.s.). X_n is said to converge in mean square to X if

$$\lim_{n\to\infty} \mathrm{E}\{|X_n - X|^2\} = 0, \tag{3}$$

that is if, for any positive ε, there is a $N_0 = N_0(\varepsilon)$ such that

$$\mathrm{E}\{|X_n - X_m|^2\} < \varepsilon,$$

for all $n, m \geq N_0$. A more compact form for referring to this mode of convergence is

$$\underset{n\to\infty}{\mathrm{l.i.m.}} X_n = X.$$

These convergence definitions may be extended, as in analysis, to refer to functions. Let us therefore consider a random function $X(t)$, where t has a continuous range.

Continuity "in the mean" or "in mean square" of a random function. The random function $X(t)$ is m.s. continuous at $t = \tau$ if

$$\underset{t\to\tau}{\mathrm{l.i.m.}} X(t) = X(\tau),$$

that is, if

$$\lim_{t\to\tau} \mathrm{E}\{|X(t) - X(\tau)|^2\} = 0. \tag{4}$$

If this is true at every point t in an entire interval $(0, T)$, the function is m.s. continuous over the interval. Eq. (4) can also be written as (Bartlett, 1956, p. 139)

$$\lim_{\substack{t\to\tau\\ s\to\tau}} \mathrm{E}\{X(t)X(s)\} \equiv \lim_{\substack{t\to\tau\\ s\to\tau}} \sigma(t,s) = \sigma^2(\tau) \equiv \mathrm{E}\{X^2(\tau)\},$$

from which, given (4), we must necessarily have

$$\mathrm{E}\left\{ \underset{t\to\tau}{\mathrm{l.i.m.}}\, X(t) \right\} = \mathrm{E}\{X(\tau)\} = \lim_{t\to\tau} \mathrm{E}\{X(t)\}, \tag{5}$$

so that the m.s. limiting operation and the expectation sign commute.

We next extend the ideas so far expounded to differentiation and integration.

Stochastic differentiation. The random function $X(t)$ is said to be m.s. differentiable at point t if the difference quotient $[X(t+h) - X(t)]/h$ converges in mean square to a value $\dot{X}(t)$, that is,

$$\lim_{h\to 0} \mathrm{E}\left\{ \left| \frac{X(t+h) - X(t)}{h} - \dot{X}(t) \right|^2 \right\} = 0, \tag{6}$$

and $\dot{X}(t)$ is said to be the m.s. differential coefficient of $X(t)$.

Stochastic integration. Given a random function $X(t)$ and a real bounded deterministic function $g(t)$, piecewise continuous in the ordinary sense, let us consider the sum

$$U_n = \sum_{k=1}^{n} g(t'_k)X(t'_k)(t_k - t_{k-1}), \tag{7}$$

where $a = t_0 < t_1 < \ldots < t_{n-1} < t_n = b$ and $t_{k-1} \le t'_k \le t_k$. In other words, we proceed as in the ordinary calculus (see, e.g., Courant, 1961, Vol. I, ch. II.2 and Appendix). Now, U_n is a stochastic variable, that we can check for m.s. convergence. If U_n converges in mean square to a stochastic limit U, then U is said to be the (Riemann) mean square integral of $g(t)X(t)$ over the interval (a, b), that is

$$\int_a^b g(t)X(t)\,\mathrm{d}t = U = \underset{n\to\infty}{\mathrm{l.i.m.}}\, U_n. \tag{8}$$

It can be shown that stochastic integrals have the same formal properties as ordinary integrals (it is therefore possible to consider infinite ranges of integration, as well as random functions in more than one real variable, etc.). For proofs we refer the reader to the works cited in footnote 6.

3.3. Theoretical aspects of the estimation method[7]

Let us consider system (1), already seen in section 3.1, and shown here for convenience

$$\mathrm{D}\boldsymbol{x}(t) = \boldsymbol{A}\boldsymbol{x}(t) + \boldsymbol{B}\boldsymbol{z}(t) + \boldsymbol{u}(t), \tag{1}$$

where $\boldsymbol{u}(t)$ is a vector of disturbances assumed of white noise type. In this case $\boldsymbol{u}(t)$ is conventionally considered to satisfy the equation (Sargan, 1976)[8]

$$\boldsymbol{u}(t) = \frac{\mathrm{d}}{\mathrm{d}t}\boldsymbol{\zeta}(t), \tag{9}$$

where $\boldsymbol{\zeta}(t)$ is generated by a homogeneous stochastic process with uncorrelated increments and with mean zero, that is

$$\begin{aligned}
&\mathrm{E}\{\boldsymbol{\zeta}(t)\} = 0, \qquad \forall t,\\
&\mathrm{E}\{[\boldsymbol{\zeta}(t_1) - \boldsymbol{\zeta}(t_2)][\boldsymbol{\zeta}(t_3) - \boldsymbol{\zeta}(t_4)]^{\mathrm{T}}\} = 0,\\
&\forall t_1 > t_2 \geq t_3 > t_4, \qquad \text{(uncorrelated increments)}\\
&\mathrm{E}\{[\boldsymbol{\zeta}(t+h) - \boldsymbol{\zeta}(t)][\boldsymbol{\zeta}(t+h) - \boldsymbol{\zeta}(t)]^{\mathrm{T}}\} = \boldsymbol{\Omega}|h|, \qquad \text{(homogeneity)}
\end{aligned} \tag{10}$$

where $\boldsymbol{\Omega}$ is a matrix of constants.

[7] The problem of estimation of system (1) could also be treated from the frequency point of view: see, for example, Robinson (1976). In our opinion, however, it is easier to handle the model in the time domain than in the frequency domain. See also the remarks by Bergstrom (in the Introduction to Bergstrom ed., 1976, p. 12) and by Phillips (1978, p. 272).

[8] Assumption (9) can be dropped without consequences. Suppose that $\boldsymbol{u}(t)$ is generated by a stochastic process such that the integral $\boldsymbol{\zeta}(t) = \int_0^t \boldsymbol{u}(s)\,\mathrm{d}s$ has the properties (10). Even if

$$\lim_{h\to 0} \mathrm{E}\left\{\left|\frac{\boldsymbol{\zeta}(t+h) - \boldsymbol{\zeta}(t)}{h} - \dot{\boldsymbol{\zeta}}(t)\right|^2\right\}$$

does not exist (so that $\boldsymbol{\zeta}(t)$ is non-m.s. differentiable and the process $\boldsymbol{u}(t)$ cannot be rigorously defined), it is possible to consider the system

$$\mathrm{d}\boldsymbol{x}(t) = \boldsymbol{A}\boldsymbol{x}(t)\,\mathrm{d}t + \boldsymbol{B}\boldsymbol{z}(t)\,\mathrm{d}t + \mathrm{d}\boldsymbol{\zeta}(t), \tag{1'}$$

where $\boldsymbol{u}(t)$ is replaced by the mean square differential of the process $\boldsymbol{\zeta}(t)$; system (1′) has the same properties as (1). See Wymer (1972, 1976).

In what follows we shall first consider the exact discrete model equivalent to (1) and then an approximate discrete analogue.

3.3.1. The exact discrete analogue

The first step is to solve the differential system (1). As it is linear and non-homogeneous, its general solution is given by the general solution of the corresponding homogeneous[9] system plus a particular solution of the non-homogeneous system itself. Formally (see, e.g., Bellman, 1953, p. 14) the general solution of a system of the type

$$\mathrm{D}\boldsymbol{y}(t) = \boldsymbol{A}\boldsymbol{y}(t) + \boldsymbol{w}(t), \qquad \boldsymbol{y}(0) = \boldsymbol{c}, \tag{11}$$

where $\boldsymbol{w}(t)$ is a vector of known functions, is given by

$$\boldsymbol{y}(t) = \boldsymbol{r}(t) + \int_0^t \boldsymbol{R}(t-\theta)\boldsymbol{w}(\theta)\,\mathrm{d}\theta, \tag{11'}$$

where $\boldsymbol{r}(t)$ is the solution of $\mathrm{D}\boldsymbol{r}(t) = \boldsymbol{A}\boldsymbol{r}(t)$, $\boldsymbol{r}(0) = \boldsymbol{c}$, and $\boldsymbol{R}(t)$ is the solution of $\mathrm{D}\boldsymbol{R}(t) = \boldsymbol{A}\boldsymbol{R}(t)$, $\boldsymbol{R}(0) = \boldsymbol{I}$. As the solution of $\mathrm{D}\boldsymbol{r}(t) = \boldsymbol{A}\boldsymbol{r}(t)$, $\boldsymbol{r}(0) = \boldsymbol{c}$, is $\boldsymbol{c}\mathrm{e}^{\boldsymbol{A}t}$,[10] and the solution of $\mathrm{D}\boldsymbol{R}(t) = \boldsymbol{A}\boldsymbol{R}(t)$, $\boldsymbol{R}(0) = \boldsymbol{I}$ is $\mathrm{e}^{\boldsymbol{A}t}$, we have

$$\boldsymbol{y}(t) = \boldsymbol{y}(0)\mathrm{e}^{\boldsymbol{A}t} + \int_0^t \boldsymbol{I}\mathrm{e}^{\boldsymbol{A}(t-\theta)}\boldsymbol{w}(\theta)\,\mathrm{d}\theta. \tag{12}$$

In the case of (1) it is enough to observe that $\boldsymbol{w}(t)$ is the sum of $\boldsymbol{B}\boldsymbol{z}(t)$ and $\boldsymbol{u}(t)$ and to remember the property of the integral of a sum. Thus

$$\boldsymbol{x}(t) = \boldsymbol{x}(0)\mathrm{e}^{\boldsymbol{A}t} + \int_0^t \mathrm{e}^{\boldsymbol{A}(t-\theta)}\boldsymbol{B}\boldsymbol{z}(\theta)\,\mathrm{d}\theta + \int_0^t \mathrm{e}^{\boldsymbol{A}(t-\theta)}\boldsymbol{u}(\theta)\,\mathrm{d}\theta. \tag{12'}$$

[9] The adjectives "homogeneous" and "non-homogeneous" are used here with the meaning that they have in the theory of differential equations, and should not be confused with the definitions concerning stochastic processes.

[10] We recall that $\mathrm{e}^{\boldsymbol{A}t}$ is defined as the matrix series

$$\mathrm{e}^{\boldsymbol{A}t} = \sum_{j=0}^{\infty} \frac{\boldsymbol{A}^j t^j}{j!}, \qquad \boldsymbol{A}^0 = \boldsymbol{I},$$

which converges uniformly in any finite interval, and the sum function is a continuous function of t for all finite t. See, for example, Gantmacher (1959, Vol. I, p. 113 and p. 122).

Given (9), we have $\boldsymbol{u}(\theta)\,\mathrm{d}\theta = \mathrm{d}\,\boldsymbol{\zeta}(\theta)$, so that the solution can be written as

$$\boldsymbol{x}(t) = \boldsymbol{x}(0)\mathrm{e}^{At} + \int_0^t \mathrm{e}^{A(t-\theta)}\boldsymbol{B}\boldsymbol{z}(\theta)\,\mathrm{d}\theta + \int_0^t \mathrm{e}^{A(t-\theta)}\,\mathrm{d}\,\boldsymbol{\zeta}(\theta), \tag{13}$$

where the last integral on the right hand side is a stochastic integral.

Suppose now that the continuous variables are observed at equispaced intervals, say every δ time units, where δ is the length of the observation interval in terms of the basic time unit of the system. Evaluating (13) at time $t - \delta$ we have

$$\boldsymbol{x}(t-\delta) = \boldsymbol{x}(0)\mathrm{e}^{A(t-\delta)} + \int_0^{t-\delta} \mathrm{e}^{A(t-\delta-\theta)}\boldsymbol{B}\boldsymbol{z}(\theta)\,\mathrm{d}\theta + \int_0^{t-\delta} \mathrm{e}^{A(t-\delta-\theta)}\,\mathrm{d}\,\boldsymbol{\zeta}(\theta). \tag{14}$$

By multiplying both members of (14) by $\mathrm{e}^{\delta A}$ and subtracting from (13) we obtain

$$\boldsymbol{x}(t) - \mathrm{e}^{\delta A}\boldsymbol{x}(t-\delta) = \int_0^t \mathrm{e}^{A(t-\theta)}\boldsymbol{B}\boldsymbol{z}(\theta)\,\mathrm{d}\theta - \int_0^{t-\delta} \mathrm{e}^{A(t-\theta)}\boldsymbol{B}\boldsymbol{z}(\theta)\,\mathrm{d}\theta + \int_0^t \mathrm{e}^{A(t-\theta)}\,\mathrm{d}\,\boldsymbol{\zeta}(\theta) - \int_0^{t-\delta} \mathrm{e}^{A(t-\theta)}\,\mathrm{d}\,\boldsymbol{\zeta}(\theta). \tag{14'}$$

Now, since $\int_0^{t-\delta} \cdots = -\int_{t-\delta}^0 \cdots$, and given the additive property of integrals, we get

$$\boldsymbol{x}(t) - \mathrm{e}^{\delta A}\boldsymbol{x}(t-\delta) = \int_{t-\delta}^t \mathrm{e}^{A(t-\theta)}\boldsymbol{B}\boldsymbol{z}(\theta)\,\mathrm{d}\theta + \int_{t-\delta}^t \mathrm{e}^{A(t-\theta)}\,\mathrm{d}\,\boldsymbol{\zeta}(\theta). \tag{14''}$$

By suitable changes of variable[11] in the last two integrals we obtain

$$\boldsymbol{x}(t) = \mathrm{e}^{\delta A}\boldsymbol{x}(t-\delta) + \int_0^{\delta} \mathrm{e}^{A\theta}\boldsymbol{B}\boldsymbol{z}(t-\theta)\,\mathrm{d}\theta + \int_0^{\delta} \mathrm{e}^{A\theta}\,\mathrm{d}\,\boldsymbol{\zeta}(t-\theta). \tag{15}$$

Let $\boldsymbol{y}_\tau$ be the discrete observation of a continuous variable $\boldsymbol{y}(t)$ at time $\tau\delta$, τ being an integer, that is $\boldsymbol{y}_\tau = \boldsymbol{y}(\tau\delta)$. Setting $t = \tau\delta$ in (15) we have

$$\boldsymbol{x}_\tau = \mathrm{e}^{\delta A}\boldsymbol{x}_{\tau-1} + \boldsymbol{\psi}_\tau + \boldsymbol{\omega}_\tau, \tag{16}$$

where

$$\psi_\tau \equiv \int_0^\delta e^{A\theta} Bz(\tau\delta - \theta)\,d\theta, \qquad \omega_\tau \equiv \int_0^\delta e^{A\theta}\,d\zeta(\tau\delta - \theta). \tag{16'}$$

Eqs. (16) can be considered as a set of stochastic difference equations generating the discrete time data x_τ over some sample period $\tau = 1, \ldots, T$. Since the observations generated by the differential system (1) will satisfy the exact discrete model (16) irrespective of the length of the interval between successive observations, the sampling properties of the differential system may be studied by considering the sampling properties of the exact discrete model.

We must now cope with two problems: the first is how to evaluate the integral ψ_τ, the second is how to deal with flow variables.

3.3.1.1. *Evaluation of the integral ψ_τ*

In general the exogenous variables $z(t)$ will not be simple integrable functions of time so that we cannot integrate out in (16′) to obtain a model that can be estimated directly. Therefore an approximation to ψ_τ is necessary. A satisfactory solution is provided by a quadratic approximation,[12] namely we approximate $z(\tau\delta - \theta)$ by a quadratic in θ for $0 \le \theta < \delta$ and express the coefficients of this quadratic in terms of three consecutive observations $z_{\tau-2}$, $z_{\tau-1}$ and z_τ.

[11]Consider, for example, the first integral on the right-hand side and make the substitution $\theta = t - s$. Then

$$\int_{t-\delta}^{t} e^{A(t-\theta)} Bz(\theta)\,d\theta = \int_\delta^0 e^{As} Bz(t-s)\frac{d\theta}{ds}\,ds = -\int_\delta^0 e^{As} Bz(t-s)\,ds$$

$$= \int_0^\delta e^{As} Bz(t-s)\,ds.$$

Given the arbitrariness of the denomination of the integration variable, we denominate s as θ [of course, this θ is not the same θ as before, but this fact has no influence on the evaluation of the integrals in (15)].

[12]See, e.g., Phillips (1976a, section 3), Wymer (DISCON Manual, section I).

Consider the vector equation $z(\tau\delta - \theta) = \boldsymbol{a}\theta^2 + \boldsymbol{b}\theta + \boldsymbol{c}$. Then

$$z_\tau = z(\tau\delta) = z(\tau\delta - \theta) \qquad \text{for } \theta = 0 \text{ and so } z_\tau = \boldsymbol{c},$$
$$z_{\tau-1} = z(\tau\delta - \delta) = \boldsymbol{a}\delta^2 + \boldsymbol{b}\delta + \boldsymbol{c}, \tag{17}$$
$$z_{\tau-2} = z(\tau\delta - 2\delta) = 4\boldsymbol{a}\delta^2 + 2\boldsymbol{b}\delta + \boldsymbol{c}.$$

By substituting $z(\tau\delta - \theta) = \boldsymbol{a}\theta^2 + \boldsymbol{b}\theta + \boldsymbol{c}$ in the expression for ψ_τ defined in (16), we have

$$\psi_\tau = \int_0^\delta e^{A\theta}\boldsymbol{B}(\boldsymbol{a}\theta^2 + \boldsymbol{b}\theta + \boldsymbol{c})\,d\theta. \tag{18}$$

If we integrate out in (18) we obtain[13]

$$\begin{aligned}
\psi_\tau &= \int_0^\delta e^{A\theta}\boldsymbol{Ba}\theta^2 d\theta + \int_0^\delta e^{A\theta}\boldsymbol{Bb}\theta\, d\theta + \int_0^\delta e^{A\theta}\boldsymbol{Bc}\, d\theta \\
&= \left[\boldsymbol{A}^{-1}\theta^2 e^{A\theta}\boldsymbol{Ba} - 2\boldsymbol{A}^{-3}e^{A\theta}\boldsymbol{Ba}(\boldsymbol{A}\theta - \boldsymbol{I})\right]_0^\delta \\
&\quad + \left[\boldsymbol{A}^{-2}e^{A\theta}\boldsymbol{Bb}(\boldsymbol{A}\theta - \boldsymbol{I})\right]_0^\delta + \left[\boldsymbol{A}^{-1}e^{A\theta}\boldsymbol{Bc}\right]_0^\delta \\
&= \left[\boldsymbol{A}^{-1}\theta^2 e^{A\theta}\boldsymbol{Ba} - 2\boldsymbol{A}^{-2}e^{A\theta}\boldsymbol{Ba}\theta + 2\boldsymbol{A}^{-3}e^{A\theta}\boldsymbol{Ba}\right]_0^\delta \\
&\quad + \left[\boldsymbol{A}^{-1}e^{A\theta}\boldsymbol{Bb}\theta - \boldsymbol{A}^{-2}e^{A\theta}\boldsymbol{Bb}\right]_0^\delta + \left[\boldsymbol{A}^{-1}e^{A\theta}\boldsymbol{Bc}\right]_0^\delta \\
&= \{[\boldsymbol{A}^{-1}\delta^2 e^{A\delta}\boldsymbol{Ba} - 2\boldsymbol{A}^{-2}e^{A\delta}\boldsymbol{Ba}\delta + 2\boldsymbol{A}^{-3}e^{A\delta}\boldsymbol{Ba}] \\
&\quad - [2\boldsymbol{A}^{-3}\boldsymbol{Ba}]\} + \{[\boldsymbol{A}^{-1}e^{A\delta}\boldsymbol{Bb}\delta - \boldsymbol{A}^{-2}e^{A\delta}\boldsymbol{Bb}] \\
&\quad - [-\boldsymbol{A}^{-2}\boldsymbol{Bb}]\} + \{\boldsymbol{A}^{-1}e^{A\delta}\boldsymbol{Bc} - \boldsymbol{A}^{-1}\boldsymbol{Bc}\}.
\end{aligned} \tag{18'}$$

In the last equation we collect terms according to the negative powers of $\boldsymbol{A}$ and using (17) obtain

$$\begin{aligned}
\psi_\tau &= \boldsymbol{A}^{-1}\left[e^{A\delta}\boldsymbol{B}(\boldsymbol{a}\delta^2 + \boldsymbol{b}\delta + \boldsymbol{c}) - \boldsymbol{Bc}\right] - \boldsymbol{A}^{-2}\left[e^{A\delta}\boldsymbol{B}(2\boldsymbol{a}\delta + \boldsymbol{b}) \right.\\
&\quad \left. - \boldsymbol{Bb}\right] + 2\boldsymbol{A}^{-3}(e^{A\delta} - \boldsymbol{I})\boldsymbol{Ba} \\
&= \boldsymbol{A}^{-1}\left[e^{A\delta}\boldsymbol{B}z_{\tau-1} - \boldsymbol{B}z_\tau\right] - \boldsymbol{A}^{-2}\left[e^{A\delta}\boldsymbol{B}(2\boldsymbol{a}\delta + \boldsymbol{b}) - \boldsymbol{Bb}\right] \\
&\quad + 2\boldsymbol{A}^{-3}(e^{A\delta} - \boldsymbol{I})\boldsymbol{Ba}.
\end{aligned} \tag{19}$$

[13] From ordinary integral calculus remember that

$$\int e^{\alpha x} x\, dx = \alpha^{-2}e^{\alpha x}(\alpha x - 1)$$

and that

$$\int e^{\alpha x}x^2 dx = \alpha^{-1}x^2 e^{\alpha x} - 2\alpha^{-1}\int e^{\alpha x}x\, dx = \alpha^{-1}x^2 e^{\alpha x} - 2\alpha^{-3}e^{\alpha x}(\alpha x - 1).$$

These rules apply to matrix integrals as well: see, for example, Gantmacher (1959, Vol. I, ch. V).

By direct substitution[14] we can check that

$$\begin{aligned}\psi_\tau = \delta\Big[&\{(\delta A)^{-3}+\tfrac{1}{2}(\delta A)^{-2}\}e^{A\delta}\\ &-(\delta A)^{-3}-\tfrac{3}{2}(\delta A)^{-2}-(\delta A)^{-1}\Big]Bz_\tau\\ +\delta\Big[&\{-2(\delta A)^{-3}+(\delta A)^{-1}\}e^{A\delta}\\ &+2(\delta A)^{-3}+2(\delta A)^{-2}\Big]Bz_{\tau-1}\\ +\delta\Big[&\{(\delta A)^{-3}-\tfrac{1}{2}(\delta A)^{-2}\}e^{A\delta}\\ &-(\delta A)^{-3}-\tfrac{1}{2}(\delta A)^{-2}\Big]Bz_{\tau-2}.\end{aligned} \tag{20}$$

The bias involved in using this approximation is of $O(\delta^4)$ for small δ.[15] Of course (20) will be exact when the elements of $z(t)$ are polynomials in t the degree of which is at most two.

For estimation purposes we may consider $\delta = 1$ (this means setting the basic time unit equal to the length of the observation interval), hence $\tau = t$.

When we come to estimate the model (16) in practice, it will often be necessary to use the derivatives of the expressions that appear in (20) with respect to the unknown elements of A and B in the computations. These derivatives give rise to quite complicated formulae which can lead to serious rounding errors. It is therefore useful to simplify the expressions before differentiating them; this simplification can be obtained by expanding A in a power series.

Setting $\delta = 1$ in (20) and calling K_1, K_2, K_3, in the order, the coefficient of Bz_t, the coefficient of Bz_{t-1} and the coefficient of Bz_{t-2}, we have

$$\begin{aligned}K_1 &= \left(A^{-3}+\tfrac{1}{2}A^{-2}\right)e^{A}-A^{-3}-\tfrac{3}{2}A^{-2}-A^{-1}\\ &= \left(I+\tfrac{1}{2}A\right)A^{-3}e^{A}-\left(I+\tfrac{1}{2}A\right)A^{-3}-A^{-2}-A^{-1}\\ &= \left(I+\tfrac{1}{2}A\right)A^{-3}(e^{A}-I)-A^{-2}-A^{-1}.\end{aligned}$$

[14] That is substituting in (20) the values of z_τ etc. defined in (17). Apart from this check, the procedure to obtain (20) is the following. Let $\psi_\tau = \alpha Bz_\tau + \beta Bz_{\tau-1} + \gamma Bz_{\tau-2}$, where α, β, γ, are to be determined. Substituting z_τ etc. from (17) and comparing the result with (19) we can determine α, β and γ. The result is (20).

[15] Phillips (1976a, p. 139). The order of magnitude symbol O is used here in the following sense: given a function $f(\delta)$, $f(\delta) = O(\delta^r)$ if $\lim_{\delta\to 0}(\delta^{-r}|f(\delta)|)$ is finite. See also Hyslop (1959, p. 14).

Since

$$\mathrm{e}^{\boldsymbol{A}} = \sum_{k=0}^{\infty} \frac{\boldsymbol{A}^k}{k!} = \boldsymbol{I} + \boldsymbol{A} + \tfrac{1}{2}\boldsymbol{A}^2 + \frac{\boldsymbol{A}^3}{3!} + \frac{\boldsymbol{A}^4}{4!} + \cdots + \frac{\boldsymbol{A}^n}{n!} + \cdots,$$

it follows that

$$\begin{aligned} \boldsymbol{A}^{-3}(\mathrm{e}^{\boldsymbol{A}} - \boldsymbol{I}) &= \boldsymbol{A}^{-2} + \tfrac{1}{2}\boldsymbol{A}^{-1} + \frac{\boldsymbol{I}}{3!} + \frac{\boldsymbol{A}}{4!} + \cdots + \frac{\boldsymbol{A}^{n-3}}{n!} + \cdots \\ &= \boldsymbol{A}^{-2} + \tfrac{1}{2}\boldsymbol{A}^{-1} + \boldsymbol{E}, \end{aligned} \tag{21}$$

where

$$\boldsymbol{E} \equiv \sum_{k=0}^{\infty} \frac{\boldsymbol{A}^k}{(k+3)!}. \tag{22}$$

Therefore we have

$$\begin{aligned} \boldsymbol{K}_1 &= \left(\boldsymbol{I} + \tfrac{1}{2}\boldsymbol{A}\right)\left(\boldsymbol{A}^{-2} + \tfrac{1}{2}\boldsymbol{A}^{-1} + \boldsymbol{E}\right) - \boldsymbol{A}^{2} - \boldsymbol{A}^{-1} \\ &= \left(\boldsymbol{I} + \tfrac{1}{2}\boldsymbol{A}\right)\boldsymbol{E} + \tfrac{1}{4}\boldsymbol{I}. \end{aligned} \tag{23}$$

Let us next consider $\boldsymbol{K}_2$:

$$\begin{aligned} \boldsymbol{K}_2 &= (-2\boldsymbol{A}^{-3} + \boldsymbol{A}^{-1})\mathrm{e}^{\boldsymbol{A}} + 2\boldsymbol{A}^{-3} + 2\boldsymbol{A}^{-2} \\ &= (-2\boldsymbol{I} + \boldsymbol{A}^2)\boldsymbol{A}^{-3}\mathrm{e}^{\boldsymbol{A}} - (-2\boldsymbol{I} + \boldsymbol{A}^2)\boldsymbol{A}^{-3} + 2\boldsymbol{A}^{-2} + \boldsymbol{A}^{-1} \\ &= (-2\boldsymbol{I} + \boldsymbol{A}^2)\boldsymbol{A}^{-3}(\mathrm{e}^{\boldsymbol{A}} - \boldsymbol{I}) + 2\boldsymbol{A}^{-2} + \boldsymbol{A}^{-1}. \end{aligned}$$

With the use of (21) we obtain

$$\begin{aligned} \boldsymbol{K}_2 &= (-2\boldsymbol{I} + \boldsymbol{A}^2)\left(\boldsymbol{A}^{-2} + \tfrac{1}{2}\boldsymbol{A}^{-1} + \boldsymbol{E}\right) + 2\boldsymbol{A}^{-2} + \boldsymbol{A}^{-1} \\ &= (-2\boldsymbol{I} + \boldsymbol{A}^2)\boldsymbol{E} - 2\boldsymbol{A}^{-2} - \boldsymbol{A}^{-1} + \boldsymbol{I} + \tfrac{1}{2}\boldsymbol{A} + 2\boldsymbol{A}^{-2} + \boldsymbol{A}^{-1} \\ &= (-2\boldsymbol{I} + \boldsymbol{A}^2)\boldsymbol{E} + \boldsymbol{I} + \tfrac{1}{2}\boldsymbol{A}. \end{aligned} \tag{24}$$

We consider finally

$$\begin{aligned} \boldsymbol{K}_3 &= \left(\boldsymbol{A}^{-3} - \tfrac{1}{2}\boldsymbol{A}^{-2}\right)\mathrm{e}^{\boldsymbol{A}} - \boldsymbol{A}^{-3} - \tfrac{1}{2}\boldsymbol{A}^{-2} \\ &= \left(\boldsymbol{I} - \tfrac{1}{2}\boldsymbol{A}\right)\boldsymbol{A}^{-3}\mathrm{e}^{\boldsymbol{A}} - \left(\boldsymbol{I} - \tfrac{1}{2}\boldsymbol{A}\right)\boldsymbol{A}^{-3} - \boldsymbol{A}^{-2} \\ &= \left(\boldsymbol{I} - \tfrac{1}{2}\boldsymbol{A}\right)\boldsymbol{A}^{-3}(\mathrm{e}^{\boldsymbol{A}} - \boldsymbol{I}) - \boldsymbol{A}^{-2}, \end{aligned}$$

whence, with (21)

$$\begin{aligned} K_3 &= \left(I - \tfrac{1}{2}A\right)\left(A^{-2} + \tfrac{1}{2}A^{-1} + E\right) - A^{-2} \\ &= \left(I - \tfrac{1}{2}A\right)E + A^{-2} + \tfrac{1}{2}A^{-1} - \tfrac{1}{2}A^{-1} - \tfrac{1}{4}I - A^{-2} \\ &= \left(I - \tfrac{1}{2}A\right)E - \tfrac{1}{4}I. \end{aligned} \tag{25}$$

Account having been taken of these transformations, system (16) can be written as

$$x_t = \mathrm{e}^{A}x_{t-1} + \sum_{i=1}^{3} C_i z_{t-i+1} + \omega_t, \tag{26}$$

where the coefficients C_i are defined as the product $K_i B$, that is

$$\begin{aligned} C_1 &\equiv \left[\left(I + \tfrac{1}{2}A\right)E + \tfrac{1}{4}I\right]B, \\ C_2 &\equiv \left[\left(-2I + A^2\right)E + I + \tfrac{1}{2}A\right]B, \\ C_3 &\equiv \left[\left(I - \tfrac{1}{2}A\right)E - \tfrac{1}{4}I\right]B, \end{aligned} \tag{27}$$

and E is defined in (22).

3.3.1.2. *Models containing flow variables*

The exact discrete analogue has been derived under the assumption that all variables are measurable at a point in time. Although this is true of certain variables like wages, prices, interest rates and stocks (which we term *instantaneous variables*), many economic variables are *flow variables* such as consumption, income, etc. or variables which are the rate of change of some instantaneously measurable variables, such as the rate of change of the money supply, of the capital stock (net investment), etc. These variables (which we term flow variables in the broad sense) are not measurable at a point in time and observations on them are usually integrals over some given interval. If we let $y(t)$ be a generic flow variable, the integral

$$y^0(t) = \frac{1}{\delta}\int_0^{\delta} y(t-\theta)\,\mathrm{d}\theta \tag{28}$$

is measurable. We denote by y_τ^0 an observation of $y^0(t)$, that is a flow over the interval $(\tau\delta - \delta, \tau\delta)$ where δ is, as before, the length of the observation interval; actually y_τ^0 is what we observe in reality.[16]

Therefore, a continuous model containing flow variables needs to be integrated over the observation interval in order to produce a model defined in terms of variables that are measurable. If we integrate (15) we have

$$\begin{aligned}\frac{1}{\delta}\int_{t-\delta}^{t} \boldsymbol{x}(\theta)\,\mathrm{d}\theta &= \mathrm{e}^{\delta \boldsymbol{A}}\cdot\frac{1}{\delta}\int_{t-\delta}^{t} \boldsymbol{x}(\theta-\delta)\,\mathrm{d}\theta \\ &\quad+\frac{1}{\delta}\int_{t-\delta}^{t}\int_{0}^{\delta}\mathrm{e}^{\boldsymbol{A}\theta}\boldsymbol{B}\boldsymbol{z}(s-\theta)\,\mathrm{d}\theta\,\mathrm{d}s \\ &\quad+\frac{1}{\delta}\int_{t-\delta}^{t}\int_{0}^{\delta}\mathrm{e}^{\boldsymbol{A}\theta}\,\mathrm{d}\boldsymbol{\zeta}(s-\theta)\,\mathrm{d}s \\ {}^{17}&= \mathrm{e}^{\delta \boldsymbol{A}}\cdot\frac{1}{\delta}\int_{t-\delta}^{t} \boldsymbol{x}(\theta-\delta)\,\mathrm{d}\theta \\ &\quad+\int_{0}^{\delta}\mathrm{e}^{\boldsymbol{A}\theta}\frac{1}{\delta}\int_{t-\delta}^{t}\boldsymbol{B}\boldsymbol{z}(s-\theta)\,\mathrm{d}s\,\mathrm{d}\theta \\ &\quad+\frac{1}{\delta}\int_{t-\delta}^{t}\int_{0}^{\delta}\mathrm{e}^{\boldsymbol{A}\theta}\,\mathrm{d}\boldsymbol{\zeta}(s-\theta)\,\mathrm{d}s. \end{aligned} \tag{29}$$

Thus the integral of a flow variable can be replaced by the observed value y_τ^0 as defined in (28), and y may be either an endogenous (x) or an exogenous (z) variable.[18]

Now, apart from the particular case of a model containing only flow variables, the integration carried out in (29) has also transformed the instantaneous variables into integrals and these we must deal with. In fact, if we now let $y(t)$ denote a generic instantaneous variable, the integral

$$\frac{1}{\delta}\int_{t-\delta}^{t} y(\theta)\,\mathrm{d}\theta$$

is not observable and has to be evaluated using, for example, the

[16] This had already been pointed out by Koopmans (1950) and Phillips (1956), and was occasionally noted in some applied econometric studies which, although using traditional methods, attempted to take account of this fact. See, for example, Houthakker and Taylor (1966, ch. 1, section III).

[17] We use here the property of the change in the order of integration in multiple integrals.

[18] Note that $\int_0^\delta y(t-\theta)\,\mathrm{d}\theta = \int_{t-\delta}^{t} y(\delta)\,\mathrm{d}\delta$. See footnote 11.

trapezoidal rule. If δ is small, an acceptable approximation is

$$\int_{t-\delta}^{t} y(\theta)\,\mathrm{d}\theta \simeq \frac{\delta}{2}[y(t)+y(t-\delta)],$$

whence, if we set $t=\tau\delta$

$$\frac{1}{\delta}\int_{t-\delta}^{t} y(\theta)\,\mathrm{d}\theta \simeq \tfrac{1}{2}[y(\tau\delta)+y(\tau\delta-\delta)], \tag{30}$$

so that an observation of this integral is approximately given by

$$y_\tau^0 = \mathrm{M}y_\tau, \qquad \mathrm{M} \equiv \tfrac{1}{2}(1+\mathrm{L}), \tag{31}$$

L being the lag operator.

It should be pointed out that when we have to deal with a variable that in principle is an instantaneous variable but that has actually been observed or defined as an average of the values over the observation period (e.g. an annual price index defined as the average of the monthly indexes) or generated in such a way as to give observations equivalent to period averages (e.g. an implicit GNP deflator), then the variable that we observe must be treated as the integral of the continuous instantaneous variable. In other words, in these cases (28) holds and not (31).

It may also happen that the model contains second order equations that determine stock variables, as in ch. 2, eqs. (42). In this case, as we know, we introduce additional variables so as to reduce the model to a first-order system. These variables will be the instantaneous rates of change of the stock variables, and observations on them can be derived from the point observations on the stock. Let $y_1(t)=\mathrm{D}y(t)$ be the new variable; then we have

$$\frac{1}{\delta}\int_{t-\delta}^{t} y_1(\theta)\,\mathrm{d}\theta = \frac{1}{\delta}[y(t)-y(t-\delta)],$$

and observations on $y_1(\tau\delta)$ are given by

$$y_{1\tau}^0 = \Delta y_\tau, \qquad \Delta \equiv \frac{1}{\delta}(1-\mathrm{L}). \tag{32}$$

Thus the exact discrete analogue of a continuous mixed stock-flow model is given by

$$\begin{aligned} \boldsymbol{x}_\tau^0 = \mathrm{e}^{\delta A}\boldsymbol{x}_{\tau-1}^0 &+ \int_0^\delta \mathrm{e}^{A\theta}\boldsymbol{B}\boldsymbol{z}^0(\tau\delta-\theta)\,\mathrm{d}\theta \\ &+ \int_{\tau\delta-\delta}^{\tau\delta}\int_0^\delta \mathrm{e}^{A\theta}\,\mathrm{d}\boldsymbol{\zeta}(s-\theta)\,\mathrm{d}s, \end{aligned} \tag{33}$$

where the variables with the superscript zero are replaced by (28), (31), or (32) as the case may be.

We must next point out that the integration carried out in order to obtain measurable variables implies that the disturbances in (29) and so in (33) are no longer serially uncorrelated. It is possible, however, to derive (see Appendix II to this chapter) an approximation to the process of formation of these disturbances that is independent of the parameters of the model and which allows a pre-whitening of the data. If we denote by $\boldsymbol{\xi}(t)$ the disturbance vector, this approximation is[19]

$$\boldsymbol{\xi}(t) \simeq (1 + 0.268\mathrm{L})\boldsymbol{\varepsilon}(t), \tag{34}$$

where $\boldsymbol{\varepsilon}(t)$ is a serially uncorrelated random disturbance. As the moving average process (34) is independent of the parameters of the model, the model can be transformed by using the inverse of this process to obtain a model with serially uncorrelated disturbances.

We have (as we are in discrete time, we use t as a subscript)

$$\boldsymbol{\varepsilon}_t = (1 + 0.268\mathrm{L})^{-1}\boldsymbol{\xi}_t. \tag{34$'$}$$

If we expand $(1 + 0.268\mathrm{L})^{-1}$ in a Taylor series[20] and truncate after the third order term which is sufficiently small for all practical purposes (Wymer, 1976), we obtain

$$\begin{aligned}\boldsymbol{\varepsilon}_t &\simeq (1 - 0.268\mathrm{L} + 0.268^2\mathrm{L}^2 - 0.268^3\mathrm{L}^3)\boldsymbol{\xi}_t \\ &= \boldsymbol{\xi}_t - 0.268\boldsymbol{\xi}_{t-1} + 0.268^2\boldsymbol{\xi}_{t-2} - 0.268^3\boldsymbol{\xi}_{t-3}.\end{aligned} \tag{35}$$

Therefore, if we transform the variables $\boldsymbol{x}^0$ and $\boldsymbol{z}^0$ in (33) by means of the same process, that is if (setting $\delta = 1$ and so $\tau = t$) we

[19] The approximation is due to the fact that the factor $e^{A\theta}$ is neglected in the disturbance term in (29) and so in (33); assuming that the observation interval is small this is acceptable because the elements of δA will be small. For a rigorous analysis of the consequences of this approximation see Phillips (1978) and Wymer (1972).

[20] As the operator L can be treated as an algebraic quantity, we use the power series expansion

$$\begin{aligned}(1+x)^\alpha &= 1 + \alpha x + \frac{\alpha(\alpha-1)}{2!}x^2 + \frac{\alpha(\alpha-1)(\alpha-2)}{3!}x^3 \cdots \\ &= \sum_{n=0}^{\infty} \frac{\alpha(\alpha-1)\cdots(\alpha-n+1)}{n!}x^n,\end{aligned}$$

which, for $\alpha = -1$, becomes $1 - x + x^2 - x^3 + \cdots$ (see Hyslop, 1959, p. 27). In our case, $x = 0.268\mathrm{L}$.

let

$$x_t^* = x_t^0 - 0.268x_{t-1}^0 + 0.268^2 x_{t-2}^0 - 0.268^3 x_{t-3}^0, \tag{36}$$

and similarly for z (remembering that the disturbance term in (33) is ξ_t), we obtain the following model with serially uncorrelated disturbances

$$x_t^* = e^A x_{t-1}^* + \int_0^1 e^{A\theta} B z^*(t-\theta)\,d\theta + \varepsilon_t, \tag{33'}$$

where the integral can be approximated as we saw previously in (18) ff.

The parameters of this model – or of model (26), if no flow variables are present – can be estimated by using a FIML method (see further on, para 3.5.1). However, as this estimation is time consuming and therefore expensive, especially if there are general restrictions on the elements of A and B, it is convenient to consider a discrete approximation to system (1).

3.3.2. *The approximate discrete analogue*

Let us integrate the system (1) over the interval $(t-\delta, t)$ and utilize the following approximations[21]

$$\frac{1}{\delta}\int_0^\delta Dy(\tau\delta-\theta)\,d\theta = \Delta y_\tau, \qquad \int_0^\delta y(\tau\delta-\theta)\,d\theta = M y_\tau, \tag{37}$$

where the operators Δ and M have already been defined in (31) and (32), y is a generic vector of continuous variables and y_τ is the discrete observation of $y(\tau\delta)$ at time $t = \tau\delta$. Thus, as $MAy_\tau = AMy_\tau$, we have

$$\Delta x_\tau = AMx_\tau + BMz_\tau + \eta_\tau, \tag{38}$$

where η_τ is a vector of disturbances that depends on u and on the errors of approximation. As we already saw in the exact discrete analogue, the disturbances η_τ will be serially uncorrelated if all the variables are measured at a point in time. In the opposite case, in

[21]Since the integral of the derivative of a function is the function itself, the first of the two relationships is exact; on the contrary, the second is approximate, as clarified in another context when dealing with (30).

particular in mixed stock-flow models, model (1) must be integrated twice, once to provide measurable variables and once to obtain the approximate discrete analogue. By performing these integrations we obtain

$$\Delta \boldsymbol{x}_\tau^0 = \boldsymbol{A}\mathrm{M}\boldsymbol{x}_\tau^0 + \boldsymbol{B}\mathrm{M}\boldsymbol{z}_\tau^0 + \boldsymbol{v}_\tau, \tag{39}$$

where the variables with a superscript zero are as defined in (28) and in (31) respectively for flow and stock variables. In this case too the disturbances $\boldsymbol{v}_\tau$ will no longer be serially uncorrelated, but the same transformation described in the exact discrete analogue – see eq. (36) – allows us to obtain a model with serially uncorrelated disturbances.

The approximate discrete model (39) – after the just mentioned transformation of the variables, if it is the case – can be estimated using a FIML estimator with any *a priori* constraint on the parameters.

Let us now examine the bias introduced by the discrete approximation; to this purpose we compare the coefficients of the approximate discrete model (38) with those of the exact discrete model (16). Given the definitions of the operators Δ and M, model (38) can be rewritten with simple passages as

$$\frac{1}{\delta}\left(\boldsymbol{I} - \frac{1}{2}\delta\boldsymbol{A}\right)\boldsymbol{x}_\tau = \frac{1}{\delta}\left(\boldsymbol{I} + \frac{1}{2}\delta\boldsymbol{A}\right)\boldsymbol{x}_{\tau-1} + \boldsymbol{B}\mathrm{M}\boldsymbol{z}_\tau + \boldsymbol{\eta}_\tau. \tag{38$'$}$$

If we premultiply both members by $\delta(\boldsymbol{I} - \frac{1}{2}\delta\boldsymbol{A})^{-1}$ and compare the matrix of coefficients of the lagged endogenous variables with the corresponding matrix, $\mathrm{e}^{\delta A}$, of the exact discrete model (16), we obtain the bias by difference

$$\begin{aligned}
&\left(\boldsymbol{I} - \tfrac{1}{2}\delta\boldsymbol{A}\right)^{-1}\left(\boldsymbol{I} + \tfrac{1}{2}\delta\boldsymbol{A}\right) - \mathrm{e}^{\delta A} \\
&\quad = \left(\boldsymbol{I} + \tfrac{1}{2}\delta\boldsymbol{A} + \tfrac{1}{4}\delta^2\boldsymbol{A}^2 + \tfrac{1}{8}\delta^3\boldsymbol{A}^3 + \cdots\right)\left(\boldsymbol{I} + \tfrac{1}{2}\delta\boldsymbol{A}\right) \\
&\qquad - \left(\boldsymbol{I} + \delta\boldsymbol{A} + \tfrac{1}{2}\delta^2\boldsymbol{A}^2 + \tfrac{1}{3!}\delta^3\boldsymbol{A}^3 + \cdots\right).
\end{aligned} \tag{40}$$

If we carry out the multiplication on the right-hand side and collect terms we obtain

$$
\begin{aligned}
&\left(I - \tfrac{1}{2}\delta A\right)^{-1}\left(I + \tfrac{1}{2}\delta A\right) - e^{\delta A} \\
&\quad = \left(I + \delta A + \tfrac{1}{2}\delta^2 A^2 + \tfrac{1}{4}\delta^3 A^3 + \cdots\right) \\
&\qquad - \left(I + \delta A + \tfrac{1}{2}\delta^2 A^2 + \tfrac{1}{3!}\delta^3 A^3 + \cdots\right) \\
&\quad = \tfrac{1}{12}\delta^3 A^3 + O(\delta^4),
\end{aligned}
\tag{40'}
$$

so that the approximation errors decrease with the cube of the observation interval. A similar result holds for the coefficients of the exogenous variables.

Monte Carlo studies carried out by Phillips (Phillips, 1974) showed that the bias is small also for quarterly models. This means that the use of the approximate discrete model should give fairly satisfactory estimates of the parameters of the continuous model, though the exact discrete model gives more precise estimates: in particular, the aforementioned studies (see also Phillips, 1976b) show that the estimates of the parameters have much smaller asymptotic standard errors than those of the estimates obtained using the approximate discrete model. However, even if one wants to obtain more precise estimates by using the exact discrete model, it is suggested that the approximate discrete analogue should previously be used for two reasons:

(1) to determine the structure of the model; this usually requires the preliminary screening of several hypotheses and so the estimation of several preliminary versions of the model, which it would be too expensive to carry out by using the exact discrete analogue, and

(2) to provide initial values for the parameters to be used as a starting point in the estimation based on the exact discrete analogue.

3.3.3. A simple illustration

It may be useful to give by way of illustration a simple example (Wymer, 1976) of what we have expounded in the previous paragraphs. Let us consider the model described in ch. 2, eqs. (47′). As it contains both instantaneous variables $[M(t), p(t), r(t)]$ and flow variables $[Y(t), m(t)]$, it must be integrated to obtain measurable variables. Therefore the variables to be used in the estimation, taking into account (28), (31)[22] and (32), are

$$\boldsymbol{x}_t^0 = \begin{bmatrix} \frac{1}{2}(\log p_t + \log p_{t-1}) \\ \frac{1}{\delta}(\log M_t - \log M_{t-1}) \\ \frac{1}{2}(\log M_t + \log M_{t-1}) \end{bmatrix}, \quad \boldsymbol{z}_t^0 = \begin{bmatrix} \frac{1}{\delta}\log Y_t \\ \frac{1}{2}(\log r_t + \log r_{t-1}) \\ \frac{1}{2}(\log p_{f_t} + \log p_{f_{t-1}}) \\ 1 \end{bmatrix}.$$

In order to eliminate the autocorrelation introduced with the integration we use transformation (36), that is

$$\boldsymbol{x}_t^* = \boldsymbol{x}_t^0 - 0.268\boldsymbol{x}_{t-1}^0 + 0.072\boldsymbol{x}_{t-2}^0 - 0.019\boldsymbol{x}_{t-3}^0, \tag{41}$$

$$\boldsymbol{z}_t^* = \boldsymbol{z}_t^0 - 0.268\boldsymbol{z}_{t-1}^0 + 0.072\boldsymbol{z}_{t-2}^0 - 0.019\boldsymbol{z}_{t-3}^0. \tag{42}$$

Note that the constant term (which corresponds to the fourth element in the vector $\boldsymbol{z}_t^0$) becomes 0.785, the algebraic sum of the coefficients of the transformation.

If we define the basic time unit as equal to the observation interval, we have $\delta = 1$ and the exact discrete analogue becomes – see eq. (33) and the following transformations, in particular eq. (33′) –

$$\boldsymbol{x}_t^* = \mathrm{e}^{\boldsymbol{A}}\boldsymbol{x}_{t-1}^* + \int_0^1 \mathrm{e}^{\boldsymbol{A}\theta}\boldsymbol{B}\boldsymbol{z}^*(t-\theta)\,\mathrm{d}\theta + \boldsymbol{\varepsilon}_t, \tag{43}$$

where the integral can be approximated using eq. (20).

The approximate discrete analogue (39) becomes

$$\boldsymbol{x}_t^* - \boldsymbol{x}_{t-1}^* = \boldsymbol{A}\tfrac{1}{2}(\boldsymbol{x}_t^* + \boldsymbol{x}_{t-1}^*) + \boldsymbol{B}\tfrac{1}{2}(\boldsymbol{z}_t^* + \boldsymbol{z}_{t-1}^*) + \boldsymbol{v}_t, \tag{44}$$

which for estimation purposes can be rewritten – see eq. (38′) – as

$$\left(\boldsymbol{I} - \tfrac{1}{2}\boldsymbol{A}\right)\boldsymbol{x}_t^* = \left(\boldsymbol{I} + \tfrac{1}{2}\boldsymbol{A}\right)\boldsymbol{x}_{t-1}^* + \boldsymbol{B}\tfrac{1}{2}(\boldsymbol{z}_t^* + \boldsymbol{z}_{t-1}^*) + \boldsymbol{v}_t, \tag{44′}$$

or, adding $-(\boldsymbol{I} - \frac{1}{2}\boldsymbol{A})\boldsymbol{x}_{t-1}$ to both members, as

$$\left(\boldsymbol{I} - \tfrac{1}{2}\boldsymbol{A}\right)\Delta\boldsymbol{x}_t^* = \boldsymbol{A}\boldsymbol{x}_{t-1}^* + \boldsymbol{B}\tfrac{1}{2}(\boldsymbol{z}_t^* + \boldsymbol{z}_{t-1}^*) + \boldsymbol{v}_t. \tag{44″}$$

[22] By the way, eq. (31) allows a clear understanding of what we said in relation to eq. (3) in ch. 1.

3.4. Analysis, forecasting and simulation

The analysis of the estimated model is carried out according to the procedures illustrated qualitatively in section 2.2, that do not need to be repeated here. Let us only recall that once one has obtained the estimates of the parameters, the computation of the characteristic roots of the matrix of the coefficients of the endogenous variables[23] and of their standard errors[24] will make it possible to ascertain the dynamic behaviour of the model (kind of movement – monotonic, oscillatory or a combination of the two – and stability); furthermore, it will be possible to perform the sensitivity analysis whose great importance for policy analysis we must stress once more.

In the case in which there are over-identifying restrictions on the parameters[25] the likelihood ratio test[26] allows us to check whether

[23]As we said in section 3.1, if the original non-linear model has a steady state but the estimates have been obtained by linearizing the model about the sample means, these estimates must be substituted in the linearization about the steady state before carrying out the stability and sensitivity analyses.

[24]For the computation of these standard errors see Wymer (1972).

[25]This is the normal case, as we said in section 3.1.

[26]It should be remembered that, if Ω is the parameter space and ω a subset of Ω, the hypothesis H_0: the parameter vector θ is a point in ω, can be tested by using the statistic $-2\log\mathfrak{L}$, where $\mathfrak{L} = L(\hat{\omega})/L(\hat{\Omega})$; $L(\hat{\omega})$ is the maximum of the likelihood function with respect to the parameters over the set ω and $L(\hat{\Omega})$ is the maximum of the likelihood function with respect to the parameters over the set Ω. This statistic is asymptotically distributed as the χ^2, and H_0 is rejected if the statistic is greater than the critical value at a given significance level in a one-tailed test in the region of the upper tail (see, e.g., Kendall and Stuart, 1973, vol. 2, ch. 24; Mood, Graybill and Boes, 1974, ch. IX). To our purposes the cases under consideration are:

(i) $\log L(\hat{\Omega})$ is the maximum of the log-likelihood function of the just-identified model (unrestricted reduced form) and $\log L(\hat{\omega})$ is the maximum of the log-likelihood function of the over-identified model being estimated. The degrees of freedom are: number of endogenous variables times number of predetermined variables minus number of parameters. This is the first of the two cases mentioned in the text.

(ii) $\log L(\hat{\Omega})$ is the maximum of the log-likelihood function of a just- or over-identified model containing p_1 parameters and $\log L(\hat{\omega})$ is the maximum of the log-likelihood function of a model containing p_2 parameters which are a subset of the parameter set of the first model. The degrees of freedom are p_1 minus p_2 (this number can also be interpreted as the number of the additional over-identifying restrictions in the second model, consisting in setting to zero all the p_1 minus p_2 parameters). This is the second of the cases mentioned in the text. It should be noted that the likelihood ratio test is valid only asymptotically and may be invalid also for samples of 100 observations.

the over-identifying restrictions are consistent with the sample or, more generally – when the parameters of a model are a subset of the parameters of another model – whether the model on which the additional over-identifying restrictions have been imposed is consistent with the less restricted model. The Carter–Nagar[27] system R_w^2 test can be used to test the hypothesis that the model as a whole is not consistent with the data (overall goodness of fit).

As regards *forecasting and simulation*, two procedures are possible in principle: (1) use of the discrete linearized model; (2) use of the original non-linear continuous model.

3.4.1. *Forecasting and simulation by the discrete linearized model*

This is the most obvious procedure: the same model that has been used for estimation will be used for forecasting and simulation. As we know, the estimation procedure involves first a linearization of the original non-linear continuous model and then the derivation of an exact or approximate discrete analogue which is the model actually used for estimation. However, the use of this same model for forecasting and simulation involves two problems pointed out by Wymer (1979):

(a) *back-transformation of the variables.* If the original model contains some flow variables, the data must be pre-whitened to eliminate the autocorrelation introduced with the integration, and this is obtained by using transformation (36). Furthermore, in a model of this kind instantaneous variables must be previously (that

[27]A measure of correlation for a simultaneous system as a whole is the positive square root of $R_w^2 = 1 - G/\mathrm{tr}[(\boldsymbol{Y}'\boldsymbol{Y})^{-1}\hat{\boldsymbol{V}}'\hat{\boldsymbol{V}}]^{-1}$, where $\boldsymbol{Y}$ is the $T \times G$ matrix of T observations on G endogenous variables and $\hat{\boldsymbol{V}}$ is the matrix of T reduced-form residuals. R_w^2 lies between zero and one and has the same interpretation as the familiar coefficient of determination used with ordinary least squares. When the system parameter estimators have the same limiting distribution as FIML, the statistic $\chi^2 = TGR_w^2/(1 - R_w^2)$ has an asymptotic chi-square distribution with p (the number of parameters) degrees of freedom. Therefore the hypothesis that the model as a whole is not consistent with the data is rejected (accepted) if the χ^2 is greater than the critical value at a given significance level in a one-tailed test in the region of the upper tail. Let us note, finally, that the measure under consideration takes account of the (over) identifying restrictions for all equations of the model. See Carter and Nagar (1977).

is, before using the transformation) averaged using the operator $M = \frac{1}{2}(1 + L)$ and variables which are the rate of change of some instantaneously measurable variables must be previously replaced by the first difference of the instantaneous variables from which they derive – see eqs. (31) and (32). Therefore back-transformation of forecasted or simulated values of variables is necessary to produce figures on the same basis as the original data. More formally, if we let y denote a generic variable, and $\beta(L) = (1 + 0.268L)$, we have

$$y_t^* = \beta^{-1}(L)y_t, \tag{45}$$

where y_t is the observed value of the integral of a flow variable $y(t)$ – see eqs. (28) and (36); or

$$y_t^* = \beta^{-1}(L)My_t, \tag{46}$$

where y_t is the observed value of an instantaneous variable $y(t)$ – see eqs. (31) and (36); or

$$y_{1t}^* = \beta^{-1}(L)\Delta y_t, \tag{47}$$

where y_t is the observed value of an instantaneous variable of which y_{1t} is the rate of change – see eqs. (32) and (36). The forecasted or simulated values (denoted by a hat) produced by the discrete model are on the same basis as the starred values; therefore, the back-transformations required to produce figures on the same basis as the original data are respectively

$$\begin{aligned} \hat{y}_t &= \beta(L)\hat{y}_t^*, \\ \hat{y}_t &= \beta(L)M^{-1}\hat{y}_t^*, \\ \Delta\hat{y}_t &= \beta(L)\hat{y}_{1t}^*. \end{aligned} \tag{48}$$

Let us note, incidentally, that it is necessary to know not only the value of all the variables at the beginning of the forecast or simulation period but also several lagged values of the same variables.

(b) *spurious improper oscillations.*[28] These oscillations may arise from the endogenous part of the model under certain conditions;

[28] For the definition of "improper" as distinguished from "proper" oscillations see Gandolfo (1980, Part. I, ch. 2). Equivalent denominations are "alternations" and "saw-tooth oscillations".

therefore in what follows the terms involving the exogenous variables will be neglected.

Supposing that the exact discrete analogue has been used,[29] the model employed for forecasting or simulation is

$$\boldsymbol{x}_t = \mathrm{e}^{\boldsymbol{A}}\boldsymbol{x}_{t-1} + \text{exogenous and error terms}, \tag{49}$$

and the dynamic behaviour of this difference system will be governed by the characteristic roots of the matrix $\mathrm{e}^{\boldsymbol{A}}$, whereas the dynamic behaviour of the differential system (11) is governed by the characteristic roots of the matrix $\boldsymbol{A}$. It is a well-known result in matrix theory that if λ_j is a root of $\boldsymbol{A}$, then e^{λ_j} is a root of $\mathrm{e}^{\boldsymbol{A}}$.

Suppose now that $\lambda_{j,j+1} = \alpha \pm \mathrm{i}\beta$ is a pair of complex conjugate characteristic roots of $\boldsymbol{A}$, with β equal to π, and let $a \pm \mathrm{i}b$ be the corresponding roots of $\mathrm{e}^{\boldsymbol{A}}$, where

$$a \pm \mathrm{i}b = \mathrm{e}^{\alpha \pm \mathrm{i}\beta} = \mathrm{e}^{\alpha}\mathrm{e}^{\pm \mathrm{i}\beta}. \tag{50}$$

As $\mathrm{e}^{\pm \mathrm{i}\beta} = \cos\beta \pm \mathrm{i}\sin\beta$, it follows that

$$\begin{aligned} a &= \mathrm{e}^{\alpha}\cos\beta, \\ b &= \mathrm{e}^{\alpha}\sin\beta. \end{aligned} \tag{51}$$

Now, if $\beta = \pi$, then $\cos\beta = -1$ and $\sin\beta = 0$, whence $a = -\mathrm{e}^{\alpha} < 0$ and $b = 0$. Therefore, in the difference system the pair of complex conjugate characteristic roots will appear as two equal negative real roots, giving rise to a spurious improper oscillation (instead of the "true" proper oscillation) in the forecasts or simulations. Note that, even if the hypothesis that the differential system has some characteristic roots with an imaginary part equal to π must be rejected, sampling errors may cause complex conjugate roots with an imaginary part close to π in the continuous model to appear as two approximately equal real negative roots in the discrete analogue.

A similar problem can arise when heavily damped, low frequency cycles are present in the continuous system: this means that α is large and negative and β is close to zero. Using the relationships between a, b and α, β seen above, and since $\sin 0 = 0$, $\cos 0 = 1$, we have $a \simeq \mathrm{e}^{\alpha} > 0$, $b \simeq 0$. Therefore in the difference system used for

[29] The results that follow hold also when the approximate discrete analogue has been used. See Wymer (1979).

forecasting or simulation we shall have two approximately equal real and positive roots (monotonic movement). More generally, large sampling errors may give rise to point estimates of real roots in the discrete system whereas the roots of the continuous system are complex (Wymer, 1979).

Finally, let us note that the spurious improper oscillations may be amplified when the data are back-transformed.

3.4.2. Forecasting and simulation by the original non-linear continuous model

Both problems treated in the previous paragraph (back-transformation of the variables and spurious improper oscillations) can be eliminated by using the differential system for forecasting. As the parameters being estimated (albeit first performing a linear approximation and then using a discrete analogue) are those of the original non-linear differential model, the non-linear model and not its linear approximation can be used directly for forecasting and simulation. Thus forecasts and simulations of the endogenous variables can be produced directly on the same basis as the raw data and no spurious improper oscillations are introduced. Furthermore the use of the original non-linear model has two additional advantages:

(1) the features of the economy which are inherently non-linear (and which therefore cannot be represented by a linear system) can be adequately investigated. Of course, the fact that a linear approximation has been used in the estimation procedure will cause biases in the estimates of the parameters of the original non-linear model, and this should be kept in mind when using these estimates.[30]

(2) Forecasts for any forecast interval can easily be produced.

When using the continuous model, continuous paths for the exogenous variables are needed. If these variables can be written as

[30] If the original model is highly non-linear, the question arises whether a situation may occur in which the linearization procedure causes such large biases in the estimates of the parameters that the non-linear model cannot be used for forecasting and simulation, or, worse still, precludes some parameters from being identified. Up to now, the question has not been satisfactorily investigated.

analytical functions of time, the system can be solved immediately. However, exogenous variables are often defined as a series of observations, and so interpolation will be needed to solve the system. Wymer (1979) suggests the use of a quadratic or a cubic polynomial for flow and instantaneous variables respectively. As regards the endogenous variables, their initial values must be given, by definition, at a point in time. This will not cause difficulties with instantaneous variables, but will with flow variables in the broad sense. Thus the initial values of flow variables will have to be approximated in some way, the particular approximation depending on the information available (Wymer, 1979).

Although the use of the continuous model for forecasting or simulation has advantages, it involves the numerical solution of a non-linear differential system, which is more expensive than using the linearized discrete analogue. Furthermore, standard errors of forecast, which are needed for much work in policy analysis, can only be obtained from the discrete linear model; however, these could be used as approximations to the standard errors of forecast for the continuous model (Wymer, 1979).

Let us conclude our treatment with some considerations on the forecasting ability of the models under consideration. A prudent assessment is to be found in Wymer (1976): "The simplicity of the models makes it unlikely that they would provide accurate short term forecasts (for say two quarters ahead) compared to the large short term forecasting models in use in many countries but, if theory is to be of any use for forecasting purposes, their more rigorous theoretical basis and emphasis on plausible long-run behaviour, would suggest that they might be preferable for medium term forecasting." Furthermore, as in our opinion forecasting is not the main use for an econometric model,[31] the advantages of continuous models for policy purposes (see ch. 2) are an important asset.

Given the novelty of the continuous time approach, there is not yet a sufficient amount of empirical results to enable us to give a

[31] This point would involve a lengthy discussion which is outside the scope of the present book. In any case, see Granger and Newbold (1977, pp. 289 ff) and Spivey and Wrobleski (1979, chs. 3 and 4) for a critical evaluation of the often disappointing forecasting ability of large scale econometric models.

fair evaluation of the forecasting ability of the models under consideration. However, the results so far obtained, both with economy-wide macroeconomic models (see, e.g., Bailey, Hall and Phillips, 1979; Bergstrom, 1978; Bergstrom and Wymer, 1976; Jonson, 1976; Jonson and Taylor, 1978; Knight and Mathieson, 1979; Knight and Wymer, 1978; Reserve Bank of Australia, 1977; and the model in Part II of the present book) and with models concerning single aspects of the economy (see, e.g., Aghevli and Khan, 1977; Armington, 1979; Brennan and Schwartz, 1979; Drollas, 1976; Heller and Knight, 1978; Khan, 1977; Knight, 1973, 1977; Laker, 1979; Richard, 1978, 1979; Wymer, 1973, 1975) are fairly good and certainly encouraging.

3.5. A note on computer programs

In order to put the new methodology dealt with in the previous sections into practice, *ad hoc* computer programs are needed. The only programs that exist are those developed by Clifford R. Wymer, and a very brief description of what they do is given here; for details the reader is referred to Wymer's manuals. The programs are indicated by the code name given them by Wymer. Their input and output is standardized, so that information can be stored on disc or tape and used in other programs. The special features of these programs allow the exact or approximate discrete analogue to be estimated and their properties analysed easily.

TRANSF. Data processing program which reads from cards, tape or disc and writes to tape or disc. Graph plotting facilities are included. Deseasonalizes the data and performs all the transformations necessary to prepare the data for the estimation of the discrete analogue, that is (31), (36), etc. Carries out quarterly interpolation from annual observations, monthly interpolation from quarterly observations, semi-annual interpolation from yearly observations, when the observations refer to continuous variables. It performs many other transformations (transcendental functions, logs, cumulation and decumulation of series, etc.).

SIMUL. Calculates two stage least squares, three stage least squares, and full information maximum likelihood estimates of a linear system of the form

$$\boldsymbol{A}(\boldsymbol{\theta})\boldsymbol{x}_t + \boldsymbol{B}(\boldsymbol{\theta})z_t = \boldsymbol{u}_t, \tag{52}$$

where $\boldsymbol{x}_t$ is a vector of endogenous variables, z_t a vector of predetermined variables, $\boldsymbol{\theta}$ a vector of parameters, and $\boldsymbol{u}_t$ a vector of disturbances generally assumed to be independently normally distributed. The elements of $\boldsymbol{A}$ and $\boldsymbol{B}$ can only be linear functions of $\boldsymbol{\theta}$. The reduced form is found if required. This program can be used to estimate the approximate discrete analogue; the log-likelihood ratio test and the Carter–Nagar R_w^2 test are calculated.

RESIMUL. Calculates full information maximum likelihood estimates of system (52) where the elements of $\boldsymbol{A}$ and $\boldsymbol{B}$ can be any functions, algebraic or transcendental, of the set of parameters. This allows non-linear restrictions within and across equations to be imposed as well as certain types of inequality constraints. Analytical first derivatives of the functions of parameters are evaluated. This program can be used to estimate the approximate discrete analogue; the log-likelihood ratio test and the Carter–Nagar R_w^2 test are calculated.

RESIMULA. Modified version of RESIMUL which calculates full information maximum likelihood estimates of model (52) with a moving average disturbance of the form $\boldsymbol{u}_t = [\boldsymbol{I} - \boldsymbol{R}(\mathrm{L}, \boldsymbol{\theta})]\boldsymbol{\varepsilon}_t$, where $\boldsymbol{R}$ is a matrix polynomial of any order in the lag operator L and $\boldsymbol{\varepsilon}_t$ is a vector of independent normally distributed disturbances.

DISCON. Calculates full information maximum likelihood estimates of the exact discrete analogue with any non-linear restrictions on the parameters within and across equations. The log-likelihood ratio test and the Carter–Nagar R_w^2 test are calculated.

CONTINEST. Calculates the characteristic roots and vectors of a matrix as well as the corresponding variance matrices and performs the sensitivity analysis. This program is used in particular with linear differential systems estimated by SIMUL, RESIMUL, or DISCON. It will also calculate the paths of the variables for non-stochastic optimal control.

PREDIC. Forecasting and simulation program for the model (52) – and so for the approximate discrete analogue – and for the exact discrete analogue. Point prediction estimates with standard errors of forecasts and prediction intervals at a given confidence level are calculated. Simulation may be either *ex post* or *ex ante*, and random normal disturbances with a given variance matrix may be included; furthermore, either the parameters or the variables in the model can be altered according to a specified control system.

ASIMUL. Calculates pseudo full information maximum likelihood estimates of a general non-linear model of the form

$$\boldsymbol{\Phi}(\boldsymbol{x}_t, z_t, \boldsymbol{\theta}) = \boldsymbol{u}_t, \tag{53}$$

where $\boldsymbol{\Phi}$ is any non-linear vector valued differentiable function. Thus the model considered is non-linear in the variables and subject to non-linear within and across equation restrictions on the parameters. The program automatically evaluates analytical first derivatives of the variable and parameter functions with respect to the parameters, and calculates the derivatives of the variable functions with respect to the endogenous variables.

APREDIC. Forecasting and simulation program for the model (53) which may be used with models estimated by ASIMUL. Facilities are similar to those of PREDIC except that standard errors of forecasts and prediction intervals are not found. Additional special features are (i) the program will accept models from any of the estimation programs, and variable functions may be introduced or altered, so that a basic non-linear model can be formed from a linearized one for simulation or prediction; (ii) the program will solve any non-linear first-order differential equation system. Therefore it can be used for forecasting and simulation with the original non-linear differential system as described in para. 3.4.2.

Appendix I. Some linearization formulae

As we saw in the text, the analysis and estimation of the model requires linearization. Since the variables are often (or must often be) expressed in logarithmic form, it may be useful to recall some formulae here.

I.1. Linearization about a point

The point may also be the steady state value, $x^0 = x^* e^{\rho t}$.

$$\log(x \pm y) \equiv \log(e^{\log x} \pm e^{\log y}) \simeq \log(x^0 \pm y^0) + \frac{1}{x^0 \pm y^0} \times \left[x^0(\log x - \log x^0) \pm y^0(\log y - \log y^0) \right]. \tag{I.1}$$

$$x \equiv e^{\log x} \simeq x^0(1 + \log x - \log x^0). \tag{I.2}$$

$$x = y \pm z. \tag{I.3}$$

Apply formula (I.2) to the three variables, then dividing by x^0 if required,

$$x^0(1 + \log x - \log x^0) \simeq y^0(1 + \log y - \log y^0) \pm z^0(1 + \log z - \log z^0),$$

and so

$$\log x \simeq \frac{y^0}{x^0}(1 + \log y - \log y^0) \pm \frac{z^0}{x^0}(1 + \log z - \log z^0) + (\log x^0 - 1).$$

If x^0, y^0, z^0 are the steady state values with the same growth rate ρ, then

$$\log x \simeq \frac{y^*}{x^*}(1 + \log y - \log y^* - \rho t) \pm \frac{z^*}{x^*}(1 + \log z - \log z^* - \rho t) + (\log x^* + \rho t - 1)$$

$$\simeq \frac{y^*}{x^*}(\log y - \log y^*) \pm \frac{z^*}{x^*}(\log z - \log z^*) + \log x^*$$

since $y^* \pm z^* - x^* = 0$.

$$\mathrm{D}x = \mathrm{D}y \pm z. \tag{I.4}$$

Dividing through by x we obtain

$$\mathrm{D}\log x = \frac{\mathrm{D}y}{\mathrm{y}} \cdot \frac{y}{x} \pm \frac{z}{x} = \frac{y}{x}\,\mathrm{D}\log y \pm \frac{z}{x}$$

$$\simeq \frac{y^0}{x^0}\,\mathrm{D}\log y + \mathrm{D}\log y^0\Big[\frac{y^0}{x^0}(\log y - \log y^0 - \log x + \log x^0)\Big]$$

$$\pm \frac{z^0}{x^0}[1 + \log z - \log z^0 - \log x + \log x^0].$$

If x^0, y^0, z^0 are the steady state values and are assumed to have the same growth rate, then $\rho x^* = \rho y^* \pm z^*$ by definition, and so

$$\mathrm{D}\log x \simeq \frac{y^*}{x^*}\,\mathrm{D}\log y + \rho\frac{y^*}{x^*}(\log y - \log y^*)$$

$$\pm \frac{z^*}{x^*}(1 + \log z - \log z^*) + \rho(-\log x + \log x^*).$$

I.2. Linearization about the sample means

A superscript bar denotes the sample mean: thus $\overline{\log x}$ is the mean of a sample of observations $\log x_t$.

$$\log(x \pm y) \equiv \log(\mathrm{e}^{\log x} \pm \mathrm{e}^{\log y})$$

$$\simeq \log\big[\mathrm{e}^{\overline{\log x}} \pm \mathrm{e}^{\overline{\log y}}\big] + \frac{1}{\mathrm{e}^{\overline{\log x}} \pm \mathrm{e}^{\overline{\log y}}}$$

$$\times\big[\mathrm{e}^{\overline{\log x}}(\log x - \overline{\log x}) \pm \mathrm{e}^{\overline{\log y}}(\log y - \overline{\log y})\big]. \tag{I.5}$$

$$x \equiv \mathrm{e}^{\log x} \simeq \mathrm{e}^{\overline{\log x}}(1 + \log x - \overline{\log x}), \tag{I.6}$$

from which the linearization of $xy \equiv \mathrm{e}^{\log x + \log y}$ and of $x/y \equiv \mathrm{e}^{\log x - \log y}$ follows directly.

$$x = y \pm z. \tag{I.7}$$

We use (I.6), then multiplying by $e^{-\overline{\log x}}$, whence

$$\log x \simeq \exp[\,\overline{\log y} - \overline{\log x}\,](1 + \log y - \overline{\log y}\,)$$
$$\pm \exp[\,\overline{\log z} - \overline{\log x}\,](1 + \log z - \overline{\log z}\,) + (\,\overline{\log x} - 1).$$

$$\mathrm{D}x = \mathrm{D}y \pm z. \tag{I.8}$$

Dividing by x we obtain

$$\begin{aligned}\mathrm{D}\log x &= \frac{\mathrm{D}y}{y}\cdot\frac{y}{x} \pm \frac{z}{x} = \frac{y}{x}\,\mathrm{D}\log y \pm \frac{z}{x}\\ &\simeq e^{\overline{\log y} - \overline{\log x}}\,\mathrm{D}\log y + \overline{\mathrm{D}\log y}\cdot\exp[\,\overline{\log y} - \overline{\log x}\,]\\ &\quad\times\left[(\log y - \overline{\log y}\,) - (\log x - \overline{\log x}\,)\right]\\ &\quad\pm \exp[\,\overline{\log z} - \overline{\log x}\,]\\ &\quad\times\left[1 + (\log z - \overline{\log z}\,) - (\log x - \overline{\log x}\,)\right],\end{aligned}$$

where $\overline{\mathrm{D}\log y}$ is the average of $\mathrm{D}\log y$, measured by $\overline{\Delta\log y}$. For the formulae concerning the logarithmic linearization of functions derived from a CES production function we refer the reader to Wymer's Supplement, on which this Appendix is based.

Appendix II. Autocorrelation in the disturbances in models containing flow variables

When flow variables are present in the model, it must be integrated over the observation interval in order to obtain a model defined in terms of measurable variables (para. 3.3.1). But in this way we introduce autocorrelation in the new disturbance term, whereas the disturbances in the original model were exempt from autocorrelation by assumption. The new disturbances, however, have the same autocorrelation properties of a certain moving average process as approximated by eq. (34) in ch. 3. Given the importance of this result and the difficulty of proof, we deal with it in a separate Appendix. Our proof requires a knowledge of the basic notions concerning generating functions and moving average processes,[32] and these we recall in the next section.

[32] See any standard textbook, in particular Granger and Newbold (1977), on which our treatment is based.

II.1. Generating functions and moving average processes

II.1.1. General principles

A *generating function* is a compact way of recording the information contained in a sequence. Consider the sequence a_0, a_1, $a_2, \ldots, a_j, \ldots$, which may be finite or infinite; its generating function, denoted by $\alpha(z)$, is

$$\alpha(z) = \sum_j a_j z^j. \tag{II.1}$$

The quantity z does not necessarily have an interpretation and is to be considered simply as the carrier of the information held in the sequence; on occasion, however, it can be given a specific interpretation. The reason for introducing (II.1) is that the function $\alpha(z)$ can often be treated in a simpler way than the original sequence.

Generating functions are widely used in statistical theory: for example, $p(z) = \Sigma p_j z^j$ is the probability generating function of a discrete random variable that can take only non-negative integer values with probability p_j; $p(\mathrm{e}^t)$ is the moment generating function because, using the power series expansion of e^t we have $p(\mathrm{e}^t) = \Sigma_j \mu_j (t)^j / j!$, $\mu_j = \mathrm{E}[X^j]$.

Generating functions have the additive property: if a_j, b_j, $j = 0, 1, \ldots$ are two sequences, then, letting $c_j = a_j + b_j$, we have

$$c(z) = \alpha(z) + \beta(z). \tag{II.2}$$

A more important property is that of *convolution*. Given two sequences, a_j and b_j, $j = 0,\ 1, \ldots,$ we define a new sequence c_j, called the convolution of a_j and b_j, by

$$c_j = a_0 b_j + a_1 b_{j-1} + a_2 b_{j-2} + \cdots + a_j b_0 = \sum_{k=0}^{j} a_k b_{j-k}. \tag{II.3}$$

In words, to obtain the jth term of the convolution we multiply the first term of the first sequence by the jth term of the second sequence, the second term of the first sequence by the $(j-1)$th term of the second sequence and so on, then add all these products. The generating functions of the three sequences are related by the equation

$$c(z) = \alpha(z)\beta(z), \tag{II.4}$$

as can be checked by multiplication. In fact, using (II.3) the terms of the convolution turn out to be

$$c_0 = a_0 b_0; \qquad c_1 = a_0 b_1 + a_1 b_0;$$
$$c_2 = a_0 b_2 + a_1 b_1 + a_2 b_0; \ldots, \tag{II.3$'$}$$

and so the generating function is

$$c(z) = a_0 b_0 + (a_0 b_1 + a_1 b_0)z + (a_0 b_2 + a_1 b_1 + a_2 b_0)z^2 + \cdots. \tag{II.4$'$}$$

Using (II.4) we obtain

$$\begin{aligned} c(z) &= (a_0 + a_1 z + a_2 z^2 + \cdots)(b_0 + b_1 z + b_2 z^2 + \cdots) \\ &= (a_0 b_0 + a_0 b_1 z + a_0 b_2 z^2 + \cdots) \\ &\quad + (a_1 b_0 z + a_1 b_1 z^2 + a_1 b_2 z^3 + \cdots) \\ &\quad + (a_2 b_0 z^2 + a_2 b_1 z^3 + a_2 b_2 z^4 + \cdots) + \cdots. \end{aligned} \tag{II.4$''$}$$

Collecting terms according to the powers of z in (II.4″) we get (II.4′).

Among the generating functions that we shall meet let us mention the autocovariance generating function. As we know (see section 3.2 in the text), a property of stationary stochastic processes is $\sigma(t,s) = \sigma_h, s = t - h$; now, we consider the sequence of the σ_h's, for h that takes on all the integer values from $-\infty$ to $+\infty$ and define the *autocovariance generating function*

$$\sigma(z) = \sum_{\forall h} \sigma_h z^h, \tag{II.5}$$

where $\forall h$ means that h runs through all integers from $-\infty$ to $+\infty$.

Generating functions may also be used in the solution of difference equations. Let us consider the equation

$$X_t = \sum_{j=1}^{p} a_j X_{t-j}, \tag{II.6}$$

that is

$$X_t - a_1 X_{t-1} - a_2 X_{t-2} - \cdots - a_p X_{t-p} = 0, \tag{II.7}$$

which is a linear homogeneous difference equation with constant coefficients, of order p. Using standard methods (see, for example, Gandolfo, 1980, Part I, ch. 6) we obtain the characteristic equation

$$f(\lambda) = \lambda^p - a_1\lambda^{p-1} - a_2\lambda^{p-2} - \cdots - a_p = 0, \qquad \text{(II.8)}$$

and the (necessary and sufficient) *stability condition* (which in the context of time series analysis is also called the *stationarity condition*) is that the roots of (II.8) all lie within the unit circle in the complex plane $|\lambda| = 1$. Let us now consider the sequence of the coefficients in (II.7), which is $1, -a_1, -a_2, \ldots, -a_p$, and its generating function

$$\alpha(z) = 1 - \sum_{j=1}^{p} a_j z^j. \qquad \text{(II.9)}$$

We show that setting $\alpha(z) = 0$ we obtain an equation whose roots are the reciprocal of the roots of $f(\lambda) = 0$. From eq. (II.8), multiplying through by λ^{-p} (this is legitimate because, as $a_p \neq 0$, there are no zero roots) we obtain

$$1 - a_1\lambda^{-1} - a_2\lambda^{-2} \cdots - a_p\lambda^{-p} = 0, \qquad \text{(II.8}')$$

whose roots coincide with the roots of (II.8). If we now consider the equation $\alpha(z) = 0$, that is

$$1 - a_1 z - a_2 z^2 \cdots - a_p z^p = 0, \qquad \text{(II.10)}$$

and compare it with eq. (II.8′), we see immediately that the two are related by the transformation $\lambda = z^{-1}$, $z = \lambda^{-1}$.

It follows from the above that the stability (stationarity) condition of the solution to (II.6) can also be expressed by saying that the roots of (II.10) all lie outside the unit circle $|z| = 1$, it being obvious that $|\lambda| < 1$ is equivalent to $|z| > 1$ and vice versa. Therefore, the stationarity condition under consideration is that the roots of the equation $\alpha(z) = 0$, where $\alpha(z)$ is the generating function of the coefficients of the difference equation, are all in modulus greater than unity.

II.1.2. Moving average processes

The stochastic process generated by the equation

$$X_t = \sum_{j=0}^{q} b_j \varepsilon_{t-j}, \qquad b_0 = 1, \qquad \text{(II.11)}$$

where ε_t is white noise with mean zero, is called a *moving average process of order* q and denoted $X_t \sim \text{MA}(q)$. Given the theorem on the mean of a linear combination, the mean of X_t is clearly zero. Let us now examine the autocovariances. From (II.11) we have

$$X_t = \varepsilon_t + b_1\varepsilon_{t-1} + \cdots + b_{h-1}\varepsilon_{t-h+1} + b_h\varepsilon_{t-h} + b_{h+1}\varepsilon_{t-h-1} + \cdots + b_q\varepsilon_{t-q},$$

$$X_{t-h} = \varepsilon_{t-h} + b_1\varepsilon_{t-h-1} + \cdots + b_{q-h}\varepsilon_{t-q} + \cdots + b_q\varepsilon_{t-q-h}.$$

As $\text{E}(\varepsilon_t\varepsilon_s) = 0$, $t \neq s$, it follows immediately that

$$\sigma_h \equiv \text{E}(X_tX_{t-h}) = \sigma_\varepsilon^2(b_h + b_1b_{h+1} + b_2b_{h+2} + \cdots + b_{q-h}b_q) \quad \text{for } |h| \leq q, \tag{II.12}$$

and

$$\sigma_h = 0 \qquad \text{for } |h| > q. \tag{II.13}$$

We can therefore conclude that a MA(q) process with q finite is always a stationary process (in the sense defined in section 3.2 of the text). A feature of the processes under consideration is that their autocorrelation generating function takes a peculiar form. Rewriting eq. (II.12) as

$$\sigma_h = \sigma_\varepsilon^2 \sum_{j=0}^{q-h} b_jb_{j+h}, \tag{II.12$'$}$$

and considering that the typical coefficient b_i is zero for $i > q$ – this follows by definition from (II.11) – we can extend the summation, for convenience of analysis, up to q, because the terms from $q - h + 1$ to q (i.e. $b_{q-h+1}b_{q+1}$, etc.) are all zero. Therefore we can write

$$\sigma_h = \sigma_\varepsilon^2 \sum_{j=0}^{q} b_jb_{j+h}. \tag{II.14}$$

Since h varies from $-q$ to $+q$, the autocovariance generating function turns out to be

$$\sigma(z) = \sum_{h=-q}^{q} \sigma_h z^h = \sigma_\varepsilon^2 \sum_{h=-q}^{q} z^h \sum_{j=0}^{q} b_jb_{j+h}. \tag{II.15}$$

Let us now consider the generating function of the sequence of the b_j's

$$\beta(z) = \sum_{j=0}^{q} b_j z^j, \qquad b_0 = 1, \tag{II.16}$$

so that eq. (II.11) can be written, in terms of the operator L, as

$$X_t = \beta(\mathrm{L})\varepsilon_t. \tag{II.17}$$

We denote by $\beta(z^{-1})$ the function that we obtain by putting z^{-1} in the place of z (and so z^{-j} in the place of z^j) in eq. (II.16), that is

$$\beta(z^{-1}) = \sum_{j=0}^{q} b_j z^{-j}, \tag{II.18}$$

and we consider the product $\beta(z)\beta(z^{-1})$, that turns out to be, as can be easily checked,

$$\beta(z)\beta(z^{-1}) = \sum_{k=0}^{q} \sum_{j=0}^{q} b_j b_k z^{k-j}. \tag{II.19}$$

In this double summation, the powers of z depend only on the difference between k and j. If we put $k - j = h$ (and so $k = j + h$), and consider that as j and k vary from 0 to q the difference $k - j$, namely h, varies from $-q$ to q, we can write

$$\beta(z)\beta(z^{-1}) = \sum_{h=-q}^{q} z^h \sum_{j=0}^{q} b_j b_{j+h}. \tag{II.20}$$

From eqs. (II.20) and (II.15) we finally have

$$\sigma(z) = \sigma_\varepsilon^2 \beta(z)\beta(z^{-1}), \tag{II.21}$$

which is the typical form of the autocovariance generating function of the MA(q) process defined by (II.11).

Let us now consider a stochastic process X_t, known to be stationary with mean zero and of which we know the theoretical autocovariances σ_h (such that $\sigma_h = 0$ for $|h| \geq q + 1$ and $\sigma_{-h} = \sigma_h$ for $|h| < q + 1$), and ask the following questions:

(1) whether and under what conditions X_t will be a MA(q) process, and, if yes,
(2) how to find the coefficients b_j of such a process given the autocovariances σ_h.

The answer to the first question is that if the σ_h's satisfy certain conditions,[33] X_t will be a MA(q) process definable in the form (II.17) – or, equivalently, in the form (II.11). The answer to the second question is a bit more complicated, and can be given along the following lines. First we find the roots of

$$\sigma(z) = \sum_{h=-q}^{q} \sigma_h z^h = 0, \tag{II.22}$$

(as the σ_h's are given by (II.15), eq. (II.22) is a reciprocal equation, and so if z_h is a root, z_h^{-1} is also a root) and, assuming for simplicity's sake that there are no roots with modulus 1, we denote by z_j^* the roots whose modulus is greater than one. Since eq. (II.22) has $2q$ roots and given the reciprocal nature of these roots, we shall have q roots with modulus greater than one and q roots, reciprocal of them, with modulus smaller than one.

Let z_j', $j = 1, \dots, q$, be a proper subset, containing q elements, of the set of the $2q$ roots of eq. (II.22), such that if z_h belongs to z_j' then z_h^{-1} does not belong to it.[34] Then the solution of our problem is

$$\beta'(z) = \sigma_\varepsilon^{-1/2} \prod_{j=1}^{q} (z - z_j'). \tag{II.23}$$

If we expand the product on the right hand side as a power series in z, compare the result with (II.16) and equate the coefficients of like powers of z,[35] we obtain the values of the b_j that we are looking for.

[33] The condition is that the spectrum $f(\omega)$, that is the function that we obtain by setting $z = e^{-i\omega}$, $-\pi \le \omega \le \pi$, in the autocovariance generating function $\sigma(z)$ must be non-negative: see Granger and Newbold (1977, p. 23). This is a necessary and sufficient condition in order for a MA(q) process corresponding to a set of "covariances" c_j, $j = 0, 1, \dots$; $c_j = 0$ for $j > q$, to exist.

[34] The reason for this choice is of course that we must also satisfy form (II.21).

[35] It is important to note that, as in (II.16) we have $b_0 = 1$, it will be necessary to reduce to 1 the constant term resulting from the product on the right hand side of (II.23). In other words, since

$$\prod_{j=1}^{q} (z - z_j') = (-1)^q z^q + a_1 z^{q-1} + \cdots + a_n,$$

where

$$a_n = (-1)^q \prod_{j=1}^{q} z_j',$$

if $a_n \neq 1$ we shall write the equation in the form $a_n[a_n^{-1}(-1)^q z^q + a_n^{-1} a_1 z^{q-1} + \cdots + 1]$, then setting $b_1 = a_n^{-1} a_{n-1}, \dots, b_q = a_n^{-1}(-1)^q$. The multiplicative constant a_n can be incorporated in the variance term in (II.23) without any problem.

But, as there are several – although at most 2^q – ways[36] of choosing the subset z'_j, it follows that there will be as many solutions of our problem, that is as many MA(q) processes with the same given sequence of autocovariances. However, only one of these has the property of *invertibility*,[37] and is therefore the one to be selected. To see this, let us write (II.17) as

$$\varepsilon_t = \frac{1}{\beta(\mathrm{L})} X_t, \tag{II.24}$$

and since $\beta(\mathrm{L})$ is $\beta(z)$ with z replaced by L, the polynomial $\beta(\mathrm{L})$ has the same roots as $\beta(z) = 0$, let them be z'_j, $j = 1, \ldots, q$. We can expand $1/\beta(\mathrm{L})$ in partial fractions[38] according to the formula

$$\frac{1}{\beta(\mathrm{L})} = \sum_{j=1}^{q} A_j \frac{1}{\mathrm{L} - z'_j}. \tag{II.25}$$

Writing the terms $1/(\mathrm{L} - z'_j)$ as $-(1/z'_j)[1/(1 - (\mathrm{L}/z'_j))]$, and expanding $1/(1 - (\mathrm{L}/z'_j))$ in a power series, we arrive at the following expression for the typical term of eq. (II.25)

$$A_j \frac{1}{\mathrm{L} - z'_j} = -\frac{A_j}{z'_j} \sum_{k=0}^{\infty} \frac{\mathrm{L}^k}{(z'_j)^k}, \tag{II.26}$$

which is the form that we were looking for, provided that the sum

[36]We say "at most" because, since the b_j must be real, any complex roots must be taken in conjugate pairs.

[37]The process (II.11) is said to be *invertible* if ε_t can be expressed as an infinite sum of present and past values of X_t, that is as an *autoregressive process* AR(∞) of the type

$$\varepsilon_t = \sum_{r=0}^{\infty} C_r \mathrm{L}^r X_{t-r},$$

where L is the lag operator and the C_r's are coefficients to be found. As we shall see in the text, the invertibility condition is that the roots are all in modulus greater than 1.

[38]Let us recall (see, for example, Turnbull, 1957, ch. III, § 19) that given the rational function $F(x)/G(x)$, where $F(x)$ is a polynomial of lower degree than the polynomial $G(x)$, we have

$$\frac{F(x)}{G(x)} = \sum_{j=1}^{n} \frac{F(x_j)}{G'(x_j)} \frac{1}{x - x_j},$$

where the x_j's are the roots of $G(x) = 0$ and $G'(x_j)$ denotes the derivative of $G(x)$ evaluated at $x = x_j$. In our case, being $F(x) = 1$, we have $A_j = 1/G'(x_j)$, that is

$$A_j = \frac{1}{(\mathrm{d}\beta/\mathrm{d}z)_{z=z'_j}}.$$

on the right hand side converges. As we know, the convergency condition is $|z_j'| > 1$. Therefore, among the moving average processes being considered, only one is invertible, and it is the one corresponding to the subset of roots z_j^*, where $|z_j^*| > 1$, $j = 1, 2, \dots, q$.

II.2. *Derivation of the process in eq. (34)*

If we consider the disturbance vector in ch. 3, eq. (33) – or, what amounts to the same thing, in eq. (29) – and neglect the term $e^{A\theta}$, we have

$$\boldsymbol{\xi}(t) = \int_{t-\delta}^{t} \int_{0}^{\delta} \mathrm{d}\boldsymbol{\zeta}(s-\theta)\,\mathrm{d}s, \tag{II.27}$$

which can also be written as[39]

$$\boldsymbol{\xi}(t) = \int_{t-\delta}^{t} \int_{s-\delta}^{s} \boldsymbol{u}(\theta)\,\mathrm{d}\theta\,\mathrm{d}s. \tag{II.28}$$

Its autocovariance generating function – see eq. (II.5) – is[40]

$$\boldsymbol{\sigma}(z) = \sum_{-\infty}^{\infty} \boldsymbol{\sigma}_h z^h \tag{II.29}$$

where

$$\boldsymbol{\sigma}_h = \mathrm{E}\{[\boldsymbol{\xi}(t)][\boldsymbol{\xi}(t+h\delta)]^{\mathrm{T}}\}. \tag{II.29'}$$

Let us now compute the autocovariances $\boldsymbol{\sigma}_h$. For $h = 1$ we have

$$\begin{aligned}\boldsymbol{\sigma}_1 &= \mathrm{E}\{[\boldsymbol{\xi}(t)][\boldsymbol{\xi}(t+h\delta)]^{\mathrm{T}}\} \\ &= \mathrm{E}\left\{\left[\int_{t-\delta}^{t} \int_{s-\delta}^{s} \boldsymbol{u}(\theta)\,\mathrm{d}\theta\,\mathrm{d}s\right]\left[\int_{t}^{t+\delta} \int_{s-\delta}^{s} \boldsymbol{u}(\theta)^{\mathrm{T}}\,\mathrm{d}\theta\,\mathrm{d}s\right]\right\}.\end{aligned} \tag{II.30}$$

The procedure that we follow consists in expressing the integrals in

[39] Remembering eqs. (15), (14″), (13) and (12′) in ch. 3, we have

$$\int_0^{\delta} \mathrm{d}\boldsymbol{\zeta}(s-\theta) = \int_{s-\delta}^{s} \mathrm{d}\boldsymbol{\zeta}(\theta) = \int_{s-\delta}^{s} \boldsymbol{u}(\theta)\,\mathrm{d}\theta.$$

[40] In what follows we use the extension to vector stochastic processes of the properties expounded in the previous section with reference to a single variable stochastic process.

a form that allows the use of properties (10) in ch. 3. Remembering the definition of integral as the limit of a sum, and dividing the integration interval δ into n sub-intervals each equal to δ/n, we have

$$\boldsymbol{\sigma}_1 = \mathrm{E}\left\{ \lim_{n\to\infty} \left[\frac{\delta}{n} \sum_{i=1}^{n} \int_{t-2\delta+\delta i/n}^{t-\delta+\delta i/n} \boldsymbol{u}(\theta)\,\mathrm{d}\theta \right] \times \left[\frac{\delta}{n} \sum_{i=1}^{n} \int_{t-\delta+\delta i/n}^{t+\delta i/n} \boldsymbol{u}(\theta)^{\mathrm{T}}\,\mathrm{d}\theta \right] \right\}. \tag{II.31}$$

Taking account of the fact that the operator E and the operator lim commute, and factoring out the multiplicative constant (δ^2/n^2) we obtain

$$\boldsymbol{\sigma}_1 = \lim_{n\to\infty} \frac{\delta^2}{n^2} \mathrm{E}\left\{ \left[\sum_{i=1}^{n} \int_{t-2\delta+\delta i/n}^{t-\delta+\delta i/n} \boldsymbol{u}(\theta)\,\mathrm{d}\theta \right] \times \left[\sum_{i=1}^{n} \int_{t-\delta+\delta i/n}^{t+\delta i/n} \boldsymbol{u}(\theta)^{\mathrm{T}}\,\mathrm{d}\theta \right] \right\}. \tag{II.32}$$

Performing a further subdivision we get

$$\boldsymbol{\sigma}_1 = \lim_{n\to\infty} \frac{\delta^2}{n^2} \mathrm{E}\left\{ \left[\sum_{i=1}^{n} \sum_{j=1}^{n} \int_{t-2\delta+\delta(i+j-1)/n}^{t-2\delta+\delta(i+j)/n} \boldsymbol{u}(\theta)\,\mathrm{d}\theta \right] \times \left[\sum_{i=1}^{n} \sum_{j=1}^{n} \int_{t-\delta+\delta(i+j-1)/n}^{t-\delta+\delta(i+j)/n} \boldsymbol{u}(\theta)^{\mathrm{T}}\,\mathrm{d}\theta \right] \right\}. \tag{II.33}$$

We shall now develop the summations. We have

$$\boldsymbol{\sigma}_1 = \lim_{n\to\infty} \frac{\delta^2}{n^2} \mathrm{E}\left\{ \left[\sum_{i=1}^{n} \left(\int_{t-2\delta+\delta i/n}^{t-2\delta+\delta(i+1)/n} \boldsymbol{u}(\theta)\,\mathrm{d}\theta + \int_{t-2\delta+\delta(i+1)/n}^{t-2\delta+\delta(i+2)/n} \boldsymbol{u}(\theta)\,\mathrm{d}\theta + \cdots + \int_{t-2\delta+\delta(i+n-1)/n}^{t-2\delta+\delta(i+n)/n} \boldsymbol{u}(\theta)\,\mathrm{d}\theta \right) \right] \right.$$

$$\times\left[\sum_{i=1}^{n}\left(\int_{t-\delta+\delta i/n}^{t-\delta+\delta(i+1)/n}\boldsymbol{u}(\theta)^{\mathrm{T}}\,\mathrm{d}\theta\right.\right.$$

$$+\int_{t-\delta+\delta(i+1)/n}^{t-\delta+\delta(i+2)/n}\boldsymbol{u}(\theta)^{\mathrm{T}}\,\mathrm{d}\theta+\cdots$$

$$\left.\left.\left.+\int_{t-\delta+\delta(i+n-1)/n}^{t-\delta+\delta(i+n)/n}\boldsymbol{u}(\theta)^{\mathrm{T}}\,\mathrm{d}\theta\right)\right]\right\}. \qquad \text{(II.34)}$$

Developing the second summation we obtain

$$\boldsymbol{\sigma}_1=\lim_{n\to\infty}\frac{\delta^2}{n^2}\mathrm{E}\left\{\left[\int_{t-2\delta+\delta/n}^{t-2\delta+2\delta/n}\boldsymbol{u}(\theta)\,\mathrm{d}\theta+\int_{t-2\delta+2\delta/n}^{t-2\delta+3\delta/n}\boldsymbol{u}(\theta)\,\mathrm{d}\theta+\cdots\right.\right.$$

$$+\int_{t-2\delta+n\delta/n}^{t-2\delta+(n+1)\delta/n}\boldsymbol{u}(\theta)\,\mathrm{d}\theta+\int_{t-2\delta+2\delta/n}^{t-2\delta+3\delta/n}\boldsymbol{u}(\theta)\,\mathrm{d}\theta$$

$$+\int_{t-2\delta+3\delta/n}^{t-2\delta+4\delta/n}\boldsymbol{u}(\theta)\,\mathrm{d}\theta+\ldots$$

$$+\int_{t-2\delta+(n+1)\delta/n}^{t-2\delta+(n+2)\delta/n}\boldsymbol{u}(\theta)\,\mathrm{d}\theta$$

$$+\cdots\cdots\cdots\cdots\cdots\cdots\cdots\cdots\cdots\cdots\cdots\cdots$$

$$+\int_{t-2\delta+n\delta/n}^{t-2\delta+(n+1)\delta/n}\boldsymbol{u}(\theta)\,\mathrm{d}\theta$$

$$+\int_{t-2\delta+(n+1)\delta/n}^{t-2\delta+(n+2)\delta/n}\boldsymbol{u}(\theta)\,\mathrm{d}\theta+\cdots$$

$$\left.+\int_{t-2\delta+(2n-1)\delta/n}^{t-2\delta+2n\delta/n}\boldsymbol{u}(\theta)\,\mathrm{d}\theta\right]$$

$$\times\left[\int_{t-\delta+\delta/n}^{t-\delta+2\delta/n}\boldsymbol{u}(\theta)^{\mathrm{T}}\,\mathrm{d}\theta+\int_{t-\delta+2\delta/n}^{t-\delta+3\delta/n}\boldsymbol{u}(\theta)^{\mathrm{T}}\,\mathrm{d}\theta\right.$$

$$+\cdots+\int_{t-\delta+n\delta/n}^{t-\delta+(n+1)\delta/n}\boldsymbol{u}(\theta)^{\mathrm{T}}\,\mathrm{d}\theta$$

$$+\int_{t-\delta+2\delta/n}^{t-\delta+3\delta/n}\boldsymbol{u}(\theta)^{\mathrm{T}}\,\mathrm{d}\theta+\int_{t-\delta+3\delta/n}^{t-\delta+4\delta/n}\boldsymbol{u}(\theta)^{\mathrm{T}}\,\mathrm{d}\theta$$

$$+\cdots+\int_{t-\delta+(n+1)\delta/n}^{t-\delta+(n+2)\delta/n}\boldsymbol{u}(\theta)^{\mathrm{T}}\,\mathrm{d}\theta$$

$$+\ldots\ldots\ldots\ldots\ldots\ldots\ldots\ldots\ldots\ldots\ldots$$

$$+\int_{t-\delta+n\delta/n}^{t-\delta+(n+1)\delta/n}\boldsymbol{u}(\theta)^{\mathrm{T}}\,\mathrm{d}\theta$$

$$+\int_{t-\delta+(n+1)\delta/n}^{t-\delta+(n+2)\delta/n}\boldsymbol{u}(\theta)^{\mathrm{T}}\,\mathrm{d}\theta+\cdots$$

$$\left.\left.+\int_{t-\delta+(2n-1)\delta/n}^{t-\delta+2n\delta/n}\boldsymbol{u}(\theta)^{\mathrm{T}}\,\mathrm{d}\theta\right]\right\}. \tag{II.35}$$

If we collect terms we get

$$\boldsymbol{\sigma}_1=\lim_{n\to\infty}\frac{\delta^2}{n^2}\mathrm{E}\left\{\left[\int_{t-2\delta+\delta/n}^{t-2\delta+2\delta/n}\boldsymbol{u}(\theta)\mathrm{d}\theta+2\int_{t-2\delta+2\delta/n}^{t-2\delta+3\delta/n}\boldsymbol{u}(\theta)\,\mathrm{d}\theta\right.\right.$$

$$+3\int_{t-2\delta+3\delta/n}^{t-2\delta+4\delta/n}\boldsymbol{u}(\theta)\,\mathrm{d}\theta+\cdots$$

$$+(n-1)\int_{t-2\delta+(n-1)\delta/n}^{t-2\delta+n\delta/n}\boldsymbol{u}(\theta)\,\mathrm{d}\theta+n\int_{t-2\delta+n\delta/n}^{t-2\delta+(n+1)\delta/n}\boldsymbol{u}(\theta)\,\mathrm{d}\theta$$

$$+(n-1)\int_{t-2\delta+(n+1)\delta/n}^{t-2\delta+(n+2)\delta/n}\boldsymbol{u}(\theta)\,\mathrm{d}\theta$$

$$+\cdots+3\int_{t-2\delta+(2n-3)\delta/n}^{t-2\delta+(2n-2)\delta/n}\boldsymbol{u}(\theta)\,\mathrm{d}\theta$$

$$\left.+2\int_{t-2\delta+(2n-2)\delta/n}^{t-2\delta+(2n-1)\delta/n}\boldsymbol{u}(\theta)\,\mathrm{d}\theta+\int_{t-2\delta+(2n-1)\delta/n}^{t-2\delta+2n\delta/n}\boldsymbol{u}(\theta)\,\mathrm{d}\theta\right]$$

$$\times\left[\int_{t-\delta+\delta/n}^{t-\delta+2\delta/n}\boldsymbol{u}(\theta)^{\mathrm{T}}\,\mathrm{d}\theta+2\int_{t-\delta+2\delta/n}^{t-\delta+3\delta/n}\boldsymbol{u}(\theta)^{\mathrm{T}}\,\mathrm{d}\theta\right.$$

$$+3\int_{t-\delta+3\delta/n}^{t-\delta+4\delta/n}\boldsymbol{u}(\theta)^{\mathrm{T}}\,\mathrm{d}\theta+\cdots$$

$$+(n-1)\int_{t-\delta+(n-1)\delta/n}^{t-\delta+n\delta/n}\boldsymbol{u}(\theta)^{\mathrm{T}}\,\mathrm{d}\theta$$

$$+ n\int_{t-\delta+n\delta/n}^{t-2\delta+(n+1)\delta/n} \boldsymbol{u}(\theta)^{\mathrm{T}}\,\mathrm{d}\theta$$

$$+ (n-1)\int_{t-\delta+(n+1)\delta/n}^{t-\delta+(n+2)\delta/n} \boldsymbol{u}(\theta)^{\mathrm{T}}\,\mathrm{d}\theta$$

$$+ \cdots + 3\int_{t-\delta+(2n-3)\delta/n}^{t-\delta+(2n-2)\delta/n} \boldsymbol{u}(\theta)^{\mathrm{T}}\,\mathrm{d}\theta$$

$$+ 2\int_{t-\delta+(2n-2)\delta/n}^{t-\delta+(2n-1)\delta/n} \boldsymbol{u}(\theta)^{\mathrm{T}}\,\mathrm{d}\theta$$

$$\left.\left. + \int_{t-\delta+(2n-1)\delta/n}^{t-\delta+2n\delta/n} \boldsymbol{u}(\theta)^{\mathrm{T}}\,\mathrm{d}\theta\right]\right\}. \qquad \text{(II.36)}$$

Remembering that, given the relations between $\boldsymbol{u}$ and $\boldsymbol{\zeta}$ one has $\int_a^b \boldsymbol{u}(\theta)\,\mathrm{d}\theta = \boldsymbol{\zeta}(b) - \boldsymbol{\zeta}(a)$, and remembering also properties (10) in ch. 3, it can easily be seen that, by carrying out the multiplications in (II.36) and taking expected values, the expected values of the products of integrals having different integration limits are zero (this derives from the assumption of uncorrelated increments), whereas the expected values of the products of integrals having the same limits of integration are equal to the matrix $\boldsymbol{\Omega}$ multiplied by the absolute value of the difference between the limits (this derives from the assumption of homogeneity). It is possible to check that no integral in the second square brackets corresponds[41] to the first n integrals in the first square brackets in eq. (II.36), whereas one, and only one, integral in the second square brackets corresponds to the successive (from $n + 1$ onwards) integrals in the first square brackets. To be precise, the integrals we are interested in are

$$(n-1)\int_{t-2\delta+(n+1)\delta/n}^{t-2\delta+(n+2)\delta/n} \boldsymbol{u}(\theta)\,\mathrm{d}\theta \quad \int_{t-\delta+\delta/n}^{t-\delta+2\delta/n} \mathbf{u}(\theta)^{\mathrm{T}}\,\mathrm{d}\theta;$$

$$(n-2)\int_{t-2\delta+(n+2)\delta/n}^{t-2\delta+(n+3)\delta/n} \boldsymbol{u}(\theta)\,\mathrm{d}\theta \quad 2\int_{t-\delta+2\delta/n}^{t-\delta+3\delta/n} \boldsymbol{u}(\theta)^{\mathrm{T}}\,\mathrm{d}\theta; \ldots;$$

$$2\int_{t-2\delta+(2n-2)\delta/n}^{t-2\delta+(2n-1)\delta/n} \boldsymbol{u}(\theta)\,\mathrm{d}\theta \quad (n-2)\int_{t-\delta+(n-2)\delta/n}^{t-\delta+(n-1)\delta/n} \boldsymbol{u}(\theta)^{\mathrm{T}}\,\mathrm{d}\theta;$$

$$\int_{t-2\delta+(2n-1)\delta/n}^{t-2\delta+2n\delta/n} \boldsymbol{u}(\theta)\,\mathrm{d}\theta \quad (n-1)\int_{t-\delta+(n-1)\delta/n}^{t-\delta+n\delta/n} \boldsymbol{u}(\theta)^{\mathrm{T}}\,\mathrm{d}\theta; \qquad \text{(II.37)}$$

[41] "Corresponds" in the sense of having the same limits of integration, as clarified above.

whose integration limits, once the simplification of the formulae that express these limits has been performed, turn out to be equal. As the integration interval is constant and equal to δ/n, we have

$$\begin{aligned}\boldsymbol{\sigma}_1 &= \lim_{n\to\infty}\frac{\delta^2}{n^2}\left\{(n-1)\boldsymbol{\Omega}\frac{\delta}{n}+(n-2)2\boldsymbol{\Omega}\frac{\delta}{n}\right.\\ &\quad\left.+\cdots+2(n-2)\boldsymbol{\Omega}\frac{\delta}{n}+(n-1)\boldsymbol{\Omega}\frac{\delta}{n}\right\}\\ &= \lim_{n\to\infty}\frac{\delta^2}{n^2}\left\{\sum_{m=1}^{n}(n-m)m\boldsymbol{\Omega}\frac{\delta}{n}\right\}\\ &= \delta^3\boldsymbol{\Omega}\lim_{n\to\infty}\frac{1}{n}\sum_{m=1}^{n}\frac{m}{n}\left(1-\frac{m}{n}\right).\end{aligned} \tag{II.38}$$

If we again recall the definition of definite integral as the limit of a sum, we have

$$\lim_{n\to\infty}\frac{1}{n}\sum_{m=1}^{n}\frac{m}{n}\left(1-\frac{m}{n}\right)=\int_0^1 x(1-x)\,\mathrm{d}x=\left[\tfrac{1}{2}x^2-\tfrac{1}{3}x^3\right]_0^1=\tfrac{1}{6}, \tag{II.39}$$

and so finally

$$\boldsymbol{\sigma}_1=\tfrac{1}{6}\delta^3\boldsymbol{\Omega}. \tag{II.40}$$

By the same procedure it can be shown – the proof is left to the reader – that

$$\boldsymbol{\sigma}_0=\tfrac{2}{3}\delta^3\boldsymbol{\Omega}, \tag{II.41}$$

and that $\boldsymbol{\sigma}_h = 0$ for $h > 1$ and, furthermore, that $\boldsymbol{\sigma}_{-j} = \boldsymbol{\sigma}_j$. Therefore the autocovariance generating function is

$$\boldsymbol{\sigma}(z)=\delta^3\boldsymbol{\Omega}\left(\tfrac{1}{6}z^{-1}+\tfrac{2}{3}+\tfrac{1}{6}z\right). \tag{II.42}$$

Now, in order to write $\boldsymbol{\xi}(t)$ as a moving average process let us apply the procedure described in the previous paragraph, beginning with the computation of the roots of $\boldsymbol{\sigma}(z) = 0$, that is, of

$$\tfrac{1}{6}z^{-1}+\tfrac{2}{3}+\tfrac{1}{6}z=0. \tag{II.43}$$

Since $z = 0$ is not a root, we can multiply through by $6z$, $z \neq 0$, obtaining the second-degree equation

$$z^2+4z+1=0, \tag{II.44}$$

whose roots are $-2 \pm \sqrt{3} \simeq -0.268, -3.732$, which are reciprocal numbers. As there are only two roots, the choice – see eq. (II.23) – has to be made between $(z + 0.268)$ and $(z + (1/0.268))$. On the basis of what we said in the previous paragraph, we must take the root with modulus greater than one and therefore choose the expression $(z + (1/0.268))$ which, rewritten in the form

$$\frac{1}{0.268}(1 + 0.268z),$$

gives the coefficients – in this case only one has to be found, as the first is always one – of the sought for MA(1) process. This process – apart from multiplicative constants – turns out to be $(1 + 0.268\mathrm{L})$. Thus we have finally

$$\xi(t) = (1 + 0.268\mathrm{L})\varepsilon(t), \tag{II.45}$$

which is eq. (34) in ch. 3. At the same time, note that 0.268 is the approximate value of $2 - \sqrt{3}$.

Appendix III. Interpolation of observations of continuous variables

As we know from the treatment in the text, the estimators are independent of the length of the observation interval. But, of course, this interval must be the same for all variables. In order to avoid the loss of information and of degrees of freedom, it may therefore be desirable or necessary to interpolate data referred to a certain observation interval so as to obtain a series that refers to a smaller observation interval.

The case may arise, for example, where quarterly observations are available for all variables except one, which is available on an annual basis, or where monthly observations are available for all variables except one, which is available on a quarterly basis. According to Wymer, "such interpolation can be justified if the time path of the variable is likely to be relatively smooth and if the variable is either exogenous or does not appear directly in the model but is a component of some other variable".

In undertaking the derivation of the interpolation formulae, we must remember that, if we are dealing with flow variables, the observed values are actually integrals. Therefore, if we use a quadratic interpolation formula, we must integrate it. In what follows, we first deal with flow variables and then with stock variables.

III.1. Quarterly interpolation from annual observations

Let y_{t-1}, y_{t-2}, y_{t-3} be three consecutive annual observations of a continuous flow variable $y(t)$. Using a quadratic approximation, namely assuming that $y(t)$ can be represented by a parabola $at^2 + bt + c$, where a, b and c are coefficients to be found, we have

$$\begin{aligned} &\int_0^1 (at^2 + bt + c)\,\mathrm{d}t = y_{t-1}, \\ &\int_1^2 (at^2 + bt + c)\,\mathrm{d}t = y_t, \\ &\int_2^3 (at^2 + bt + c)\,\mathrm{d}t = y_{t+1}. \end{aligned} \tag{III.1}$$

Since

$$\int_\alpha^\beta (at^2 + bt + c)\,\mathrm{d}t = \left[\tfrac{1}{3}at^3 + \tfrac{1}{2}bt^2 + ct\right]_\alpha^\beta,$$

by integrating out in eqs. (III.1) we have

$$\begin{aligned} &\tfrac{1}{3}a + \tfrac{1}{2}b + c = y_{t-1}, \\ &\tfrac{7}{3}a + \tfrac{3}{2}b + c = y_t, \\ &\tfrac{19}{3}a + \tfrac{5}{2}b + c = y_{t+1}. \end{aligned} \tag{III.2}$$

After solving this linear system for the unknowns a, b and c we get

$$\begin{aligned} &a = 0.5y_{t-1} - 1.0y_t + 0.5y_{t+1}, \\ &b = -2.0y_{t-1} + 3.0y_t - 1.0y_{t+1}, \\ &c = \tfrac{11}{6}y_{t-1} - \tfrac{7}{6}y_t + \tfrac{1}{3}y_{t+1}, \qquad \tfrac{11}{6} = 1.8\bar{3};\ \tfrac{7}{6} = 1.1\bar{6};\ \tfrac{1}{3} = 0.\bar{3}. \end{aligned} \tag{III.3}$$

Now, the quarterly figures within any year t must in turn satisfy the conditions

$$\begin{aligned} &y_t^{(1)} = \int_{1.0}^{1.25} (at^2 + bt + c)\,\mathrm{d}t, \qquad y_t^{(2)} = \int_{1.25}^{1.50} (at^2 + bt + c)\,\mathrm{d}t, \\ &y_t^{(3)} = \int_{1.50}^{1.75} (at^2 + bt + c)\,\mathrm{d}t, \qquad y_t^{(4)} = \int_{1.75}^{2} (at^2 + bt + c)\,\mathrm{d}t, \end{aligned} \tag{III.4}$$

because, given the additive property of integrals, $y_t = \Sigma_{i=1}^{4} y_t^{(i)}$. By performing the integrations in (III.4) and then by substituting the values of a, b and c found above, we obtain

$$y_t^{(1)} = \frac{0.953125}{3}a + 0.28125b + 0.25c$$

$$= \left(\frac{0.953125}{6}y_{t-1} - \frac{0.953125}{3}y_t + \frac{0.953125}{6}y_{t+1}\right)$$

$$+ (-0.5625y_{t-1} + 0.84375y_t - 0.28125y_{t+1})$$

$$+ \left(\frac{11}{24}y_{t-1} - \frac{7}{24}y_t + \frac{1}{12}y_{t+1}\right)$$

$$= \left(\frac{0.953125}{6} - 0.5625 + \frac{11}{24}\right)y_{t-1}$$

$$+ \left(-\frac{0.953125}{3} + 0.84375 - \frac{7}{24}\right)y_t$$

$$+ \left(\frac{0.953125}{6} - 0.28125 + \frac{1}{12}\right)y_{t+1}$$

$$= \frac{1.3125}{24}y_{t-1} + \frac{5.625}{24}y_t - \frac{0.46875}{12}y_{t+1}$$

$$= 0.0546875y_{t-1} + 0.234375y_t - 0.0390625y_{t+1}. \qquad \text{(III.5)}$$

$$y_t^{(2)} = \frac{1.421875}{3}a + 0.34375b + 0.25c$$

$$= \left(\frac{1.421875}{6}y_{t-1} - \frac{1.421875}{3}y_t + \frac{1.421875}{6}y_{t+1}\right)$$

$$+ (-0.6875y_{t-1} + 1.03125y_t - 0.34375y_{t+1})$$

$$+ \left(\frac{11}{24}y_{t-1} - \frac{7}{24}y_t + \frac{1}{12}y_{t+1}\right)$$

$$= \left(\frac{1.421875}{6} - 0.6875 + \frac{11}{24}\right)y_{t-1}$$

$$+ \left(-\frac{1.421875}{3} + 1.03125 - \frac{7}{24}\right)y_t$$

$$+ \left(\frac{1.421875}{6} - 0.34375 + \frac{1}{12}\right)y_{t+1}$$

$$= \frac{0.1875}{24}y_{t-1} + \frac{6.375}{24}y_t - \frac{0.28125}{12}y_{t+1}$$

$$= 0.0078125y_{t-1} + 0.265625y_t - 0.0234375y_{t+1}. \qquad \text{(III.6)}$$

$$
\begin{aligned}
y_t^{(3)} &= \frac{1.984375}{3}a + 0.40625b + 0.25c \\
&= \left(\frac{1.984375}{6}y_{t-1} - \frac{1.984375}{3}y_t + \frac{1.984375}{6}y_{t+1}\right) \\
&\quad + (-0.8125y_{t-1} + 1.21875y_t - 0.40625y_{t+1}) \\
&\quad + \left(\frac{11}{24}y_{t-1} - \frac{7}{24}y_t + \frac{1}{12}y_{t+1}\right) \\
&= \left(\frac{1.984375}{6} - 0.8125 + \frac{11}{24}\right)y_{t-1} \\
&\quad + \left(-\frac{1.984375}{3} + 1.21875 - \frac{7}{24}\right)y_t \\
&\quad + \left(\frac{1.984375}{6} - 0.40625 + \frac{1}{12}\right)y_{t+1} \\
&= -\frac{0.5625}{24}y_{t-1} + \frac{6.375}{24}y_t + \frac{0.09375}{12}y_{t+1} \\
&= -0.0234375y_{t-1} + 0.265625y_t + 0.0078125y_{t+1}. \qquad \text{(III.7)}
\end{aligned}
$$

$$
\begin{aligned}
y_t^{(4)} &= \frac{2.640625}{3}a + 0.46875b + 0.25c \\
&= \left(\frac{2.640625}{6}y_{t-1} - \frac{2.640625}{3}y_t + \frac{2.640625}{6}y_{t+1}\right) \\
&\quad + (-0.9375y_{t-1} + 1.40625y_t - 0.46875y_{t+1}) \\
&\quad + \left(\frac{11}{24}y_{t-1} - \frac{7}{24}y_t + \frac{1}{12}y_{t+1}\right) \\
&= \left(\frac{2.640625}{6} - 0.9375 + \frac{11}{24}\right)y_{t-1} \\
&\quad + \left(-\frac{2.640625}{3} + 1.40625 - \frac{7}{24}\right)y_t \\
&\quad + \left(\frac{2.640625}{6} - 0.46875 + \frac{1}{12}\right)y_{t+1} \\
&= -\frac{0.9375}{24}y_{t-1} + \frac{5.625}{24}y_t + \frac{0.65625}{12}y_{t+1} \\
&= -0.0390625y_{t-1} + 0.234375y_t + 0.0546875y_{t+1}. \qquad \text{(III.8)}
\end{aligned}
$$

III.2. Monthly interpolation from quarterly observations

Let y_{t-1}, y_t, y_{t+1} be three successive quarterly observations of a continuous flow variable $y(t)$. The quadratic passing through these points must have the same properties (III.1) and so the coefficients a, b and c are the same as in (III.3); of course we must remember that the time unit is now the quarter.

The monthly figures within any quarter t must in turn satisfy the conditions

$$\begin{aligned} {}^{(1)}y_t &= \int_1^{4/3} (at^2 + bt + c)\,\mathrm{d}t, \\ {}^{(2)}y_t &= \int_{4/3}^{5/3} (at^2 + bt + c)\,\mathrm{d}t, \\ {}^{(3)}y_t &= \int_{5/3}^{2} (at^2 + bt + c)\,\mathrm{d}t, \end{aligned} \tag{III.9}$$

because $y_t = \Sigma_{i=1}^{3}\, {}^{(i)}y_t$. By performing the integrations in (III.9) and by using the values of a, b and c found above, we have

$$\begin{aligned} {}^{(1)}y_t = \frac{37}{81}a + \frac{7}{18}b + \frac{1}{3}c &= \left(\frac{37}{162}y_{t-1} - \frac{37}{81}y_t + \frac{37}{162}y_{t+1}\right) \\ &\quad + \left(-\frac{7}{9}y_{t-1} + \frac{7}{6}y_t - \frac{7}{18}y_{t+1}\right) \\ &\quad + \left(\frac{11}{18}y_{t-1} - \frac{7}{18}y_t + \frac{1}{9}y_{t+1}\right) \\ &= \left(\frac{37}{162} - \frac{7}{9} + \frac{11}{18}\right)y_{t-1} + \left(-\frac{37}{81} + \frac{7}{6} - \frac{7}{18}\right)y_t \\ &\quad + \left(\frac{37}{162} - \frac{7}{18} + \frac{1}{9}\right)y_{t+1} \\ &= \frac{10}{162}y_{t-1} + \frac{52}{162}y_t - \frac{8}{162}y_{t+1} \\ &= 0.061728395y_{t-1} + 0.320987654y_t - 0.04938271y_{t+1}. \end{aligned} \tag{III.10}$$

$$
\begin{aligned}
{}^{(2)}y_t &= \frac{61}{81}a + \frac{1}{2}b + \frac{1}{3}c = \left(\frac{61}{162}y_{t-1} - \frac{61}{81}y_t + \frac{61}{162}y_{t+1}\right) \\
&\quad + \left(-y_{t-1} + \frac{3}{2}y_t - \frac{1}{2}y_{t+1}\right) \\
&\quad + \left(\frac{11}{18}y_{t-1} - \frac{7}{18}y_t + \frac{1}{9}y_{t+1}\right) \\
&= \left(\frac{61}{162} - 1 + \frac{11}{18}\right)y_{t-1} + \left(-\frac{61}{81} + \frac{3}{2} - \frac{7}{18}\right)y_t \\
&\quad + \left(\frac{61}{162} - \frac{1}{2} + \frac{1}{9}\right)y_{t+1} \\
&= -\frac{2}{162}y_{t-1} + \frac{58}{162}y_t - \frac{2}{162}y_{t+1} \\
&= -0.012345679y_{t-1} + 0.358024691y_t - 0.012345679y_{t+1}.
\end{aligned}
\tag{III.11}
$$

$$
\begin{aligned}
{}^{(3)}y_t &= \frac{91}{81}a + \frac{11}{18}b + \frac{1}{3}c = \left(\frac{91}{162}y_{t-1} - \frac{91}{81}y_t + \frac{91}{162}y_{t+1}\right) \\
&\quad + \left(-\frac{11}{9}y_{t-1} + \frac{11}{6}y_t - \frac{11}{18}y_{t+1}\right) \\
&\quad + \left(\frac{11}{18}y_{t-1} - \frac{7}{18}y_t + \frac{1}{9}y_{t+1}\right) \\
&= \left(\frac{91}{162} - \frac{11}{9} + \frac{11}{18}\right)y_{t-1} + \left(-\frac{91}{81} + \frac{11}{6} - \frac{7}{18}\right)y_t \\
&\quad + \left(\frac{91}{162} - \frac{11}{18} + \frac{1}{9}\right)y_{t+1} \\
&= -\frac{8}{162}y_{t-1} + \frac{52}{162}y_t + \frac{10}{162}y_{t+1} \\
&= -0.049382716y_{t-1} + 0.320987654y_t + 0.061728395y_{t+1}.
\end{aligned}
\tag{III.12}
$$

III.3. Further considerations

With similar procedures it is possible to interpolate quarterly figures from semi-annual observations or semi-annual figures from annual data.

The treatment in the previous paragraphs is valid for *flow* variables only. When we have to deal with *stock* variables, the procedure suggested is to take first differences to obtain a series of changes in stocks over the period. As changes in stock can be treated as flow variables, we can use the formulae expounded in paragraphs III.1 and III.2 to interpolate changes over the intermediate periods; these changes can then be cumulated to find the new stock series. As regards non-stock instantaneous variables, a standard cubic interpolation formula can be used.

The procedure described in paragraphs III.1 and III.2 requires T + 2 annual observations $y_0, y_1, \ldots, y_T, y_{T+1}$ to generate a series of 4T quarterly observations, or T + 2 quarterly observations to generate a series of 3T monthly observations. Since the initial (annual or quarterly) observation y_0 and the final (annual or quarterly) observation y_{T+1} enter only in the quarterly (or monthly) interpolation of y_1 and of y_T respectively, and since the weights of these observations are relatively small, approximate values for y_0 and y_{T+1} may be used if necessary.

References to Part I

Aghevli, B. B. and Khan, M. S., 1977, Inflationary Finance and the Dynamics of Inflation: Indonesia, 1951–1972, *American Economic Review* **67**, 390–403.

Armington, P., 1979, A Multilateral Dynamic Model of Exchange Rates and Short-Term Interest Rates, paper presented at the 6th International Conference of Applied Econometrics, Rome, Feb. 7–10, 1979.

Bartlett, M. S., 1956, *An Introduction to Stochastic Processes, With Special Reference to Methods and Applications* (Cambridge University Press).

Baumol, W. J., 1970, *Economic Dynamics*, 3rd ed. (Macmillan, New York).

Bailey, R. E., Hall, V. B. and Phillips, P. C. B., 1979, A Model of Output, Employment and Inflation in an Open Economy, paper presented at the Australia and New Zealand Association for the Advancement of Science, 29th Congress, Auckland, 1979.

Bellman, R., 1953, *Stability Theory of Differential Equations* (McGraw-Hill, New York).

Bentzel, R. and Hansen, B., 1954, On Recursiveness and Interdependency in Economic Models, *Review of Economic Studies* **22**, 153–68.

Bergstrom, A. R., 1967, *The Construction and Use of Economic Models* (The English Universities Press, London); U.S. edition: *Selected Economic Models and Their Analysis* (Elsevier, New York, 1967).

Bergstrom, A. R., ed., 1976, *Statistical Inference in Continuous Time Economic Models* (North-Holland, Amsterdam).

Bergstrom, A. R. and Wymer, C. R., 1976, A Model of Disequilibrium Neoclassical Growth and its Application to the United Kingdom, in: Bergstrom, A. R., ed., 1976, 267–327.

Bergstrom, A. R., 1978, Monetary Policy in a Model of the United Kingdom, in: Bergstrom, A. R., Catt, A. J. L., Peston, M. H. and Silverstone, B. D. J., eds., *Stability and Inflation: Essays in Memory of A. W. H. Phillips* (Wiley, New York), 89–102.

Brennan, M. J. and Schwartz, E. S., 1979, A Continuous Time Approach to the Pricing of Bonds, *Journal of Banking and Finance* **3**, 133–56.

Carter, R. A. L. and Nagar, A. L., 1977, Coefficients of Correlation for Simultaneous Equation Systems, *Journal of Econometrics* **6**, 39–50.

Clements, K. W. and Jonson, P. D., 1979, Unanticipated Money, Disequilibrium Modelling and Rational Expectations, *Economics Letters* **2**, 303–308.

Coddington, E. A. and Levinson, N., 1955, *Theory of Ordinary Differential Equations* (McGraw-Hill, New York).

Courant, R., 1961, *Differential and Integral Calculus*, Vol. I and Vol. II (Blackie & Son, London).

Cramér, H. and Leadbetter, M. R., 1967, *Stationary and Related Stochastic Processes* (Wiley, New York).

Drabicki, J. Z. and Takayama, A., 1979, The General Equilibrium Framework of Economic Analysis: Stocks and Flows – With Special Application to Macroeconomic Models, in: Green, J. R. and Scheinkman, J. A. eds., *General Equilibrium*,

Growth and Trade – Essays in Honor of Lionel McKenzie (Academic Press, New York), 355–401.

Drollas, L. P., 1976, The Foreign Trade Sector in Disequilibrium: A Comparative Study of Sixteen Developed Economies, unpublished Ph.D. thesis (London School of Economics).

Fisher, F. M., 1966, *The Identification Problem in Econometrics* (McGraw-Hill, New York).

Foley, D. K., 1975, On Two Specifications of Asset Equilibrium in Macroeconomic Models, *Journal of Political Economy* **83**, 303–24.

Frazer, R. A., Duncan, W. J. and Collar, A. R., 1938, *Elementary Matrices and Some Applications to Dynamics and Differential Equations* (Cambridge University Press, London).

Frisch, R., 1933, Editorial, *Econometrica* **1**, 1–3.

Gandolfo, G., 1980, *Economic Dynamics: Methods and Models* (North-Holland, Amsterdam).

Gantmacher, F. R., 1959, *The Theory of Matrices*, Vol. I and Vol. II (Chelsea, New York).

Gillespie, R. P., 1959, *Integration* (Oliver and Boyd, Edinburgh and London).

Goodwin, R. M., 1948, Secular and Cyclical Aspects of the Multiplier and the Accelerator, in: *Income, Employment and Public Policy: Essays in Honor of A. H. Hansen* (Norton, New York).

Granger, C. W. J. and Newbold, P., 1977, *Forecasting Economic Time Series* (Academic Press, New York).

Grenander, U. and Rosenblatt, M., 1967, *Statistical Analysis of Stationary Time Series* (Wiley, New York).

Heller, H. R. and Knight, M., 1978, *Reserve-Currency Preferences of Central Banks* (Essays in International Finance No. 131, International Finance Section, Princeton University).

Houthakker, H. S. and Taylor, L. D., 1966, *Consumer Demand in the United States 1929–70, Analysis and Projections* (Harvard University Press)

Hyslop, J. M., 1959, *Infinite Series* (Oliver and Boyd, Edinburgh and London).

Intriligator, M. D., 1978, *Econometric Models, Techniques, and Applications* (North-Holland, Amsterdam).

Jonson, P. D., 1976, Money and Economy Activity in the Open Economy: The United Kingdom, 1880–1970, *Journal of Political Economy* **84**, 979–1012.

Jonson, P. D. and Taylor, J. C., 1978, Inflation and Economic Stability in a Small Open Economy: A Systems Approach, in: *The Problem of Inflation*, Vol. 8 in Carnegie-Rochester Series on Public Policy (A Supplementary Series to the Journal of Monetary Economics), 289–323.

Kalman, R. E. and Bertram, J. E., 1960, Control System Analysis and Design Via the "Second Method" of Lyapunov, I (Continuous-Time Systems), *Journal of Basic Engineering* (Transactions of the ASME), 371–93.

Kendall, M. G. and Stuart, A., 1969, 1973, 1976, *The Advanced Theory of Statistics*, Vol. 1, Vol. 2, Vol. 3, third ed. (Griffin & Co., London).

Kenkel, J. L., 1974, *Dynamic Linear Economic Models* (Gordon and Breach, New York).

Khan, M. S., 1977, Variable Expectations and the Demand for Money in High-Inflation Countries, *Manchester School* **45**, 270–93.

Knight, M., 1973, A Continuous Disequilibrium Econometric Model of the Domestic and International Portfolio Behaviour of the U.K. Banking System, in:

Parkin, M. and Nobay, A. R., eds., *Essays in Modern Economics*, Proceedings of the 1972 AUTE Conference (Longman, London), 266–290.

Knight, M., 1977, Euro-Dollars, Capital Mobility and the Forward Market, *Economica* (n.s.) **44**, 1–21.

Knight, M. D. and Mathieson, D. J., 1979, Model of an Industrial Country under Fixed and Flexible Exchange Rates, in: Martin, J. P. and Smith, A., eds., 1979, *Trade and Payments Adjustment Under Flexible Exchange Rates* (Macmillan, London), 86–119.

Knight, M. D. and Wymer, C. R., 1975, A Monetary Model of an Open Economy with Particular Reference to the United Kingdom, in: Artis, M. J. and Nobay, A. R., eds., *Essays in Economic Analysis*, Proceedings of the 1975 AUTE Conference (Cambridge University Press), 153–71.

Knight, M. D. and Wymer, C. R., 1978, A Macroeconomic Model of the United Kingdom, *IMF Staff Papers* **25**, 742–78.

Koopmans, T. C., 1950, Models Involving a Continuous Time Variable, in: Koopmans, T. C., ed., *Statistical Inference in Dynamic Economic Models*, Cowles Commission for Research in Economics, Monograph 10 (Wiley, New York), 384–89.

Krasovskiĭ, N. N., 1963, *Stability of Motion: Applications of Lyapunov's Second Method to Differential Systems and Equations with Delay* (Stanford University Press).

Laughton, M. A., 1964, Sensitivity in Dynamical System Analysis, *Journal of Electronics and Control* **1**, 577–91.

Laker, J. F., 1979, Continuous Disequilibrium Adjustment Model of the Labour Market with Particular Reference to Australia, 1964–76, unpublished Ph.D. thesis (London School of Economics).

Malinvaud, E., 1969, *Méthodes statistiques de l'économétrie*, 2me éd. (Dunod, Paris).

Marschak, J., 1950, Statistical Inference in Economics: An Introduction, in: Koopmans, T. C., ed., *Statistical Inference in Dynamic Economic Models*, Cowles Commission for Research in Economics, Monograph 10 (Wiley, New York), 1–50.

May, J., 1970, Period Analysis and Continuous Analysis in Patinkin's Macroeconomic Model, *Journal of Economic Theory* **2**, 1–9.

Mood, A. M., Graybill, F. A. and Boes, D. C., 1974, *Introduction to the Theory of Statistics*, 3rd ed. (McGraw-Hill, New York).

Phillips, A. W., 1956, Some Notes on the Estimation of Time-Forms of Reactions in Interdependent Dynamic Systems, *Economica* (n.s.) **23**, 99–113.

Phillips, E. G., 1961, *Functions of a Complex Variable* (Oliver and Boyd, Edinburgh and London).

Phillips, P. C. B., 1973, The Problem of Identification in Finite Parameter Continuous Time Models, *Journal of Econometrics* **1**, 351–62. Reprinted in: Bergstrom, A. R., ed., 1976, 123–34.

Phillips, P. C. B., 1974, A Finite Sample Experiment with an Incomplete Continuous System, mimeo.

Phillips, P. C. B., 1976a, The Estimation of Linear Stochastic Differential Equations with Exogenous Variables, in: Bergstrom, A. R., ed., 1976, 135–73.

Phillips, P. C. B., 1976b, Some Computations Based on Observed Data Series of the Exogenous Variable Component in Continuous Systems, in: Bergstrom, A. R., ed., 1976, 175–214.

Phillips, P. C. B., 1978, The Treatment of Flow Data in the Estimation of Continuous Time Systems, in: Bergstrom, A. R., Catt, A. J. L., Peston, M. H. and Silverstone, B. D. J., eds., *Stability and Inflation: Essays in Memory of A. W. H. Phillips* (Wiley, New York), 257–74.

Reserve Bank of Australia, 1977, *Conference in Applied Economic Research* (Reserve Bank of Australia, Sydney).

Richard, D. M., 1978, A Dynamic Model of the World Copper Industry, *IMF Staff Papers* **25**, 779–833.

Richard, D. M., 1979, A Global Adjustment Model of Exchange and Interest Rates: Empirical Analysis, mimeo (forthcoming in: Bigman, D. and Taya, T. eds., *The Functioning of Floating Exchange Rates: Theory, Evidence and Policy Implications*, Ballinger, Cambridge, Mass.).

Robinson, P. M., 1976, Fourier Estimation of Continuous Time Models, in: Bergstrom, A. R., ed., 1976, 215–66.

Robinson, P. M., 1977, The Construction and Estimation of Continuous Time Models and Discrete Approximations in Econometrics, *Journal of Econometrics* **6**, 173–97.

Sansone, G. and Conti, R., 1964, *Non-Linear Differential Equations* (Pergamon Press, London).

Sargan, J. D., 1976, Some Discrete Approximations to Continuous Time Stochastic Models, in: Bergstrom, A. R., ed. 1976, 27–79. Previously published (1974) in abridged form in *Journal of the Royal Statistical Society*, Series B, **36**, 74–90.

Spivey, W. A. and Wrobleski, W. J., 1979, *Econometric Model Performance in Forecasting and Policy Assessment* (American Enterprise Institute, Washington).

Strotz, R. H., 1960, Interdependence as a Specification Error, *Econometrica* **28**, 428–42.

Strotz, R. H. and Wold, H. O., 1960, Recursive Vs. Nonrecursive Systems: An Attempt at Synthesis, *Econometrica* **28**, 417–27.

Turnbull, H. W., 1957, *Theory of Equations* (Oliver and Boyd, Edinburgh and London).

Turnovsky, S. J., 1977, On the Formulation of Continuous Time Macroeconomic Models with Asset Accumulation, *International Economic Review* **18**, 1–28.

Wilks, S. S., 1962, *Mathematical Statistics*, 2nd ed. (Wiley, New York).

Wold, H. O., 1959, Ends and Means in Econometric Model Building: Basic Considerations Reviewed, in: Grenander, U., ed., 1959, *Probability and Statistic* (The Harald Cramér Volume), (Almqvist & Wiksell, Stockolm; Wiley, New York), 355–434.

Wymer, C. R., 1968, The Computation of the Eigensystem of an Econometric Model: A Note, unpublished manuscript.

Wymer, C. R., various dates, Program Manuals and Supplements, mimeo.

Wymer, C. R., 1972, Econometric Estimation of Stochastic Differential Equation Systems, *Econometrica* **40**, 565–77. Reprinted in: Bergstrom, A. R., ed., 1976, 81–95.

Wymer, C. R., 1973, A Continuous Disequilibrium Adjustment Model of United Kingdom Financial Market, in Powell, A. A. and Williams, R. A., eds., 1973, *Econometric Studies of Macro and Monetary Relations* (North-Holland, Amsterdam), 301–34.

Wymer, C. R., 1975, Estimation of Continuous Time Models with an Application to the World Sugar Market, in Labys, W. C., ed., 1975, *Quantitative Models of Commodity Markets* (Ballinger, Cambridge, Mass.), 173–91.

Wymer, C. R., 1976, Continuous Time Models in Macro-Economics: Specification and Estimation, mimeo (Paper prepared for the SSRC-Ford Foundation Conference on "Macroeconomic Policy and Adjustment in Open Economies" at Fanhams Hall, Ware, England, April 28–May 1, 1976).

Wymer, C. R., 1979, The Use of Continuous Time Models in Economics, unpublished manuscript.

Yaglom, A. M., 1952, *An Introduction to the Theory of Stationary Random Functions* (Prentice-Hall, Englewood Cliffs, New Jersey).

PART II

A MACRODYNAMIC GENERAL DISEQUILIBRIUM MODEL FOR THE DETERMINATION OF THE EQUILIBRIUM EXCHANGE RATE

CHAPTER 4

The equilibrium exchange rate: A critical survey*

4.1. Introduction

Recent events on the exchange markets have led the majority of industrialized countries to adopt managed flexibility in exchange rates.[1] This raises the problem of how the equilibrium value (or equilibrium path) may be determined, so as to estimate the amount of deviation of the current rate from the equilibrium rate itself.[2] The need to determine this and the consequent interventions on the exchange-rate arises from the fact that the exchange markets have often proved themselves incapable, if left to fluctuate freely, of converging towards equilibrium values over the medium and long term.[3] It should be noted, however, that the problem of the determination of the exchange-rate is not peculiar to a system of flexible exchange-rates, but is of equal importance in a system of fixed rates. In the latter case the problem is to create a solid base which might prevent the occurrence of foreign-exchange disturbances which could lead to a fundamental disequilibrium in the balance of payments.

The aim of the present chapter is to examine and critically assess the explanations developed in recent and also earlier literature on the subject, regarding the formation of the equilibrium exchange-rate. Even if, in the following treatment of the subject, there will be

*By Giancarlo Martinengo

[1]In the present work the rate of exchange is taken as the quantity of national currency per unit of foreign currency.

[2]For an analysis of alternative methods, see Artus (1978).

[3]This is the dominant theme in recent works on exchange-rates. For an extended critical analysis of the problems posed by the need for control and of the causes of instability, see Artus and Crockett (1978).

no lack of references to descriptions of models which aim to explain the current rate, it is necessary to keep the latter distinct from the equilibrium rate. In fact, their determinants can be different and in any case the current rate can diverge from the equilibrium rate, understood as the rate which keeps the balance of payments to zero when the entire economic system is in equilibrium. This work starts from the theories of flexible exchange-rates in the classical formulations of the purchasing power parity approach (PPP) and the standard model. Afterwards it will be necessary to extend our analysis and dwell in particular on the most recent formulations, such as the monetary or the asset-market approach and on eclectic formulations, as both the PPP and the standard model are far better known. All this serves to compare the view which these embody with regard to the determination of the exchange-rate and the type of equilibrium which they are meant to describe.

4.2. The theory of purchasing power parity (PPP)

The theory of purchasing power parity, taken up once more in recent times by the followers of the monetary approach to the balance of payments, is enjoying its second youth in current literature. The reasons for this will be clear further on; at this point we wish only to deal briefly with the contents of the theory and the problems which arise from its application.

In the first place there are various versions of the PPP. The absolute version affirms that the equilibrium exchange-rate is given by the ratio between the level of national and foreign prices. The relative version on the other hand puts the variations (or level) of the exchange-rate into relation with the ratio between the variations (or level) of the national price-index and the variations (or level) of the foreign price-index. In other words this latter version obtains the long-term rate of exchange (or its variations) from the product between the current exchange-rate and the ratio between the national and foreign price-index (or its variations[4]).

[4] The relative version starts from the idea that, given a period in which the exchange-rate was in equilibrium, its variations – and therefore the equilibrium rate in any subsequent period – can be calculated on the basis of variations in the levels of prices between the two countries. In this regard, see Balassa (1964).

In both versions the PPP is put forward as a long-term theory capable of explaining the equilibrium exchange-rate. The problems and divergences arise when an attempt is made to decide how to arrive at the price-indexes necessary to test the theory itself. In fact this entails stating which forces effectively act upon the current exchange-rate, so as to bring it in line with its equilibrium value.

Those who maintain that a price-index based on internationally traded goods only should be used, believe that the validity of the PPP is based on the arbitrage that the economic agents are induced to carry out whenever the price of traded goods shifts from that prevailing on the international market (the law of one price). Furthermore, it is assumed that there exists a constant ratio between the prices of goods traded internationally and those not so traded. Literature on the subject defines this as the PPP in the narrow sense. Conversely, those who maintain the necessity of utilizing the general price-index think that the equilibrium exchange-rate depends strictly on monetary equilibrium, insofar as every variation in the purchasing power between different currencies would lead to corrective variations in the exchange-rate. Others again put forward the idea of utilizing cost-of-production indexes as indexes of competitiveness, in particular, those of labour costs. In this proposal there is clearly the idea that what counts – given the total productivity, or particularly that of labour, for the determination of the value of one currency with respect to another – is the relative behaviour of costs or wages. Finally, there are those who hold that the variation rate in the actual (or expected) exchange-rate depends approximately on the observed (or expected) inflation differentials. That is to say, it is assumed that the agents in allocating their wealth between national and foreign assets will take into consideration the differentials between the nominal interest-rates.

The hypothesis implicit in this is that such operators do not behave in a manner that favours or is adverse to the exchange risk, but rather assume risk neutrality. Now, if it is assumed that the nominal interest-rates are given by the sum of the real rate (by hypothesis levelled internationally) and the rate of inflation, it follows that it is the differentials of expected inflation which assume importance with regard to decisions as to how the operator will divide his wealth between national and foreign assets.

While the criticisms and the difficulties involved in each formulation of the PPP as an expression of the equilibrium exchange-rate are well known,[5] it is sufficient for us here to remember that the costs necessary for the acquisition of information, for the reallocation of funds or for transactions in general, can represent elements sufficient to cause substantial disparities in purchasing power between the different currencies. In addition, with regard to the formulation which utilizes price-indexes only of traded goods, it is necessary to emphasize the fact that many industrial products are greatly differentiated and not homogeneous goods. It follows that, by utilizing the price-indexes of these products, the ratio between these indexes can show considerable deviations from the current exchange-rate. It should be pointed out that this last observation concerns the view that the proponents of this version of the PPP have of the international economy. For them the prevailing element consists in the fact that the economic systems are highly integrated and therefore exchange homogeneous, not clearly differentiated, goods. This hypothesis, as we shall see, departs from that of the standard model.

Cassel himself, as Officer points out (1976, p. 9), identifies several causes of divergence between the current exchange-rate and the PPP. These are: trade restrictions, speculation on the foreign exchange market, anticipations of greater inflation inside a country than abroad, changes in relative prices, long-term capital movements and government interventions on the foreign exchange market.

As was mentioned at the outset, the PPP is offered anew today, by scholars who follow the monetarist approach to the balance of payments (BP), as a valid explanation of the exchange-rate in long-term equilibrium, and as such it is incorporated in their models. It seems opportune, therefore, to take a closer look at the result obtained by Frenkel (1978, p. 188), in a work which inquires into the empirical applicability of the PPP to the system of flexible exchange-rate in force during the first half of the Twenties. He comes to the conclusion that: "The relationship embodied in the traditional formulations of the PPP should not be viewed as a

[5] See Officer (1976).

theory of the determination of exchange-rates. Rather, it describes an equilibrium relationship between two endogenous variables. As such, the PPP relationship should be viewed as a short-cut, rather than a substitute for a complete model of the determination of prices and equilibrium exchange-rates." In fact, the analysis shows that the series of prices utilized by this author are not econometrically exogenous to the series of exchange-rates. Thus the statistical causality in a uni-equational model tends to place the prices as dependent variables and the exchange rates as independent variables.[6] This type of causality is in agreement, according to Frenkel, with the hypothesis that the speed of adjustment of the various financial markets exceeds that of the commodity market. It follows from this that, insofar as the exchange-rates and the commodity-prices are influenced by common factors, the differential in speed of adjustment may produce the type of causality observed.

It therefore seems opportune, in the light of these conclusions, to pass to the analysis of the models and theories which attempt to explain the formation of the exchange-rate in a more articulated context. We shall examine therefore the standard model, which constituted the basic framework during the Fifties and Sixties, to pass afterwards to the monetary approach to the BP which is the prevailing theory in recent works.

4.3. The standard model

The standard model is fundamentally a Keynesian model for the determination of income in an open economy. There are different formulations, each of which attempts to place the emphasis on particular problems and aspects. What interests us here and now, however, is to examine the essential aspects of this model and the view of the world which it proposes with exclusive reference to the exchange-rate.

It should be emphasized at the outset that it embodies the fundamental elements of the elasticity approach and of the multiplier in an open economy. In fact, it incorporates the proposition of the former, according to which the variations in the exchange-rate

[6]See Frenkel (1978, pp. 181–183).

can have an influence on the in-flow of imports and exports. Of the latter it includes the effect that the variations in income induce on the trade-balance. If we look at the markets present in this standard formulation, these are: the commodity market, the money market (bonds being excluded by Walras' law), and finally that of foreign exchange, which is identified with the balance constraint of the "rest of the world" operator or, in other words, with the BP equation. If we assume, hypothetically, that national and foreign commodity prices are fixed and the quantity of money is given, the model determines the level of income, the rate of interest and the exchange rate.[7]

When the exchange-rate has the task of keeping the BP in equilibrium (in other words, when one assumes that no positive or negative excess demand for foreign currency occurs), then the rate reflects the reciprocal choices of the domestic and foreign operators. These choices regard the expenditure on the respective foreign commodities, and also the allocation of wealth between domestic and foreign assets. (Capital movements are normally treated as a net balance between those on the credit and the debit side; they are, in other words, a change in the net demand for foreign financial assets.) Furthermore, it is a widely-held opinion in the literature on the subject that, with flexible exchange-rates and perfect mobility of capital, monetary policy acquires greater autonomy in seeking internal equilibrium (level of employment), as the external equilibrium can be left to the flexibility of the exchange. Thus the economic policy objectives pursued by the central authorities have an influence on the solution for the equilibrium exchange-rate.

The theory of the standard model is commonly considered a general (short-term) equilibrium theory; in it figures the equilibrium both of (real) flows and of (financial) stocks. What characterizes it is the emphasis placed on the autonomy of commercial and financial *flows* (which affect the BP) with regard to the adjustment of the respective *stocks*. This is a first element of sharp contrast with the monetary approach to the BP, in which the *flows* originate exclusively from *stock adjustments*. However, in order fully to understand the diversities between the standard theory, on the one hand, and

[7]Many formulations might be referred to. See, for example, Mundell (1968, chs. 17–18) and Gandolfo (1970, ch. V).

the PPP and subsequent monetary theories for the determination of the exchange-rate, on the other, it is necessary also to take other aspects into consideration. In particular, we should dwell on the fact that the standard theory – especially in those aspects most directly derived from the elasticity approach – makes no explicit hypothesis regarding the world price-structure. In fact, as Kravis and Lipsey emphasize (1978, p. 194), prices (obviously expressed in a common unit) may or may not be the same for identical goods in different countries. The basic hypothesis of this theory is that the variations in the exchange-rate alter the prices of one country in relation to those of another, and cause variations in the quantities which adjust the values of imports and exports and therefore the trade-balance.

Thus, in the standard model, what is mainly emphasized is the "expenditure-switching" effect on internationally traded commodities (exports and imports), due to variations in the exchange-rate; as we shall see later, the emphasis of the monetary approach to the BP, based on the PPP, is on the contrary placed on the "expenditure-reducing" effect of devaluation.

4.4. The monetary approach to the BP and the asset-market approach to the determination of the exchange-rate

4.4.1. Exchange-rate determinants: the role of money and of expectations

Frenkel, in the Preface to the volume, *The Economics of Exchange-Rates*,[8] stresses the way in which the asset-market approach to the determination of the exchange-rate represents, in a regime of flexible exchange-rates, the counter-part of the monetary approach to the BP in a regime of fixed exchanges.

A simple model proposed by Bilson (1978) may help to clarify the above statements. Bilson affirms, among other things, that this model is in line with the main ideas of Johnson and Mundell, who are regarded as the leading exponents of the monetary approach to

[8]See Frenkel and Johnson (1978).

the BP.

$$M = PK(i, Y), \tag{1}$$

$$M^* = P^*K(i^*, Y^*); \tag{2}$$

$$P = SP^*, \tag{3}$$

where: M = the money-supply; P = the general price level; i = the (exogenous) nominal interest-rate; Y = the (exogenous) real level of income; S = the exchange-rate; the asterisk denotes the variables concerning the foreign country. The first two equations connect the real demand for money negatively to the nominal interest-rate and positively to the income level. The third equation – the condition for PPP to hold between the two currencies – connects the exchange-rate to the ratio between the general domestic and foreign price-levels.

If the foreign country is large, relative to the national economy, so that any repercussions can be ignored, the second equation determines the foreign country's price-level. In the case of fixed exchange-rates, the third equation determines the national price-level, thus leaving the first to determine the stock of national money. In the case of flexible exchange-rates, the money-supply is exogenous and the first equation therefore determines the general domestic price-level, while the third determines the exchange-rate. Consequently, Bilson continues, the particular system of exchange-rates decides the set of dependent variables, but does not alter the underlying structure of the model. The connection between the two approaches, which Frenkel had stressed, thus becomes quite evident.

The solution for the exchange-rate is:

$$S = \frac{M}{M^*} \frac{K(i^*, Y^*)}{K(i, Y)}. \tag{4}$$

The equilibrium exchange-rate is therefore, as many supporters of this approach maintain, the relative price between the two currencies. In fact (4) shows that it is determined by the relative supplies and demands for the two currencies. In addition, it follows:

(a) that an increase in the money supply on the national market will lead to a proportional depreciation in the exchange-rate,
(b) that an increase in real income will lead to an appreciation in the exchange-rate,

(c) that an increase in the nominal interest-rate will cause a depreciation in the exchange-rate.

These results, Frenkel observes, arouse interest for the monetary approach, because they are different from those that derive from the traditional analysis of the balance of payments.

As we have already seen above, the PPP takes on an important role in this type of analysis. The monetary approach is not therefore in conflict with this theory, but may constitute both a development and an up-dating of it. In fact, as we shall see more clearly below, the PPP is accepted as the solution of the long-term equilibrium exchange-rate in a general equilibrium framework. On the other hand, if we want to put a finger on the essential difference between the monetary approach to the exchange-rate (or to the BP) and the standard model, we must look at the fact that, in the monetary models, autonomous expenditure flows, both national and foreign, lose their importance, as they are models which assume full employment. Even in models in which the national expenditure – but never the flow of exports – is endogenized, this will depend essentially on the adjustments in financial stocks, thus losing any autonomous character with respect to portfolio decisions.

Before coming to grips with these comparisons it is, however, better to examine some of the more significant contributions of the monetary approach to the exchange-rate, so as to identify the more important ingredients which make up the models of this kind.

Frenkel (1976), in an analysis of German inflation between the two World Wars, proposes a simple interpretative model in which the expectations of inflation play a principal role in the determination of the exchange-rate. As in Bilson's model, the PPP is the relationship which determines the exchange-rate; the foreign price-level is given, the national price-level is explained on the basis of the equilibrium between money supply and demand and the latter is made to depend negatively on the expected inflation-rate. This last hypothesis is based on the consideration that, during a period of hyperinflation, the variations in the demand for money are dominated by the variations in expectations of inflation, so that the effects of changes in production, or in the real interest-rate can be ignored. On the same basis, the hypothesis of a constant level of foreign prices is justified. From this derives the fact that the exchange-rate depreciates in direct relation to the money-supply and to the expected inflation-rate.

The determination of the expected inflation-rate is, finally, derived from the interest parity theory, according to which, in equilibrium, the premium on a forward contract for foreign exchange for a given maturity is roughly equal to the differential between the national and the foreign nominal interest-rates. As, by hypothesis, the real rates are equal, the interest differential coincides with the expected inflation-rate.

Frenkel himself points out that the results obtained on the basis of his model are different from those of a certain type of analysis which has become widely diffused. In fact, according to one of the first formulations of the latter, a rise in the expected inflation-rate increases the nominal interest-rate, which induces a surplus in the capital account, and thus the exchange-rate appreciates. The same thing happens according to a variant of the same approach, which takes the effect of the rise in the interest-rate on expenditure and therefore on the trade-balance. If the national expenditure falls, the result will be a surplus, which leads to an appreciation in the exchange-rate. Another variant places the emphasis instead on the interest parity condition. A rise in the national interest-rate involves a higher forward premium, which may be reached with a rise in the forward exchange-rate and/or a fall in the spot rate. In each case, according to the traditional theory, a rise in the expected inflation-rate leads to an appreciation in the exchange-rate.

The logic of the Frenkel model, on the other hand is as follows: a rise in the expected rate of inflation causes a reduction in the demand for money which, with the given nominal supply, leads to a rise in the general price-level, so that the asset equilibrium will be guaranteed. As the national price-level is connected through the PPP to the foreign level and as the latter is assumed to be constant, the required increase in prices leads to a depreciation in the exchange-rate.

A reconcilement of the two different results[9] would be possible, however, according to Frenkel, if it is accepted that the inverse

[9]For a model which attempts this reconcilement and for the related econometric estimates, see Frankel (1979).

connection between the interest-rate and the exchange-rate refers to the short term (when the liquidity effect of a contraction in the money-supply prevails), while the direct connection between the interest-rate and the exchange-rate represents the correct result over the long term (when the Fisher effect – a rise in the expected inflation-rate, as a consequence of a rise in the rate of monetary expansion, which has a direct effect on expectations – prevails over the interest-rate). From this exposition it emerges that in monetary models the (long-term) equilibrium exchange-rate is arrived at essentially from the equilibrium of the money-stock and that this equilibrium is affected to a considerable degree by expectations of inflation. Furthermore, a strong emphasis is placed on the role played by the general price-level as an adjustment variable of monetary equilibrium.

A prominent place is reserved for a work by Dornbusch (1976 b), for the analysis of the role played by the exchange-rate expectations in a real and financial framework.[10]

Dornbusch starts from the idea that the money-market determines the rate of interest once the following are given: the quantity of the money supply, the level of full-employment income and the general level of prices. As he assumes that the economy in question is characterized by great mobility of capital and that the financial markets are quick to adjust, he states that the national interest-rate (r) is equal to the foreign rate (r^*) increased by the expected rate of depreciation in the exchange-rate (x). The latter is made to depend, according to a coefficient of expectations (ϑ), on the difference between the long-term equilibrium exchange-rate ($\bar{e}$), which is by hypothesis well known to operators, and the current one (e). If the income (y), the general level of prices (p) and the

[10] For the introduction in Dornbusch's model of monetary and fiscal policy, in the presence of alternative hypotheses concerning the formation of expectations, see Mathieson (1977). For the formulation along the lines traced by both writers mentioned for a model in which the PPP is proposed as a guideline for the intervention of the authorities on the exchange-market, according to the rules suggested in the OPTICA report (1977), see De Grauwe, Steinherr and Basevi (1978). For a discussion of the exchange-rate expectation in the field of stochastic models which aim to formalize the short-term fluctuations, see Mussa (1976) and Barro (1978).

nominal money demand (m) are expressed in logarithms, the financial relations are:

$$r = r^* + x, \tag{5}$$

$$x = \vartheta(\bar{e} - e), \tag{6}$$

$$m - p = \vartheta y - \lambda r. \tag{7}$$

After various substitutions, Dornbusch obtains an inverse relation between e and p which satisfies the equilibrium on the financial markets:

$$e = \bar{e} - \frac{1}{\lambda\vartheta}(p - \bar{p}). \tag{8}$$

The rate of increase in the current price-level ($\dot{p}$) is put into relation with the excess demand for the national output which depends positively on the real exchange-rate and on income and, negatively, on the interest-rate:

$$\dot{p} = \pi \log(D/Y) = \pi[\mu + \delta(e - p) + (\gamma - 1)]y - \sigma r, \tag{9}$$

where D represents aggregate demand.

From the real equilibrium (nil rate of increase in the prices of goods) he obtains a positive relation between e and p which, together with eq. (8), permits him to study the process of adjustment towards stationary state equilibrium. Obviously, as the financial markets are always in equilibrium – in this respect he finds the expression for the expectations coefficient, which ensures that the expectations themselves are those which guarantee the equilibrium (perfect foresight) – even in the process of adjustment, it occurs that the exchange over the short term exclusively reflects monetary and financial choices, while only in the long-term real variables, like income, assume importance. Dornbusch arrives at the conclusion that the ultimate effect of monetary expansion is an equiproportional increase in prices and the exchange-rate. However, in the short term, the monetary expansion does exert real effects on interest-rates, the terms of trade and the aggregate demand.

Dornbusch also examines the case in which the aggregate demand determines the level of income, and prices vary in relation to discrepancies between actual income and full-employment income

($\bar{Y}$). Specifically, he puts

$$Y = \log D = \mu + \vartheta(e - p) + \gamma y - \sigma r \tag{10}$$

in place of (9) and

$$\dot{p} = \pi(y - \bar{y}) \tag{11}$$

for the price-adjustment.

He concludes that the effect of monetary policy on the interest-rate and on the exchange-rate depends on the behaviour of real output:

(a) if output is fixed, in the short term, the monetary expansion will lower interest-rates and cause the current exchange-rate to overshoot the long-term depreciation;
(b) if output is variable, the changes in the interest-rate and in the exchange-rate will be dampened.

It must be recognized that, among all the works examined, this is the first model which also considers a context which is not one of full employment.

From what has been said so far we can deduce that the change of view with respect to the standard model and to the elasticity approach is total. In the latter what counts for the determination of the exchange-rate are both the real variables and the financial ones, and the changes in the exchange-rate lead to lasting effects on expenditure flows and on trade (expenditure switching effect). In the models so far examined on the other hand the exchange-rate is strictly of a monetary nature and its changes cannot induce substitutions in the trade with foreign countries. This failure derives from the introduction of the PPP, which – with its assumption of alignment of national with foreign prices through variation in the rate of exchange – precludes any distinction between imported and exported goods. The price of each commodity produced in the economy will be aligned with the world price and a variation in the exchange-rate will not have any effect, insofar as both the prices of imports and those of exports are modified so as to keep the exchange-rate unaltered. On the contrary, as we shall see, the aggregation proposed by the monetary models is based on the distinction between traded and non-traded goods and the exchange-rate acts as an adjustment variable which determines the allotment of expenditure between the two categories of goods.

4.4.2. The role of relative prices in the determination of the equilibrium exchange-rate

This type of aggregation is in fact present in Dornbusch (1976 a) where the long-term exchange-rate emerges, in any case, as a magnitude which is not strictly monetary. In fact, besides the national and foreign demand for money, the relative prices of traded and non-traded goods, both of the country under consideration and of the rest of the world, contribute to its determination. To obtain this however the author assumes that the PPP is valid in the narrow sense. This means that the exchange-rate is not to be arrived at from the relation between the general level of national prices and that of the rest of the world, but rather from the relation between the level of prices of traded goods by the country in question and the analogous level in force in the rest of the world. In other words, it is assumed that arbitrage does not concern those goods produced in sectors that are not exposed to international competition. Dornbusch emphasizes the fact that the real component of the exchange-rate (relative prices) makes it possible to pick up the effects to which they are subjected by the absorption changes, the shifts in demand and the biased output growth. The model assumes complete flexibility of supply relative to the goods. Furthermore, Dornbusch notes that the exchange-rate reflects in the long-term the general equilibrium situation of all markets, both of stocks and flows, and that this is obtained on a non-Keynesian basis, insofar as complete specialization between imports and exports is not assumed. On the contrary, it is assumed that the internationally traded goods are homogeneous. In the short-term, on the other hand, the exchange-rate is determined essentially by the asset markets insofar as the PPP can be verified only in the long-term. The shift in funds is effected by arbitragers, who work by covering themselves in the forward market so as to gain the interest-rate differential. It is also effected by the activity of speculators in the forward market, who as the prevalent element in the market, determine the forward exchange-rate in relation to their expectations about the future spot exchange-rate (their expectations according to Dornbusch's hypothesis being formed in an adaptive manner). These are the ingredients on which the author bases his explanation of the discrepancy between the current (or short-term) exchange-rate and the long-term equilibrium rate. In order to arrive more precisely at the nub of this situation, which in some ways differs from the simplified monetary explanation of the equilibrium exchange-rate, it will be useful to examine Dornbusch's model.

The economic system under consideration is that of a small country, in which the interest-rate and the price of internationally traded goods are given by the rest of the world. The arbitrage for internationally traded goods is continuously maintained and the flexibility of prices and of factor cost ensures the equilibrium of markets and full employment. In addition to the internationally traded goods, the country produces and consumes non-traded goods. The equilibrium of this system can be formalized as follows:

$$N(P_{\mathrm{T}}/P, r, g) = 0, \qquad N_{P_{\mathrm{T}}/P} > 0, \quad N_r < 0, \quad N_g = 1, \tag{12}$$

$$r = r(M/P, Y), \qquad r_{M/P} < 0, \quad r_Y > 0, \tag{13}$$

$$P_{\mathrm{T}} = eP_{\mathrm{T}}^*, \tag{14}$$

$$r = r^* + \frac{(\bar{e} - e)}{e}, \tag{15}$$

$$\bar{e} = \pi e + (1 - \pi)e_{-1}, \qquad 0 < \pi < 1, \tag{16}$$

where: (12) represents the excess demand on the market for non-traded goods, which is a function of the ratio between the price of the goods traded and produced nationally (P_{T}) and the general level of national prices (P), of the interest rate (r) and the public expenditure (g). Eq. (13), by describing the equilibrium on the money market, makes it possible to express r as a function of the real quantity of money (M/P) and of the full employment income level (Y); (14) is the expression of the PPP in the narrow sense which makes it possible to determine the exchange-rate (e), given the level of prices of internationally traded goods (P_{T}^*). Eq. (15) shows the relationship between the national and foreign interest-rates (r^*) through covered interest arbitrage. Eq. (16) postulates that the forward exchange-rate ($\bar{e}$) is set by speculators in a perfectly elastic manner at the level of the expected future spot rate and that expectations about the latter are formed in an adaptive manner. It is possible to reduce the previous model to just two relations, that of the equilibrium of the home goods market and that of the covered interest arbitrage by carrying out the appropriate substitutions:

$$N(eP_{\mathrm{T}}^{*}/P, r(M/P; Y), g) = 0, \tag{17}$$

$$r(M/P) - (1-\pi)(e_{-1}/e - 1) = r^{*}. \tag{18}$$

As P_{T}^{*}, M, Y and g are given, (17) provides an infinity of combinations between P and e which ensure equilibrium of the goods market. The same goes for (18), as M, π, e_{-1} and r^{*} are known. The equilibrium of (17) is ensured by a direct relation between P and e. In fact, an increase in the general price level causes a fall in the real value of liquid assets, an increase in the interest-rate and therefore a reduction in expenditure which requires a fall in the prices of non-traded goods (modification of relative prices) with respect to the general price-level. Such a result can be obtained only by an increase of e in the numerator of the ratio (eP_{T}^{*}/P). The devaluation of the exchange-rate, far from affecting imports and exports, as a version of the PPP is present, has therefore a substitution effect in the demand between traded and non-traded goods. On the contrary, the equilibrium of (18) requires an inverse relation between P and e. An increase of e, in fact, creates a forward discount (because, for (16), $\bar{e}$ increases less than proportionally), which must be compensated by a fall in the national interest-rate with respect to the foreign rate. This fall occurs if the national price-level falls, thus increasing the real quantity of money. Obviously (17) and (18) together determine the equilibrium value for P and e.

From an analysis carried out by the author on disturbances of a monetary nature which shift the system from one equilibrium to another, one can see the philosophy behind the model. First of all an increase in the quantity of money does not alter the real variables over the long-term, therefore the system converges towards neutrality. The effects over the short-term on real variables are due solely to errors in the formation of expectations. If economic agents were to use the equilibrium exchange-rate (rational expectations) as a basis for the formation of their expectations regarding the future exchange-rate, instead of adaptive models, then the system would experience neutrality even over the short-term. The same argument is valid in the case in which it is the price-level of goods traded by the rest of the world that increases. In fact, the price-level of these goods is modified nationally only within short-term equilibrium, while in the long-term it returns to its initial level and the exchange-rate is revalued until it is in balance with the increase in foreign prices.

The process of adjustment toward the long-term equilibrium following an increase in the quantity of money on the national market can be illustrated with a diagram (see fig. 1). If the exchange-rate is placed along the abscissa and the general price-level along the ordinate, the slope of the vector OR denotes the national price-structure, while $\overline{N}\overline{N}$ represents the schedule of the market-equilibrium of the non-traded goods and *aa* the equilibrium on the financial market (covered interest arbitrage). The initial position of equilibrium is at point *A*. The increase in the nominal quantity of money at initial levels of the equilibrium price and exchange-rate, causes the interest rate to fall and so an excess demand for non-traded goods occurs and the covered interest arbitrage is not satisfied. In order to re-establish the long-term equilibrium on the goods-market, the exchange-rate and prices must increase in the same proportion as the nominal quantity of money (shift of $\overline{N}\overline{N}$ to $\overline{N}'\overline{N}'$). In the short term, on the other hand, on account of the type of exchange-rate expectation, the schedule of the financial market does not shift sufficiently and thus there is temporary equilibrium at *B*. In fact, the price-increase and the exchange-rate are proportionally smaller than the increase in the quantity of money. The process

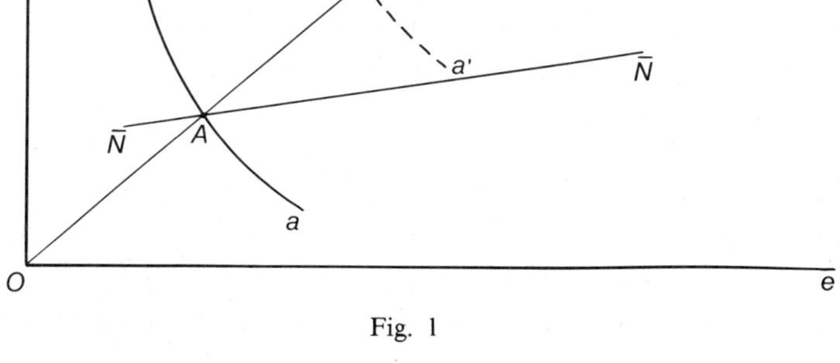

Fig. 1

which leads to B is as follows: the fall in the interest-rate, which derives from an increase in the nominal quantity of money, leads, via capital outflows, to a depreciation in the spot exchange-rate, which causes expectations of further depreciations of lesser entity and, given the behaviour of speculators on the forward market, there is a forward discount which makes it possible to verify the covered interest-arbitrage. In this sense the equilibrium formed on the financial markets determines the short-term exchange-rate. However, the general price-level may increase nationally – both because of the persistent excess demand due to the fall in the interest-rate and because of the increase in foreign demand caused by the devaluation of the exchange-rate over the short term leading to a fall in the real quantity of money and an increase in the interest rate. In this case speculators will be induced to adjust their expectations to the exchange-rate in such a way as to permit a continual verification of the arbitrage condition with a growing interest-rate. The price-increase and the devaluation of the long-term exchange-rate cause a shift of $a'a'$ schedule to point C, where the long-term equilibrium occurs and where neutrality of the monetary policy is found, insofar as the depreciation in the exchange-rate exactly balances the growth in prices, leaving the ratio between the price of traded goods and the general price-level unaltered. Among Dornbusch's conclusions one regards the inefficacy of the isolating power of flexible exchange-rates with respect to national and foreign money disturbances, at least over the shorter-term. Another conclusion which is of greater concern to us, is that this model, contrary to the usual monetary analysis, also includes real variables among the determinants of the equilibrium exchange-rate. In other words, neutrality is respected if the disturbances are of monetary origin. According to Dornbusch, this does not exclude the possibility that relative prices concur in determining the equilibrium exchange-rate.

However in the opinion of the present writer the view embodied in the model seems less convincing with regard to structural elements, like the hypothesis of full employment, which derives from full flexibility of wages and prices and the irrelevance of foreign demand, as an autonomous element which conditions the opportunities for an outlet onto foreign markets. It should be emphasized that, even in this model, as in the previous ones, the acceptance of the PPP makes it impossible to catch this point. In fact, if on the one side the introduction of the narrow form of this theory and the consequent type of disaggregation permit the introduction of a real element in the determination of the exchange-rate, the relative prices, on the other hand, make it impossible to make room for the flow of foreign demand[11] and its effects, via exports, on the exchange-rate.

4.4.3. The interaction between current and capital accounts of the BP

The importance of foreign demand was recognized by Branson (1976), who developed a work of Kouri's (1976) along different lines. Though still moving within the view of the portfolio approach to the exchange-rate, Branson does not accept the PPP as a relation which determines the long-term exchange-rate. On the contrary, he assumes that the latter is determined by the equilibrium of the balance of payments.

Before considering the characteristic aspects of the works, it will be opportune to put appropriate emphasis on the fact that these authors assume that the markets for financial assets reach equilibrium more rapidly than the real markets. This conclusion is reached on the assumption that the costs of financial transactions are slight or non-existent. The different speeds of adjustment thus make it possible to work with recursive relations between the various subsets of the model: first the financial markets reach equilibrium and determine the exchange-rate in a context of partial equilibrium, then the real markets undergo the effect of the exchange-rate determined on the basis of financial logic. The feedback of the real on the financial equilibrium is obtained by considering the effect of the balance of payments current account on the accumulation of foreign financial assets, hence on the general

[11] A contribution which deals with the connections between the monetary and the traditional approach, leaving room for foreign demand in a context in which, however, the equilibrium exchange-rate is represented by the PPP in its narrow form, is that of Minford (1978, Ch. 6). See also Michaely (1978) for a comparative analysis of the various approaches and their attitude in dealing with real or monetary disturbances.

equilibrium of the portfolio. The changed conditions of the financial markets then determine the new exchange-rate and so on towards stationary state equilibrium. In substance these authors study the relation between the current account and the capital account, in particular in the case of Kouri, on the assumption that the latter determines the former. This last is a position which contrasts markedly with that which in former years, under a fixed exchange-rate regime, saw the movements of capital as adjustment variables with respect to the current account. Kouri tackles the problem just described on the basis of a simple model. The hypotheses which characterize it are: the economy under examination is small; it produces only internationally traded goods (this hypothesis eliminates the problem of relative prices); prices and wages are flexible and full employment is always guaranteed.

The assets considered are national and foreign money; there is no accumulation of real capital, nor any equity claims on real capital. Kouri's is essentially no more than a portfolio model in which financial equilibrium alone determines the current account balance and any possible real component of an autonomous nature is absent. Therefore, he proposes an equilibrium exchange-rate which exclusively represents the equilibrium exchange ratio between the two financial assets: national and foreign money. It is clear then that the critical conditions for the stability of the model are tied to the substitution effects between the assets and the nature of the formation of expectations regarding the exchange-rate, rather than to the relative prices of exports and imports. The logic of Kouri's model is the following: given the full-employment income (Y), then the trade surplus (B) depends on the consumption level (C), taken as a function of disposable income ($Y - T$) and the stock of real financial wealth (A), given by the sum of the national money (M/P) and the foreign money (F), and the government expenditure (G). In the short-term, given the expected depreciation in the exchange-rate (π), the stock of foreign money and the nominal money supply, the money-market determines the national price-level and therefore the exchange-rate – as, for simplicity, the foreign price-level has been taken as equal to one (here the PPP is present in the version of the theory connected to the portfolio). In addition, it is assumed that government expenditure in real terms depends on the (exogenous) real tax revenue and the growth-rate of money (m). Formally:

$$B = Y - C(Y - T, A) - G, \tag{19}$$

$$A = \frac{M}{P} + F, \tag{20}$$

$$\frac{M}{P} = L\Big(\underset{(-)}{\pi}, \underset{(+)}{Y}, \underset{(+)}{A}\Big), \tag{21}$$

$$G = T + m\frac{M}{P}, \tag{22}$$

Since $B = \dot{F}$, by substituting the other equations in (19) we get:

$$\dot{F} = Y - C\left(Y - T, \frac{M}{P} + F\right) - T - m\frac{M}{P}$$

$$= B\Big(\underset{(+)}{Y}, \underset{(-)}{T}, \underset{(-)}{F}, \underset{(+)}{\pi}, \underset{(-)}{M}\Big), \tag{23}$$

which, together with (21), outlines a temporary equilibrium in the system in which the monetary sector determines the current exchange-rate and the latter concurs in determining the flow of foreign assets which the economy acquires abroad, as the money balance which flows in from abroad is determined by the current account. The latter depends on absorption with regard to full employment output and the degree of absorption is in exclusive relation to the desire to accumulate financial assets. The author affirms that the hypothesis of continuous equilibrium in the money markets inhibits the use of the relation of equilibrium of the BP, as one that determines the exchange-rate. It should be emphasized however that this particular conclusion is essentially tied to the view of the model, which, as we have pointed out on more than one occasion, is simply a portfolio one. It is in fact possible to consider the stock adjustment flows, both real and financial, alongside the autonomous flows and to determine the exchange-rate from the constraint of the balance of payments equilibrium. As we shall see, this way has been followed independently by Branson and the present writer,[12] but this involves a partial or total removal from the monetarist view-point for the determination of the equilibrium

[12] See Martinengo (1978a, Part II, para. 10).

exchange-rate. Then in Kouri's model, we pass from the temporary equilibrium to that of the stationary state, seeing that the accumulation of foreign currency (in consequence for example of a trade surplus from the previous period) breaks the financial equilibrium by determining a lower exchange-rate level (appreciation). The new exchange level and the increase in foreign balance acts on national absorption and increases it on account of the wealth effect, which derives both from the quantity and the price. In this way the conditions are created for a reduction in the trade surplus and therefore reduced acquisition of foreign currency. The stationary state reached is characterized, in fact, by the complete absorption of the full-employment national output on the part of private consumption and public expenditure, by the subdivision of wealth between the two assets in the proportions desired. In addition, the expected depreciation rate, which coincides with that expected from inflation under the hypotheses of the model, must equal the current rate ($\dot{P}/P$) which is also equal to the monetary expansion rate. Thus:

$$Y = C(Y - T, \overline{M} + F) + T + \overline{M}, \tag{24}$$

$$\overline{M} = L(\pi, Y, \overline{M} + F), \tag{25}$$

$$\pi = \dot{P}/P = m, \tag{26}$$

where $\overline{M} = M/P$ indicates a constant.

Kouri deals at length with the stability of the model and studies the convergence of temporary equilibrium sequences to the stationary equilibrium under various hypotheses regarding the formation of expectations. As problems of this type are present in works of other authors considered and as the results obtained by him are perfectly in line with the typical results of the monetarist school, it is superfluous to deal with the matter here.

What substantially distinguishes Branson's model from Kouri's is the view which the former has for the determination of the equilibrium exchange-rate. In fact he assumes, for the same reasons hypothesized by Kouri – high speed of adjustment of financial markets with respect to low speed of adjustment of real markets – that portfolio equilibrium determines the current exchange-rate over the short term, but over a longer period the equilibrium of the current balance determines the equilibrium exchange-rate. In this work therefore the PPP is not proposed as a relation which determines the long-term equilibrium exchange-rate. That is to say, Branson, unlike Kouri, does not assume that it is the portfolio equilibrium which over the long-term dominates the model and the reality which it proposes to interpret. Furthermore, the fact is also stressed that the trade account is independent of the portfolio even if it comes under the influence of the short-term exchange-rate. Let us take a closer look at the logic behind the functioning of Branson's model. He starts from a description of the portfolio model in which, besides money, are included national and foreign government bonds. The following are given: the interest-rate on foreign bonds, the expectations, the income-level, etc. The current exchange-rate and the national interest-rate are the variables determined by the portfolio equilibrium. After examining the stability, Branson passes to an examination of the effects that increases in the stock of assets have upon the interest-rate and on the short-term exchange-rate. He distinguishes, on the one side, the effects which derive from net accumulation of stocks and, on the other, those that derive from interventions by the monetary authorities on the open market, money against national bonds, and those that derive from the exchange of money for foreign assets. In this way he catches the effect of an autonomous surplus in the current account (which, under a flexible exchange system, is identical in absolute value to the balance of capital movements) on the exchange-rate. In order to be accepted in the portfolio of those who possess a country's assets, an increase in financial assets, deriving from a surplus, must be accompanied by a reduction in the exchange-rate. This revaluation determines a new trade balance which, when added to the flow of net interest from abroad and varied because of the increase of the net foreign assets, will determine the current balance, or the new variation in net foreign assets. If W represents financial wealth, M the money stock, B that of national bonds, F that of foreign bonds, r and $\bar{r}$ the fixed yield on national and foreign bonds respectively and e the exchange-rate, we have:

$$\overline{M} = m(r, \bar{r})W, \tag{27}$$

$$\overline{B} = b(r, \bar{r})W, \tag{28}$$

$$e\overline{F} = f(r, \bar{r})W, \tag{29}$$

$$W = eF + B + M, \tag{30}$$

where one of the equations which express the equilibrium on the financial markets is redundant, as the wealth constraint has been explicitly included. The variables determined are: e, r, W.

From the results of comparative statics we obtain a reduced form for the behaviour of the exchange-rate with respect to the change in the stocks of financial assets and the foreign interest-rate:

$$e = e(F; M, B, \bar{r}), \qquad \text{with } e_F < 0, \tag{31}$$

where only the behaviour of the exchange-rate has been indicated with respect to F.

Considering eq. (31) together with the following equation for the BP:

$$\dot{F} = X(e/P) + rF, \tag{32}$$

we arrive at the time-path of the exchange-rate. It should be noted that Branson's reasoning is the opposite of Kouri's. For both authors the portfolio determines the short-term exchange-rate. But for Branson the trade account, defined by the difference between exports and imports, determines the variation of foreign financial assets autonomously, and this subsequently alters the equilibrium of the portfolio. For Kouri on the other hand the trade account, equal to the variation in the net foreign financial assets, is not determined autonomously by the logic of the portfolio, because it constitutes a residual phenomenon. In fact the trade-balance is the divergence between the full-employment product and the degree of absorption determined by the level of wealth. When this varies – because a new flow of foreign assets arises, and consequently the exchange-rate varies so as to bring the portfolio into equilibrium – there is a variation in the degree of absorption and therefore in the foreign assets balance. To sum up, in Branson's model the long-term equilibrium exchange-rate, even if it cannot be said to be determined independently of the portfolio equilibrium, is also the result of real and autonomous elements with respect to financial logic. In Kouri's model, on the contrary, the long-term exchange-rate is totally dominated by financial considerations and by the PPP in the broad version.[13] In Branson's model, the adjustment mechanism of the short-term equilibrium to the long-term one takes into consideration the following effects: (a) on the trade balance deriving from variations in the exchange-rate; (b) on the current account as it stands after the net variations in foreign financial assets. An increase in these assets, on the basis of a given foreign interest-rate, increases the net inflow of interest from abroad and therefore has a destabilizing effect (because, far from reducing, it actually increases the current surplus). The appreciation in the exchange-rate following this same increase in the balance in net financial activities abroad, leads to a reduction in the surplus, if the Marshall–Lerner condition holds. Indeed, to prevent the destabilizing effect from prevailing, it is necessary that the sum of the critical elasticities should not only be greater than one, but sufficiently above it to overcome the effect that derives from the net inflow of interest from abroad.

In the second part of his work, Branson also introduces the general price-level into the adjustment process. In other words, he assumes that the trade surplus depends directly on the relation between exchange-rate and general price-level. His intent is to prove that the adjustment-path of the exchange-rate is dominated by that of prices. In fact he assumes that the exchange-rate will move rapidly as a logical outcome of portfolio adjustment, as already said, and that prices will adjust more slowly in response to disturbances of a monetary or real nature. In any case, he maintains that it is the path of the latter which is the reference-point for the long-term equilibrium.

He dwells on the question of connecting the variation in the quantity of money with that of prices. He emphasizes the fact that the speed and degree of reaction of prices depend on the level of utilization of the (available) resources. He comes to the conclusion that – given the general agreement in the profession on the fact that

[13] Other models which consider the problem of the interaction between the current account and the capital account are those of Calvo–Rodriguez (1977) and Niehans (1977). The former assumes that foreign demand is irrelevant, the latter takes it into consideration. However, both works come to the conclusion that prices and exchange-rate are homogeneous after the process of adjustment, following an increase in the money supply. This result does not characterize Branson's model, as we shall see below.

prices increase, but with great uncertainty regarding the speed and the amounts involved – all that can be done is to hypothesize a gradual price-adjustment to the increase of prices over the long-term, which is at most proportional to the increase in money-stock.

On this basis he passes to an examination of the effects that an expansionary monetary-policy has on the long-term equilibrium of the system. He considers an open market operation. Initially, on the hypothesis of a more rapid adjustment of the exchange-rate, he finds a decisive depreciation which on the one hand guarantees that asset-holders will maintain the new money balances, on the other, as prices are still unchanged, the conditions for the appearance of a real surplus will be created. The consequent accumulation of financial assets leads, as we have previously seen, to a progressive appreciation in the exchange-rate. Since prices subsequently begin to rise, as the exchange-rate is revalued, there will be a point at which the exchange-rate/prices ratio will be the same as at the start.

This ratio, however, cannot be that of the new long-term equilibrium because in the meantime the accumulation of net foreign assets will have determined a flow of net interests greater than that of the previous equilibrium. By imposing the condition of a stationary state (that is, that the total interest inflow from abroad is equal to the trade balance) then there will be a deficit and therefore the exchange-rate/price ratio will necessarily be lower in the new equilibrium compared to the previous one. Branson also shows that the process of adjustment cannot be monotonic because the speed of reaction of the exchange-rate is too great compared to that of prices. In this case the dominant role of the price trend compared to the exchange-rate appears even clearer.

But especially in the case in which prices move first, following a real variation (that is to say, one not connected with the money-supply), the author recognizes that the price-path acts as an anchor for the exchange-rate path and he makes it clear that the fluctuations in the rate of exchange will be proportionately greater than those of the prices that brought them into being and that the adjustment of the exchange-rate to prices will be gradual and monotonic, contrary to that brought about by money disturbances.

Branson's conclusion is therefore to recognize a distinct independence and domination in the long-term of the price-path compared to the exchange-rate path, while the short-term fluctuations of the exchange-rate prove to be tied to conditions of equilibrium on the assets market. Branson's conclusion is connected with the idea that the flexible exchange regime enjoys a certain amount of insulating power with regard to the formation of national prices. The monetary policy determines the trend of national prices and in the end the time-path of the exchange-rate adjusts itself in such a way as to determine the terms of trade. These guarantee the current balance equilibrium, that is a balance on trade account equal in absolute value and of opposite sign to the balance of net foreign interest. We agree with Branson that over the long-term the exchange-rate is to be connected to real factors. (It is this author who observed that in the period 1971–76 the exchange-rate showed ample short-term oscillations, while it followed the movement of relative prices (terms of trade) over the long-term and therefore he took the view that, in the long run, the exchange-rate is determined by the equilibrium of the current balance, not by some sort of PPP.) However we are not entirely happy about what he says about the independence of the price-formation from the exchange-rate. For example, Artus and Crockett (1978) maintain the necessity of an intervention by the public authorities in the exchange market for two reasons.

Firstly, because the exchange-rate does not always reflect the underlying economic conditions, but is often the result of speculative behaviour. Secondly, because movements in the exchange-rate are often balanced by equal (or proportional) variations in national prices with grave consequences for the objective of price-stability. This latter thesis is the well-know "vicious circle". Contrary to what Branson maintains it lays stress upon the depreciation-inflation connection (or appreciation-deflation in the case of a "virtuous circle"), pointing to the exchange-rate as one of the causes of the movement in prices. The logic by which it is possible to reverse Branson's causation is, for example, that the entrepreneurs, when fixing prices, take into account, among other things, the variations in costs in national currency of the factors of production bought abroad and/or that there is a direct effect on the general price-level following the variation in the price of imported final goods. This last type of causation has been introduced by the present writer into a long-term model in which a study is made of the connection between the rate of growth of a (small) economy and the exchange-rate.[14] The view in this model is not strictly monetarist, even though it derives some informing principles from it. Possibly it is nearer to the Keynesian position, among other things for the connection between the level of activity of a system and the amount of employment. Yet, in effect, it is an eclectic view-point. Reference is made to the relative paragraph.

4.5. The eclectic approach to the equilibrium exchange-rate

There is a widely-held opinion that the principal merit of the monetarist approach is that is calls attention to the importance of the equilibrium of stocks compared to that of flows, as stressed by the standard model. Following Cooper (1976, p. 150), it can be said that this shift in view has become necessary in that in the standard model, for example, movements of capital are introduced exclusively in flow terms, as the equilibrium of stocks is specified so as not to constrain the duration in time of these flows. In other words, capital movements are not specified as adjustment flows of the stocks of securities. Further, Kuska (1978) goes so far as to maintain that the standard model is contradictory, when, for example, in a fixed exchange regime, monetary equilibrium is postulated with a non-zero balance of the BP. Kuska bases his argument on the introduction of a balance constraint for the economic system which ensures compatibility of real and financial equilibria, however with the complete elimination of the problem of autonomy of foreign demand. In fact, if it is true that in an economic system the sum of the excess of domestic demand for goods, securities and money must be zero, it is not necessarily true that the BP is given by the sum of the first two excess demands, unless it is supposed that the trade balance is entirely absorbed by the rest of the world. In other words, the BP coincides with the desired variations in money balances only if simplifying hypotheses contained in the monetary approach models are made, including that according to which, in a fixed exchange regime, the rest of the world is ready to absorb the

[14] See Martinengo (1978a, Part II, para. 10).

excess of goods produced by a country in order to satisfy its desire for liquidity.

The same criticism can be extended to a flexible exchange regime. In this case the exchange-rate is not determined by the equilibrium of the money market, unless it is assumed that the trade flows are not essential for the determination of the equilibrium exchange-rate. As we have seen in the monetary models, the recourse to the PPP and its assumptions are the elements which make it possible to consider the trade flows and therefore foreign demand to be irrelevant.

In particular, it is the hypothesis made with regard to the absence of differentiation between goods produced in different economies which leads one to consider the exchange-rate, either as the adjustment variable between the movement of prices of homogeneous goods traded internationally by different countries or else as the variable which puts the money market into equilibrium. It seems possible to doubt the soundness of this hypothesis if one thinks that the central problem of many industrial economies, including that of Italy, lies in exporting a range of products totally different from their imports. The oil deficit and that of agricultural products and foodstuffs throw into dramatic relief, for Italy, the problem of having an industrial structure which produces sufficiently differentiated goods which can be offered in geographical areas where Italy's technological level allows her to satisfy the price conditions imposed by her competitors. If this is true, it does not seem possible to propose, for countries like Italy, models in which the equilibrium exchange-rate is to be put in relation with what is expressed in the monetary models, which are in substance models dominated by the portfolio and in which full employment is always present. In our opinion, on the contrary, it is foreign demand and the rate of capital accumulation which assume the maximum importance, both because of the influence which these variables have on the structure of production and for the effect they have on the level of employment.

In this part of the work we shall deal briefly with those models which with various intents have attempted to consider the most valid elements from both approaches.

In a partial context and with empirical ends in view, the matter has been studied by Gandolfo *et al.* (1976). The problem posed is that of the estimation of the equilibrium exchange-rate for Italy with reference to the trade balance and to that of current account.

To this purpose a model of partial equilibrium was formulated whose significance and results these authors offer as an alternative to models based on the PPP. This study-group recognizes the limitations of a partial equilibrium approach, and stresses the fact that it is far preferable to have a general stock-flow equilibrium model in which adequate account is taken of all the interrelations between the exchange-rate and the real and monetary variables. The present volume is oriented precisely in this direction. The utilization of the BP equation to determine the equilibrium exchange-rate is a feature of Gandolfo's work. More precisely in the case of the trade balance the problem may be posed in the following terms: since imports and exports depend on a series of exogenous variables, (partial equilibrium logic) besides the exchange-rate, it is possible, given these functions, to determine the exchange-rate which brings the trade balance to zero. Alternatively it is possible to determine the depreciation or appreciation necessary to eliminate an imbalance in this account.

With regard to the functions of imports and exports, these are both considered as functions of demand, a fact which places this model in conflict with those that take a monetary approach to the exchange-rate. In fact the trade balance, when considered at all in monetary approach studies, is derived essentially from a logic based on supply.

The function of imports depends also on the degree of utilization of productive capacity, as well as on classic variables (global demand, relative price of national and foreign goods). Alternatively, it has been hypothesized that the degree of capacity utilization influences the propensity to import (or elasticity) with respect to income. The export function is formulated in share terms, that is, the share of world import demand which is satisfied by the exports of the country under consideration. This share is put into relation with an index of competitiveness given by the ratio between the price-index of imports from the rest of the world and the price-index of exports from the country itself. Recent estimates have been carried out on the basis of this model by Gandolfo (1979), better results have been obtained and some refinements have been introduced.

Instead of starting from an analysis of the monetary contributions regarding the BP and economic growth, in which the dominant paradigm in a fixed exchange situation is that the trade balance depends on the level of national absorption which in turn has to be put into relation with the desire to acquire foreign financial assets on the part of residents, Martinengo (1978a) specifies a model of stocks and flows in which the trade balance assumes instead a totally autonomous role. The central feature consists of the fact that exports, and in part imports, not being entirely destined for consumption, are independent of the financial accumulation of the country.

Furthermore, though he accepts the idea proposed by monetary-approach scholars (by which financial flows derive from a process of adjustment between desired and existing stocks) he introduces the Keynesian topic of effective demand, as recognition that the investment flow also gives origin to a similar process.

In the case of fixed exchange-rates it is the movement of income (that is, its growth-rate), which reconciles the national decisions regarding portfolio growth, real accumulation and demand on the country's economy for real resources by the rest of the world.

In the case of flexible exchange-rates, a further problem arises, that of the connection between the exchange-rate and national price-levels in a growth context. From this derives the fact that financial accumulation is no longer induced by real income growth alone, but also by variations in prices. Real accumulation is influenced in an analogous way, and consequently so is the capital account, insofar as it is assumed that investment is financed by the issue of securities.

The equilibrium exchange-rate, in this context, is that which makes the overall balance of the BP equal to zero. In fact, the divergence between the value of exports – which depends on the income of the rest of the world and on the terms of trade (or real exchange-rate) – and the value of imports, which depends on the national income and on the terms of trade is taken into consideration. In addition the movements of capital, which depend on the divergence between the structural parameters that characterize the supply of and demand for securities and on the increases in real income and prices, are taken into consideration.

The model in its compact form is composed of three relations: (33) which makes the movement of prices (p_t) dependent on changes in the exchange-rate (Z_t)

$$p_t = p_t(Z_t), \qquad p_t' > 0, \tag{33}$$

(34), in which the flow of the demand for money, prompted both by the growth in income ($\dot{X}$) and by the increase in prices ($\dot{p}$), is equal to the issue of money which goes to finance government expenditure, assumed to be proportional to money income

$$lp_t\dot{X} + l\dot{p}X_t = gp_tX_t, \tag{34}$$

and (35) which expresses the equilibrium of the BP in national currency terms

$$pE\left(p_mY, \frac{p_mZ}{p}\right) - Zp_m\mathrm{IMP}\left(pX, \frac{p_mZ}{p}\right)$$

$$= Zp_F(f - \beta)(\dot{p}X + p\dot{X}) \tag{35}$$

As regards the symbols, l indicates the structural parameter for the money demand and g that of supply: f and β indicate the structural parameters for demand and supply of securities, while p_m, p_F and Y represent prices of imports and securities, by assumption given by the international market, and the income of the rest of the world.

It should be noted that in (35) the functions of exports and imports assume the presence of money illusion. This is because of the hypothesis that both real investment and real saving, and therefore also consumption depend on money income. The variables determined (and therefore their time-paths) are p_t, Z_t and X_t. The condition of flow equilibrium (real equilibrium) is eliminated by Walras' law, while the security market gives the value of capital movements as a residual. In this model the exchange-rate is affected by real and financial choices and the expression of its proportional rate of variation is:

$$\frac{\dot{Z}}{Z}=\frac{\left(\pi\frac{\text{IMP}}{\text{E}}\varepsilon_{\text{IMP},pX}+\frac{\text{MC}}{p\text{E}}\varepsilon_{\text{MC},pX}\right)\frac{g}{l}-\varepsilon_{\text{E},pmY}\mu}{(1-\eta_{p,z})\left(\eta_{\text{E},\pi}+\pi\frac{\text{IMP}}{\text{E}}\eta_{\text{IMP},\pi}-1\right)},\qquad(36)$$

which depends: (a) on the Marshall–Lerner condition in its general form, valid in the case in which there is no equilibrium in the trade balance ($\eta_{\text{E},\pi}+\pi(\text{IMP}/\text{E})\eta_{\text{IMP},\pi}-1$), (b) on the value in relation to one of the elasticity of prices with respect to exchange-rates ($1-\eta_{p,z}$), (c) by the divergence between the growth rate of the money income of the small economy (g/l) and that of the rest of the world (μ), both weighted. In the weighting coefficient of the growth-rate of national income appears the sum of two elasticities: that of imports with respect to money income of the country ($\varepsilon_{\text{IMP},pX}$), corrected by the ratio in value between imports and exports ($\pi(\text{IMP}/\text{E})$) and that of capital movements, always with respect to the monetary income of the country ($\varepsilon_{\text{MC},pX}$), corrected by the ratio between the value of the capital movements and the value of exports ($\text{MC}/p\text{E}$). The weighting coefficient of the rate of increase in the income of the rest of the world is instead made up by the elasticity of exports with respect to the money income of the rest of the world ($\varepsilon_{\text{E},pmY}$). The relation obtained is quite general in that it makes it possible to obtain, as special cases, the expressions which are valid both in the case of trade equilibrium, and where there is an absence of effects of the exchange-rate, variations on the general price-level or when the effect is complete.

In the models examined so far the topic of the equilibrium exchange-rate is tackled with reference to a single country (versus the rest of the world). However, this theme can be proposed even in the context of simultaneous determination of the equilibrium exchange-rate for each nation which participates in international trade. Along the same lines it is also conceivable to find an exchange-rate between different countries, belonging to a particular economic area which as a whole suffers a deficit with regard to another area.

A concrete example is that of the OECD countries' oil deficit with regard to oil-producing countries; obviously there arises a problem of distribution of the adjustment costs among the various countries. The range of exchange-rates to be adopted should show the effects of a definite policy, since, if it were simply a case of economic forces resolving the problem, the equilibrium that can be achieved would run the risk of being extremely unstable on account of the implicit social conflict.[15] The weakest countries, in an attempt to avoid huge deficits should make a heavy reduction in their activity levels, thus creating enormous problems of unemployment. A different solution might be arrived at, namely that the OPEC countries, by importing goods and services for a value corresponding to that of their total oil surplus, would bring about a substantial equilibrium between the two areas. However, experience has shown that this method is not feasible, at least over the short-term.

The alternative way therefore is for the economic conditions in the two areas to become such as to induce stable flows in the movement of capital from the oil-producing areas towards the oil-importing countries of such an amount as to finance the deficits and thus ensure the stability of the equilibrium exchange-rate between the two areas. Obviously, in this second case, the further problem arises of the division of financial flows, besides that of the division of the adjustment burdens between the various OECD countries.

Following the first hypothesis, once the division of the deficit between the OECD members has been fixed, the search for the equilibrium exchange-rate can proceed on the same methodological bases as those followed when the problem does not arise, namely that of a simultaneous attempt to find equilibrium exchange-rates between the countries considered.

A work which has been carried out inside the view of the simultaneous search for equilibrium exchange-rates for several countries is that by Berner *et al.* (1977 a, b). It proposes an extremely detailed real and financial model for several countries (the USA, Canada, Germany, Japan and the UK) in which the equilibrium exchange-rates are determined by equilibrium conditions of the BP.

[15] For a formal analysis of the contribution to the stability of the trading system made by the expansionary policies of countries with a surplus and the restrictive policies of the countries with a deficit in a flexible exchange regime, see Martinengo (1978 b).

4.6. Conclusions

As Lindbeck (1976, pp. 138–141) stresses in his introduction to the number of the *Scandinavian Journal of Economics* dedicated to the theories of flexible exchange-rates, each historical period has put forward a different model for the interpretation of the formation of the equilibrium exchange-rate. He attempts to show in a diagram – in which are synthesized the repercussions which occur between strategic economic variables, which the various schools of thought have emphasized – the relevant paradigm for each of these. For the comparison between the classics, that is, old-school and latter-day monetarists, we refer the reader directly to Lindbeck's work. We do likewise for the motivations which led in the different historical periods to the placing of more emphasis on the capital account or on the current account of the BP – even if this, historically, was realized via radically different theories – but we should like to take up his conclusions here. In substance he demonstrates the need for a model that is general enough to include within it all the approaches which historically have been formulated, even if this includes the need to adapt the scheme of analysis to the type of problem that the scholar is dealing with. This, in our opinion, is to be considered as an invitation towards an approach which is legitimately eclectic and not an improvised jumble, and takes account, as well as possible, of a complex reality. However, if we look at more recent production on the subject of the exchange-rate, it does not appear that the dominant current of thought is making much effort in this direction.[16] This Lindbeck himself (1976, pp. 137–138) stresses, when speaking of the different market-reaction speeds hypothesized in the monetary models to justify the deviation of the current exchange-rate from PPP. He points out that in these models variations of income and employment never occur. He proposes that the obsession with long-term stationary full-employment equilibria should be abandoned, which is certainly not the most appropriate context for the analysis of short-term stabilization policies (that is, those policies which are aimed against fluctuations in production and employment, including "involuntary unemployment" aspects which he sees as of primary importance).

[16] Here in addition to the works presented in the paragraphs dedicated to eclectic models, account needs to be taken of Kenen (1978) and Allen and Kenen (1979).

If Lindbeck's invitation is certainly one to be accepted (and, as we have seen in the paragraph on eclectic models, there have in fact been some contributions in this sense), it seems to us that his vision regarding the description of the capitalist system is of the following type: for the short-term, models are needed which explain distortions in the exchange-rate and in other variables in the system, while over the long-term the models of the consolidated theory (PPP) are suitable. Perhaps the problem should be approached from the opposite end, as we have attempted to do in the present book, namely to start from models which describe situations in which operators attempt to adjust the effective variables to those desired, in order to verify whether this simultaneous adjustment leads towards the general equilibrium of the system.

But the methodological aspect certainly does not exhaust all the problems. In fact an even more crucial point, at least for the analysis of the equilibrium exchange-rate, is that of the behaviour of the decisional centres, or typical operators, which it is wished to describe in the model. We refer to the role played by real accumulation and in general by all those economic variables which are independent of financial accumulation and in general of portfolio decisions, such as exports. In this work we have persistently shown that all monetary models for the determination of the equilibrium exchange-rate are dominated by the portfolio, in the same way that the real neo-classical theory is dominated by the idea that the consumer is sovereign. In other words the monetarists eliminate earlier in the process every problem of autonomous flows from the portfolio and/or from financial accumulation.

Investment can be regarded as a capital stock adjustment flow and imports can represent the adjustment of the capital stock and consumption by way of goods imported from abroad with, in the case of consumption, a connection with financial accumulation.

However, not for this reason can we assume that the demand will always be at the full-employment level, accepting that investment coincides with saving,[17] and when it does not coincide, this is caused by the fact that the community wishes to accumulate financial assets and is able to do so because the rest of the world is

[17] Obviously this implies, in the simplified hypothesis of a zero balance of payments, a zero balance of trade.

prepared to absorb these surpluses of goods. There is in fact foreign demand, that is, the flow of exports, which particularly in a small country, has a heavy effect on national activity. The monetarist writers, as has been emphasized, assume that the economies are perfectly integrated and trade homogeneous goods, thus avoiding the problem that many economies, including Italy, have to face, namely the search for market outlets in which foreign demand is influenced by the terms of trade and therefore by the exchange-rate and the prices of traded goods.

This call to realism ought not to seem spurious with respect to the sophistication of the theory. It is well known that each model expresses a *Weltanschauung* in which the ideologies of the economist are to be detected. Therefore to use one model or another to explain the equilibrium exchange-rate is by no means a neutral position, especially when, from the model in question, one can deduce prescriptions for economic policy. This general consideration, can be applied as we have said, to the specific field of the equilibrium exchange-rate, which is the price derived from all the economic and financial, and at times political, relations with the rest of the world (or with a more limited group of countries). This leads one to the conclusion that a model which aims to interpret as correctly as possible the functioning of an open capitalist economy (in which the degree of intervention of the state and that of the banking system are often not neutral with regard to the private sector), must be one in which the central problem to be faced ought at least to be that of real accumulation, besides that of financial accumulation. This is because growth is one of the ways of resolving the problems of blocked economies, like that of Italy. It will be understood, therefore, why a correct formulation of theory for the exchange-rate – the end-product of all these interconnections – is essential, since the rate of growth of an economy is conditioned by this variable.

In conclusion we wish to examine a problem of a more strictly technical nature, namely that according to which the results of an approach should not differ from those of another in that – if the models are effectively general equilibrium models – to eliminate one market or another as redundant by Walras's law ought not to change anything. This is acceptable in theory, but in real situations the various models put forward as a general equilibrium model are very far from being that and so it is not possible to apply to them the theoretical principle just mentioned. On the contrary what we have said regarding the different views foreseen in the various approaches takes on particular relevance as a distinguishing factor.

In fact the answer was given above when it was affirmed that the monetarist approach essentially expresses a portfolio equilibrium, while the other approaches put the emphasis on other aspects. This is a further confirmation of the fact that the general model which Lindbeck hopes to see formulated does not in fact exist.

On the contrary there exist theories which are strongly biased in favour of financial aspects or of aspects of international trade. In other words, the general model, if it can be formulated at all, constitutes an objective for research in the near future if we wish to arrive at a correct estimation of the equilibrium exchange-rate.

References

Allen, P. R. and Kenen, P. B., 1979, *The Balance of Payments, Exchange-Rates, and Economic Policy* (Reprints in International Finance No. 19, International Finance Section, Department of Economics, Princeton University).

Armington, P., 1978, Exchange-Rate Dynamics and the Management of Currency Exposure, mimeo.

Artus, J. R., 1978, Methods of Assessing the Long Run Equilibrium Value of an Exchange-Rate, *Journal of International Economics* **8**, 277–299.

Artus, J. R. and Crockett, A. D., 1978, *Floating Exchange-Rates and the Need for Surveillance* (Essays in International Finance No. 127, International Finance Section, Princeton University).

Balassa, B., 1964, The Purchasing Power Parity Doctrine: a Reappraisal, *Journal of Political Economy* **72**, 584–596. Reprinted in: Cooper, R. N., ed., 1969, *International Finance* (Harmondsworth, Penguin Books), 191–211.

Barro, R. J., 1978, A Stochastic Equilibrium Model of an Open Economy under Flexible Exchange-Rates, *Quarterly Journal of Economics* **92**, 149–164.

Basevi, G. and De Grauwe, P., 1978, Vicious and Virtuous Circles and the OPTICA Proposal: A Two Country Analysis, in: Fratianni, M. and Peeters, T., eds., *One Money for Europe* (Macmillan, London), 144–157.

Bernauer, K., 1978, *Relative M1 Growth as a Determinant of Short-Run Exchange Rate Movement* (Research Paper No. 7814, Federal Reserve Bank of New York).

Berner, R., Clark, P., Howe, H., Kwack, S. and Stevens, J., 1977a, Modeling the International Influence on the U.S. Economy: a Multi-Country Approach (International Finance Division Discussion Paper, No. 93, Washington, Federal Reserve Board) mimeo.

Berner, R., Clark, P., Howe, H., Kwack, S. and Stevens, J., 1977 b, A Multi-Country Model of International Influences on the U.S. Economy: Preliminary Results (International Finance Discussion Paper, No. 115, Washington, Federal Reserve Board) mimeo.

Bilson, J. F. O., 1978, The Current Experience with Floating Exchange Rates: An Appraisal of the Monetary Approach, *American Economic Review, Papers and Proceedings* **68**, 392–397.

Branson, W. H., 1976, *Asset Markets and Relative Prices in Exchange-Rate Determination* (Seminar Paper No. 66, Institute for International Economic Studies, University of Stockholm).

Calvo, G. A. and Rodriguez, C. A., 1977, A Model of Exchange-Rate Determination under Currency Substitution and Rational Expectations, *Journal of Political Economy* **85**, 617–626.

Cooper, R. N., 1976, Monetary theory and Policy in an Open Economy, *Scandinavian Journal of Economics* **78**, 146–163.

De Grauwe, P., Steinherr, A. and Basevi, G., 1978, The Dynamics of Intervention in Foreign Exchange Markets: Purchasing Power Parity as a Guideline, unpublished manuscript.

Dornbusch, R., 1976a, The Theory of Flexible Exchange-Rate Regimes and Macroeconomic Policy, *Scandinavian Journal of Economics* **78**, 255–275. Reprinted in: Frenkel, J. A. and Johnson, H. G., eds., 1978, 27–46.

Dornbusch, R., 1976b, Expectations and Exchange-Rate Dynamics, *Journal of Political Economy* **84**, 1161–1176.

Dornbusch, R., 1978, Monetary Policy under Exchange-Rate Flexibility, in: *Managed Exchange-Rate Flexibility: the Recent Experience* (Conference Series No. 20, Federal Reserve Bank of Boston), pp. 90–122.

Frankel, J. A., 1979, On the Mark: A Theory of Floating Exchange Rates Based on Real Interest Differentials, *American Economic Review* **69**, 610–622.

Frenkel, J. A., 1976, A Monetary Approach to the Exchange-Rate: Doctrinal Aspects and Empirical Evidence, *Scandinavian Journal of Economics* **78**, 200–224. Reprinted in: Frenkel, J. A. and Johnson, H. G., eds., 1978, 1–25.

Frenkel, J. A., 1978, Purchasing Power Parity-Doctrinal Perspective and Evidence from the 1920s, *Journal of International Economics* **8**, 169–192.

Frenkel, J. A. and Johnson, H. G., eds., 1978, *The Economics of Exchange-Rates: Selected Studies* (Addinson-Wesley Publishing Company, London).

Gandolfo, G., 1970, *Aggiustamento della Bilancia dei Pagamenti ed Equilibrio Macroeconomico* (F. Angeli, Milano).

Gandolfo, G. *et al.*, 1976, *Il Tasso di Cambio di Equilibrio, Aspetti Teorici e Risultati Empirici* (ISEDI, Milano).

Gandolfo, G., 1979, The Equilibrium Exchange-Rate: Theory and Empirical Evidence, in: Sarnat, M. and Szegö, G. P., eds., *International Finance and Trade*, Vol. I (Ballinger Publishing Co., Cambridge, Mass.), 99–130.

Helliwell, J. F., 1979, *Policy Modelling of Foreign Exchange-Rates* (Seminar Paper No. 123, Institute for International Economic Studies, University of Stockholm).

Houthakker, H. S., 1978, *Purchasing Power Parity as an Approximation to the Equilibrium Exchange-Ratio* (Discussion Paper No. 623, Harvard Institute of Economic Research, Harvard University).

Isard, P., 1978, *Exchange-Rate Determination: a Survey of Popular Views and Recent Models* (Princeton Studies in International Finance, No. 42, International Finance Section, Princeton University).

Kenen, P. B., 1978, New Views of Exchange-Rates and Old Views of Policy, *American Economic Review, Papers and Proceedings* **68**, 398–405.

King, D. T., Putnam, B. H. and Wilford, D. S., 1977, *A Currency Portfolio Approach to Exchange-Rate Determination: Exchange-Rate Stability and the Independence of Monetary Policy* (Research Paper No. 7733, Federal Reserve Bank of New York).

Kouri, P. J. K., 1976, The Exchange-Rate and the Balance of Payments in the Short Run and in the Long Run. A Monetary Approach, *Scandinavian Journal of Economics* **78**, 280–304.

Kravis, I. B. and Lipsey, R. E., 1978, Price Behavior in the Light of Balance of Payments Theories, *Journal of International Economics* **8**, 193–246.

Kreinin, M. E. and Officer, L. H., 1978, *The Monetary Approach to the Balance of Payments: a Survey* (Princeton Studies in International Finance No. 43, International Finance Section, Department of Economics, Princeton University).

Kuska, E. A., 1978, On the Almost Total Inadequacy of Keynesian Balance of Payments Theory, *American Economic Review* **68**, 659–670.

Lindbeck, A., 1976, Approaches to Exchange-Rate Analysis: An Introduction, *Scandinavian Journal of Economics* **78**, 133–145.

Martinengo, G., 1976, Moneta, Inflazione e Bilancia dei Pagamenti, *Note Economiche* **9**, 122–133.

Martinengo, G., 1978a, *Crescita e Bilancia dei Pagamenti* (Pubblicazioni della Facoltà di Economia e Commercio delll'Università di Roma, XLI, Giuffrè, Milano).

Martinengo, G., 1978b, Cambi Flessibili e Collaborazione tra Paesi Deficitari ed Eccedentari nell'Aggiustamento degli Squilibri, *Quaderni Sardi di Economia* **8**, 127–135.

Martinengo, G., 1979, Schemi Teorici per la Determinazione del Tasso di Cambio di Equilibrio, *Rivista di Politica Economica* **69**, 533–581.

Mathieson, D. J., 1977, The Impact of Monetary and Fiscal Policy under Flexible Exchange-Rates and Alternative Expectations Structures, *IMF Staff Papers* **24**, 535–568.

McKenzie, G. W., 1977, Devaluation and the Real-Balance Effect, *Zeitschrift für Nationalökonomie* **37**, 109–122.

Michaely, M., 1978, *Analysis of Devaluation: Purchasing Power Parity, Elasticities and Absorption* (seminar Paper No. 112, Institute of International Economic Studies, University of Stockolm).

Miller, N. C., 1978, Monetary vs. Traditional Approaches to Balance of Payments Analysis, *American Economic Review, Papers and Proceedings* **68**, 406–411.

Minford, P., 1978, *Substitution Effects, Speculation and Exchange-Rate Stability* (North-Holland, Amsterdam).

Mundell, R. A., 1968, *International Economics* (Macmillan, New York).

Mundell, R. A., 1971, *Monetary Theory: Inflation, Interest and Growth in the World Economy* (Goodyear Publishing Company, Inc., Pacific Palisades, California).

Mussa, M., 1976, The Exchange Rate, the Balance of Payments and Monetary and Fiscal Policy under a Regime of Controlled Floating, *Scandinavian Journal of*

Economics **78**, 229–248. Reprinted in: Frenkel, J. A. and Johnson, H. G., eds., 1978, 47–65.

von Neumann Whitman, M., 1975, Global Monetarism and the Monetary Approach to the Balance of Payments, *Brookings Papers on Economic Activity*, No. 3, 491–536.

Niehans, J., 1977, Exchange-Rate Dynamics with Stock-Flow Interaction, *Journal of Political Economy* **85**, 1245–1258.

Officer, L. H., 1976, The Purchasing-Power-Parity Theory of Exchange Rates: a Review Article, *IMF Staff Papers* **23**, 1–60.

OPTICA Report 1976, 1977, *Inflation and Exchange Rates: Evidence and Policy Guidelines for the European Community* (Commission of the European Communities, Bruxelles).

Putnam, B. H. and Woodbury, J. R., 1977, *Exchange Rate Stability and Monetary Policy: a Case Study* (Research Paper No. 7718, Federal Reserve Bank of New York).

CHAPTER 5

A minimal model: The theoretical framework

5.1. Introduction and overview

This model, which takes into account the results of the survey on the determinants of the equilibrium exchange rate (ch. 4) as well as previous work by the author (Gandolfo *et al.*, 1976; Gandolfo, 1979), aims to be a first step in the construction of a general macrodynamic framework for the determination of the equilibrium exchange rate and in its application to Italy.

The model considers stock-flow behaviour in an open economy in which both price and quantity adjustments take place. Stocks are introduced only relatively to the real sector, where adjustments of fixed capital and inventories to their respective desired levels are present, while no financial stock behaviour is considered explicitly. There are no theoretical reasons for this choice, which merely stems from dimension constraints that we decided to impose on this version of the model and from data problems (see below). The only monetary and financial variables present are the (endogenous) proportional rate of increase in the money supply and the (exogenous) ratio of capital inflows to capital outflows. A more satisfactory approach would have consisted in taking explicit account of all the relevant financial magnitudes and of the behavioural equations, both private and public, which determine them (banking sector, government finance, interest rates and their structure, etc.). This choice would have produced an expansion of the model (and subsequent theoretical and data problems[1]) which we preferred to

[1]Data problems are particularly serious in Italy when interest rates are concerned. It is often impossible to find data with a reasonable agreement between their statistical "content" and the theoretical "content" of the variable of which they should be the numerical manifestation. Furthermore, periods of pegging of bond prices, lack of relationship between demand for (or supply of) credit and its "price" for institutional reasons, etc. etc., add to the difficulties of this situation.

avoid at this stage. There is, however, a minimal presence of monetary effects in the model, via the feed-back between the policy reaction function of the monetary authorities and the other behavioural equations. Government expenditure is also present since aggregate consumption and net capital formation include both public and private expenditure.

Quantity behaviour equations are considered for the traditional macroeconomic variables in real terms (consumption, net fixed investment, imports and exports of goods and services, inventories, net domestic product). Two separate equations for consumption and net fixed investment, rather than a single equation for aggregate expenditure, are considered, because we believe that the difference between the processes of formation of these two variables is crucial in a modern capital-accumulating economy. Expectations are included through an adaptive mechanism[2] concerning expected output.

A price block is included, which determines the domestic price level, the nominal wage rate, and the export price level. Endogenous determination of the last was considered crucial for an export-led economy such as Italy's, while wage–price spiral effects are explicitly taken into account.

Price and quantity variables interact both directly and indirectly (through the monetary variable behaviour) while a terms-of-trade effect *à la* Laursen and Metzler (1950) on consumption is considered.

The (apparently) traditional macroeconomic setting should not convey the impression that quantities are entirely demand determined. Although our model does not include a production function,[3] supply constraints are fed back into the model, as capital formation takes place, on both domestic and foreign demand.

[2]We do not wish to enter here into the controversy concerning rational vs. adaptive (or other types of) expectations. Arguments in favour of adaptive expectations (including the cases in which, under general and realistic circumstances, the "rational" expectation-formation process is an adaptive mechanism) can be found, e.g., in B. Friedman (1979), Gordon (1976), Granger and Newbold (1977), Knight (1976), Mussa (1978), Muth (1961), Sargent and Wallace (1973).

[3]This omission is deliberate, because fundamentally we agree with the so-called "Anglo-Italian" school of thought (J. Robinson, 1953; Sraffa, 1960; Garegnani, 1970; Pasinetti, 1977, ch. 6; etc.) which denies the general theoretical validity of the

The choice not to consider explicitly the financial sector leaves out many relevant links in the analysis of the accumulation process in an open industrial country. No connection is considered, for example, between internal capital formation and net capital outflows which, according to some investigations,[4] can be very important for a developed country. In order to fill such a gap, endogenous capital flow behaviour should have been considered. But this, again, would have required a fully-fledged financial sector specification, in which interest rate formation, in addition to the behaviour of stocks, could have been analyzed and complete intervention on the part of the monetary authorities thoroughly considered.

The equations that we shall discuss in the next section have been written down keeping in mind the above limitations and are a tentative compromise between the ideal "general" model and dimension and data constraints.

5.2. The model

The model is a closely interlocked system of stochastic differential equations specified according to the principles expounded in Part I of this volume, with which the reader is assumed to be familiar. For convenience of exposition, the model is first laid out in tabular form and then each equation is commented on; for economy of notation, the disturbance terms are omitted and the model is described in deterministic terms. A hat ($\hat{}$) refers to the partial equilibrium level or desired value of the hatted variable, a tilde ($\tilde{}$) to expectations;

---

standard neoclassical aggregate production function and of the ensuing marginal productivity conditions of factor-price determination. Therefore, we try to avoid using these tools in empirical research. Notwithstanding theoretical objections, many justify their use as helpful descriptive or empirical relations in applied econometric work. But, before accepting this, we prefer to ascertain whether a model in which they are absent can give a satisfactory fit and be consistent with the data (in the sense of not being rejected by them). This is the line that we decided to follow.

[4]An *ex ante* excess of saving over investment can produce a net capital outflow due to the lack of investment opportunities in the domestic economy (see, for example, Borts and Kopecky, 1972).

the symbol D denotes the differential operator d/dt, and log the natural logarithm. All variables are defined at time t. All parameters are assumed positive, unless otherwise specified.

In eq. (1), *real aggregate consumption*, C, adjusts to its desired level $\hat{C}$, which is given by the average propensity to consume applied to real net domestic income.[5] This propensity may vary over the trade cycle, that is, according to the rate of growth of Y, and is also a function of the terms of trade (proxied by the ratio of P to $PMGS$). As regards the first argument, if a "ratchet effect" is operating, β_1 should be negative, but a pro-cyclical variation in the average propensity to consume is also possible; therefore any sign can be expected for β_1 on *a priori* grounds.

The terms of trade are not usually included in consumption functions, but we believe their presence to be important in a model of an open economy. Actually, their inclusion was advocated 30 years ago in the seminal contribution by Laursen and Metzler (1950), and this is why we have called it the "Laursen and Metzler effect". Given the level of domestic prices, and given that the short-run consumption function is non-proportional (so that the average propensity to consume varies inversely with real income), it follows that "as import prices fall and the real income corresponding to a given money income increases, the amount spent on goods and services out of a given money income will fall. The argument is applicable in reverse, of course, to a rise in import prices. In short, our basic premise is that, other things being the same, the expenditure schedule of any given country rises when import prices rise and falls when import prices fall" (Laursen and Metzler, 1950, p. 286). The Laursen and Metzler effect has important consequences on the stability conditions and the comparative statics properties of open models under flexible exchange rates (see, for example, Gandolfo, 1980, Part II, ch. 9, §5; Part III, ch. 1, § 7.2), and this explains why we stated above that the presence of the terms of trade as an argument of the consumption function is important in an open economy.

Strictly speaking, the Laursen and Metzler reasoning, which leads to the assumption $\beta_2 < 0$, is applicable only to a model, like theirs,

[5]Since $\hat{C}$ includes both private and public consumption expenditure, Y seems more appropriate than disposable income. On the fact that private and public consumption are merged, see below in the text.

Table 1.
Equations of the model.

$$D\log C = \alpha_1 \log\frac{\hat{C}}{C} + \alpha_2 m, \tag{1}$$

where

$$\hat{C} = \gamma_1 e^{\beta_1 D\log Y}\left(\frac{P}{PMGS}\right)^{\beta_2} Y, \qquad \beta_1, \beta_2 \gtrless 0, \tag{1.1}$$

$$Dk = \alpha_3\left(\alpha'\frac{\hat{K}}{K} - \alpha' - k\right) + \alpha_4 m, \tag{2}$$

where

$$\hat{K} = \gamma_2 \tilde{Y}, \qquad \gamma_2 = \kappa/u, \tag{2.1}$$

and

$$D\tilde{Y} = \eta(Y - \tilde{Y}), \tag{3}$$

$$D\log MGS = \alpha_5 \log\frac{M\hat{G}S}{MGS} + \alpha_6 \log\frac{\hat{V}}{V}, \tag{4}$$

where

$$M\hat{G}S = \gamma_3\left(\frac{P}{PMGS}\right)^{\beta_3}\left(\frac{\gamma_2 Y}{K}\right)^{\beta_4} C^{\beta_5}(DK)^{\beta_6} XGS^{\beta_7},$$

$$\beta_4 \gtrless 0,$$

$$\hat{V} = \gamma_4 \tilde{Y}, \tag{4.1}$$

$$D\log XGS = \alpha_7 \log\frac{X\hat{G}S}{XGS}, \tag{5}$$

where

$$X\hat{G}S = \gamma_5\left(\frac{PXGS}{PF}\right)^{-\beta_8} YF^{\beta_9}\left(\frac{\gamma_2 Y}{K}\right)^{-\beta_{10}}, \tag{5.1}$$

$$D\log Y = \alpha_8 \log\frac{\tilde{Y}}{Y} + \alpha_9 \log\frac{\hat{V}}{V}, \tag{6}$$

$$D\log P = \alpha_{10} \log\frac{\hat{P}}{P} + \alpha_{11} m, \tag{7}$$

where

$$\hat{P} = \gamma_6 PMGS^{\beta_{11}} W^{\beta_{12}} PROD^{-\beta_{13}}, \tag{7.1}$$

$$D\log PXGS = \alpha_{12} \log\frac{PX\hat{G}S}{PXGS}, \tag{8}$$

where

$$PX\hat{G}S = \gamma_7 P^{\beta_{14}} PF^{\beta_{15}} W^{\beta_{16}} PROD^{-\beta_{17}}, \qquad \beta_{14} \gtrless 0, \tag{8.1}$$

$$D\log W = \alpha_{13} \log\frac{\hat{W}}{W}, \tag{9}$$

where

$$\hat{W} = \gamma_8 P^{\beta_{18}} e^{\lambda_5 t}, \tag{9.1}$$

$$Dm = \alpha_{14}(\hat{m} - m), \tag{10}$$

where

$$\hat{m} = \delta_1 \log \frac{PXGS \cdot XGS}{\gamma_9 PMGS \cdot MGS} + \delta_2 D \log \frac{PXGS \cdot XGS}{\gamma_9 PMGS \cdot MGS}$$
$$- \delta_3 D \log \frac{P}{PMGS} + \delta_4(\lambda_y - D \log Y) + \delta_5 \log \frac{1}{\gamma_{10}} N$$
$$+ \delta_6 D \log \frac{1}{\gamma_{10}} N, \qquad \delta_1, \delta_2, \delta_5, \delta_6, \gtrless 0, \tag{10.1}$$

$$D \log K = k, \tag{11}$$

$$DV = Y + MGS - C - DK - XGS. \tag{12}$$

Table 2.
Variables of the model.†

	Endogenous
C	= real consumption expenditure of the private and public sector
K	= stock of fixed capital
k	= proportional rate of increase of fixed capital
$\tilde{Y}$	= expected real net domestic product and income
MGS	= real imports of goods and services
XGS	= real exports of goods and services
Y	= real net domestic product and income
V	= inventories
P	= domestic price level
$PXGS$	= export price level
W	= money wage rate
m	= proportional rate of increase of domestic nominal money stock
	Exogenous
$PMGS$	= import price level
PF	= foreign competitors' export price level
YF	= real world income
$PROD$	= labour productivity
N	= ratio of autonomous capital inflows to capital outflows, in nominal terms
t	= time

†Details of the variables and sources of data are given in Appendix II to ch. 6. The sample period is 1960-I to 1975-IV.

in which the domestic price level is assumed to be constant. If, on the contrary, the terms of trade increase because the domestic price level rises, given *PMGS*, then real income decreases, thus increasing the propensity to consume (hence $\beta_2 > 0$). If both *P* and *PMGS* vary, the outcome cannot be assessed on *a priori* grounds; therefore, the coexistence of conflicting effects makes the sign of the final effect of the terms of trade on consumption ambiguous.[6]

The speed at which C adjusts to $\hat{C}$ is not considered a constant but is a function of monetary variables (proxied by m, the proportional rate of growth of the money stock; this variable will be dealt with more fully later). If we take account of this, the specification of the consumption adjustment equation is non-linear and is expressed as follows

$$\mathrm{D}\log C = h(m)\log\frac{\hat{C}}{C}, \qquad h'(m) > 0. \tag{13}$$

The specification presented in table 1 is a suitable linear approximation of eq. (13). Such a specification is of course also compatible with other theoretical considerations, such as the role played by money balances as a buffer in the private sector asset portfolio, allowing unexpected variations in income and expenditure (Wymer, 1979, section 4) or the inclusion of a monetary variable (proxied by m) as an additional explanatory variable in $\hat{C}$.

The *investment function* implicit in eq. (2) is a development of the capital stock adjustment principle, which in turn is sufficiently general to accommodate any investment theory. The traditional version of this principle states that actual net fixed investment I is a function of the difference between desired capital stock $\hat{K}$ and actual stock K

$$I \equiv \mathrm{D}K = \alpha'(\hat{K} - K), \qquad \alpha' > 0, \tag{14}$$

where $\hat{K}$ is related to current output and/or other explanatory variables. In our opinion, the difference $(\hat{K} - K)$ does not give rise directly to actual investment, but rather is the determinant of *desired* investment $\hat{I}$, namely

$$\hat{I} \equiv \hat{\mathrm{D}}K = \alpha'(\hat{K} - K), \tag{15}$$

[6]Theoretical discussion and empirical evidence on this effect in macroeconometric models is contained in Deardoff and Stern (1978).

whence we obtain the desired rate of growth of the capital stock

$$\frac{\hat{I}}{K} = \alpha'\left(\frac{\hat{K}}{K} - 1\right). \tag{15.1}$$

We then assume that the relevant economic agents adjust the actual rate of growth of the capital stock[7] to the desired rate according to a partial adjustment equation

$$D\frac{I}{K} = \alpha_3\left(\frac{\hat{I}}{K} - \frac{I}{K}\right), \qquad \alpha_3 > 0, \tag{16}$$

that is, defining $k \equiv \mathrm{D}K/K \equiv I/K$,

$$\mathrm{D}k = \alpha_3\left(\alpha'\frac{\hat{K}}{K} - \alpha' - k\right), \tag{16.1}$$

which is eq. (2) in table 1.

Now, to give operational content to eq. (16.1), it is necessary to specify how the desired capital stock is determined. In the traditional capital stock adjustment principle, $\hat{K}$ is usually related to current output, but we think it more plausible to relate it to *expected* output[8] $\tilde{Y}$, whose determination is discussed below. In particular, $\hat{K}$ is a function of $\tilde{Y}$ given the capital/output ratio κ and the desired degree of capacity utilization u. Therefore we have

$$\hat{K} = \gamma_2\tilde{Y}, \qquad \gamma_2 = \kappa/u. \tag{16.2}$$

As in the consumption function, the speed at which k adjusts to its desired value is assumed to be an increasing function of m; a suitable linear approximation then gives eq. (2). This specification is, however, also compatible with other theoretical considerations, such as the inclusion of a monetary variable (credit conditions, and the like), proxied by m, as an additional argument in $\hat{I}/K$.

It should be pointed out that, since data are not available on the public sector net investment expenditure, I is net capital formation of the whole economy. For symmetry, we did not take public

[7]The assumption that the dependent variable in the investment function is not I but I/K has a pedigree that dates at least as far back as 1933: see – though in another context – Kalecki (1933); more recent references are Bergstrom and Wymer (1976) and Knight and Wymer (1978).

[8]Expected output in turn can be considered as a variable of which expected profits are a function, then letting $\hat{K}$ depend on expected profits; but we do not wish to pursue these chinese boxes further.

consumption expenditure out of C (see above), also because (this part of) government expenditure would then have had to be considered exogenous (whereas it very much follows the trend in private consumption expenditure). In fact, endogenization of government expenditure (and of direct tax receipts) through a policy function in the usual way, is not advisable, because the standard tenet that in Italy a fiscal policy worthy of its name does not (yet?) exist (so that practically all the burden of economic policy-making rests on monetary policy) is, unfortunately, true.

Equation (3) expresses the *formation of expectations* on output according to an adaptive mechanism,[9] where $\eta > 0$ is the coefficient of expectations.

The specification of the behaviour of *real imports* for goods and services (MGS) in eq. (4) has two determinants. Imports adjust to their desired value $M\hat{G}S$, which is a function of total domestic expenditure as well as of exports (XGS), all in real terms. This specification seems preferable to the income and to the total expenditure specifications, because it relates the demand for imports to total sales and it recognizes that exports are produced, at least in part, with imported inputs. As the elasticity of import demand may be different according to which is the component of total sales involved, we considered them separately. The propensity to import – given total sales and their structure – varies according to the terms of trade and to a "capacity effect". The latter is determined by the ratio of the amount of capital which is needed (given γ_2 as defined above) to produce current output to the amount of existing capital. The reason for this effect is twofold. On the one hand, as the utilization of productive capacity increases, a larger amount of domestic demand will tend, *ceteris paribus*, to be met by foreign rather than by domestic supply. On the other hand, the greater the utilization of productive capacity, the greater domestic output, and consequently the lesser the need, *ceteris paribus*, to have recourse to foreign output to meet an increase in domestic demand. Therefore the sign of β_{14} is indeterminate.

The second determinant is due to the adjustment of inventories V to their desired level $\hat{V}$. The level of inventories is a residual in the

[9]See above, footnote 2, and below in the text, where eq. (6) is examined.

goods market (see eq. (12) in table 1, and below in the text), but it is assumed that the relevant economic agents have a desired ratio γ_4 of inventories to expected output[10] and that they will increase both output – see below, eq. (6) – and imports whenever inventories are below the desired level. Thus, inventories play the role of a buffer between supply and demand in the goods market. Furthermore, the presence of inventories in the import adjustment equation might also reflect "speculative" considerations, and this also would justify a different adjustment speed, whence the separate consideration of inventories instead of their inclusion in $M\hat{G}S$ as a further explanatory variable (in any case, this inclusion would tend to obscure their role as buffer discussed above, and, therefore, it is not advisable).

Real exports of goods and services – eq. (5) – adjust to their partial equilibrium level, $X\hat{G}S$, which is determined by (foreign) demand for exports and by a supply constraint. More precisely, foreign demand depends in the usual way on relative competitiveness (given by the ratio of domestic export prices, $PXGS$, to foreign competitors' export prices in world markets, PF), and on world income YF (which can be considered by itself or as a proxy for world demand). Given the effect of foreign demand, the partial equilibrium level of exports reflects the influence of domestic supply represented by the ratio of the amount of capital which is needed (given γ_2 as defined above) to produce current output to the amount of existing capital. In other words, as the utilization of productive capacity approaches its maximum level, the (negative) impact of a supply constraint will be felt on exports.

This specification is not entirely satisfactory: in fact, a more correct treatment of the export sector of the economy should consider separately a supply and a demand equation for exports in a disequilibrium framework.[11] Therefore, a mongrel equation such as

[10] That is, the *desired* level of inventories is related to *expected*, and not to actual, output. The reason for this is the same as that which prompted us to assume that the desired stock of capital is related to expected output rather than to actual output. It would be too naive to adjust stocks (of fixed capital and of inventories) to the level that just matches current output: as we take it that entrepreneurs look ahead in the future, the levels to which these stocks are being adjusted by them are, more plausibly, related to expected output.

[11] Studies in this sense – for the moment limited to a submodel consisting of the export sector only – are being carried out by our research group, with particular

eq. (5) might not give very good results; an alternative might then be, in the meanwhile,[12] to drop the supply constraint and to resort to the traditional pure demand equation.

Eq. (6) specifies the behaviour of the supply side, that is of *real output*, according to two components. Firstly, producers adjust current output towards expected output.[13] Secondly, as already observed in relation to eq. (4), although the level of inventories is a residual in the goods market, we assume that producers have a desired ratio (γ_4) of inventories to expected output and that they will increase output (as well as imports) whenever inventories are below their desired level. This is the role of inventories as a buffer between supply and demand in the goods market. Furthermore, inventories have another fundamental role to play in eq. (6), which is best seen by assuming that they are absent there. If so, given the adaptive expectations mechanism defined in eq. (3), eqs. (3) and (6) would form a self-contained submodel which would determine Y and $\tilde{Y}$ independently of the rest of the model. This undesirable dichotomy is avoided by the presence of inventories in eq. (6), which link Y and $\tilde{Y}$ to the rest of the model through eq. (12).

We wish to stress here the fundamental role of expected output in the model. In addition to being a determinant of the supply of current output, it is also a determinant of the accumulation of real stock (of both fixed capital and inventories), thus capturing the crucial role played by behaviour of firms in an open economy.

We now turn to the price sector of the model.

The *domestic price level* P – eq. (7) – adjusts according to both cost push and monetary factors. The latter, however, do not enter in the determination of the partial equilibrium level $\hat{P}$ (as a monetarist approach would suggest), but rather influence the speed at which the actual price level adjusts to $\hat{P}$, in a way similar to that already

---

regard to the problem of attributing sample data either to the demand or to the supply curve by an "endogenous" procedure (that is, simultaneously with the estimation of the model and not beforehand on *a priori* grounds, as is usually done). See Petit (1979).

[12] That is, until the "ideal" procedure mentioned in the previous footnote is set up.

[13] While so doing, they might run into capacity problems, which are dealt with in eq. (2).

considered for the consumption and investment equations. However, the specification of eq. (7) is also compatible with the presence of m in $\hat{P}$.

The determinants of $\hat{P}$ are both domestic and foreign. The latter are represented by import prices capturing both the effect of a rise in the cost of imported factors of production and a possible "foreign competitiveness effect" according to which domestic producers limit the rise in the prices of their products according to the prices of competing imported goods. The push from domestic costs is represented both by the level of the nominal wage rate W and, with an inverse relationship, by the level of productivity $PROD$ (exogenously given). We allowed for separate influences of wages and productivity rather than considering the familiar ratio $W/PROD$, because they might each influence $\hat{P}$ differently: if there are frictions, non-competitive situations etc., the same proportional increase in W and in $PROD$ does not necessarily leave $\hat{P}$ unaltered.

The nominal wage rate, in turn – eq. (9) – adjusts to a partial equilibrium level $\hat{W}$, which is a direct function of the domestic price level. Institutional factors (as for example an increasing bargaining power by wage-earners unions; a dominant "social pressure" – in Hicks' sense, 1974, ch. III – for rising wages, etc.) suggest for many industrial countries that target nominal wages exceed a level determined only by the domestic price behaviour. These factors have been taken into account by the introduction of a trend among the determinants of $\hat{W}$.[14] Eqs. (7) and (9) considered together represent a wage–price spiral situation and take account, albeit approximately, of the wage indexation effect for the Italian economy.

The introduction of a separate equation for *export prices* – eq. (8) – is justified by the consideration that firms which operate in the competitive sector, i.e. in the sector exposed to foreign competition, fix prices according to different behavioural patterns than those followed in the sheltered sector of the economy.[15] The partial

[14] It is often assumed that this trend coincides with the trend of productivity. But, in our opinion, such an assumption is not necessarily warranted by the institutional factors, etc. which underlie the trend in question. Therefore we allowed the trend in W to be different from the trend in $PROD$.

[15] This feature has been emphasized, though in a context different from ours, by the so-called "Scandinavian model of inflation". A recent reference is Lindbeck ed. (1979).

equilibrium level $PX\hat{G}S$ to which the actual level adjusts is a function of the nominal wage rate, of productivity[16] – the reasons for their separate consideration are the same as in eq. (7) – and of the foreign competition barrier represented by PF, as defined in the export equation, which has a positive effect on the level of $PX\hat{G}S$. We also introduced an influence of P, the domestic price level, in order to take account of two effects. The first is general domestic cost rise (i.e. push from costs which are external to the competitive sector but internal to the economy). The second is a "trade-off" between export prices and domestic prices, in the sense that – insofar as firms produce for both domestic and foreign markets – an increase in domestic prices may induce them to decrease export prices in order to increase their share in the world export market, given that, *ceteris paribus*, the smaller profit from export sales is compensated by the greater profit from domestic sales made possible by the increase in P. Therefore the sign of β_{14} is ambiguous.

Since export prices are charged by domestic producers in foreign markets, there is no reason to believe – contrary to the domestic price level adjustment equation – that the speed of adjustment is a function of a domestic monetary variable. It could, at most, be a function of a world monetary variable, which, however, is not included in the model.

Equation (10) is a policy function and describes the monetary authorities' adjustment of the *proportional rate of change of (nominal) money stock* to its target value $\hat{m}$. The choice – already discussed in section 5.1 – of keeping the monetary and financial sector to a minimal dimension, required to solve the problem of which single variable could least incorrectly represent monetary effects. In addition, such a variable should have been one over which monetary authorities had some form of control. The choice fell on a "quantity" rather than on a "price" variable for both theoretical and empirical considerations. In fact, the choice of a nominal rate of interest, that is of a "price" variable, as the "representative" monetary variable, would have given rise to insurmountable prob-

[16]A more correct specification would have required the consideration of the productivity in the export sector, possibly different from *PROD* appearing in $\hat{P}$. Different productivity behaviour in the sheltered and unsheltered sectors is, in fact, a basic assumption in the already mentioned "Scandinavian model of inflation". At this stage of our work, however, we decided not to introduce this refinement.

lems. Firstly, there is no single interest rate, at least in the Italian experience, which can be considered as representative. Secondly, in many of the years of the sample period, medium and long-term interest rates were pegged by the monetary authorities in order to give stability to the prices of public debt and assimilated bonds.[17] Thirdly, "quantity" effects (such as rationing, in the wide sense, both by monetary authorities and by the banking sector) have often been more important than "price effects". Fourthly, there are the data problems already discussed in footnote 1. Having excluded "price" variables, the proportional rate of change of money stock rather than the money stock itself seemed the most suitable variable, because a "restrictive" monetary policy is usually considered as one which causes a slowing down in the proportional rate of increase of the money stock (and not, or not necessarily, an absolute decrease in the level of this stock); a similar consideration holds for an "expansionary" monetary policy.

Let us now turn to the determinants of $\hat{m}$. The specification of $\hat{m}$ reflects, although in a completely different context, Phillips-type integral and proportional policies (Phillips, 1954; Gandolfo, 1980, Part II, ch. 5, § 1 and ch. 7, § 1). As can be seen from eq. (10.1), a large number of variables enter into this determination, contradicting the well-known one-to-one target-instrument assignment principle. However, our equation aims to reflect the actual behaviour of the Italian monetary authorities over the sample period. Now, due to the lack – already remarked above – of an effective fiscal policy, the monetary authorities have been burdened by a large amount of targets for them to take care of, although obviously not always at the same time and with the same weights (represented by the δ's).

The first two and the last two terms represent balance of payments effects. The reason for considering the goods and services balance separately from the capital movements balance stems from both theoretical and empirical considerations. In the first place, in general these balances might have different weights in the monetary authorities' policy preference function. Secondly, Italian monetary authorities were indeed concerned differently with the goods and services and capital accounts in the period considered.

[17]For a description of Italian monetary policy in the period under consideration, see, for example, Allen and Stevenson (1974, ch. 5), Baffi (1971), Fazio (1979), Hodgman (1974, ch. V), OECD (1973).

Both balances come in as levels and as (proportional) rates of change, because the monetary authorities do not only care about the state (deficit of surplus) of a balance, but also about the direction in which it is changing. The parameters γ_9 and γ_{10} can be interpreted as the ratio of exports to imports and of capital inflows to outflows, respectively, aimed at by the policy-maker, and so give the desired structure of the balance of payments. Therefore, whenever they take on values different from one, the monetary authorities do not wish to have either a goods and services or a capital account equilibrium (or both). The parameters δ_1, δ_2 and δ_5, δ_6 also reflect the sterilization coefficients. The third term in eq. (10.1) represents the anti-inflationary target of monetary policy, which however does not aim at absolute, but at relative price stability. Put differently, the monetary authorities' target rate of inflation is not zero, but is the foreign rate of inflation, proxied by the proportional rate of increase in $PMGS$. The fact that the monetary authorities, *ceteris paribus*, decrease $\hat{m}$ to cope with, say, too high a rate of inflation, reflects their opinion that this decrease should have an effect on P. This opinion, generally shared by monetary authorities, is (in part) validated by eq. (7).

The fourth term in the policy reaction function reflects a real growth target, according to which an expansionary monetary policy is called for whenever the rate of growth of real income falls short of a target rate of growth λ_y.

As we said above, the δ's represent the different weights given to the different targets. The sign is unambiguous for δ_3 and δ_4, whereas the remaining ones, since they also reflect the sterilization coefficients, in principle could have either sign depending on the monetary authorities' attitudes.

Since we are dealing with policy functions, we should notice that no direct exchange rate policy has been introduced. Our sample period covers both fixed exchange rates and managed float, and while the first case is taken care of through the balance of payments components in eq. (10.1), the second would have required the introduction of an additional policy function to explain direct intervention in the foreign exchange market. This function should probably be non-linear, in order to account for the "switch" in behaviour when the fixed exchange rate regime was abandoned for the managed float (the way to deal with such switches is described in Wymer, 1979). However, the period of managed float covered by our sample is too short, and data on the monetary authorities' intervention (directly or through a third party) on the foreign exchange market are not publicly available (this is due, of course, to the fact that one of the ingredients of a well-managed "dirty" float is the secrecy of these interventions, of their timing and amount).

Equation (11) defines the *proportional rate of change of the capital stock* and eq. (12) defines the *change in inventories* as a residual in the goods market.

Finally, let us note that both foreign prices ($PMGS$ and PF) are defined in domestic currency terms, i.e. no exchange-rate is explicitly introduced at this stage. This might seem surprising in a model aimed at the determination of the equilibrium exchange-rate. Actually, both $PMGS$ and PF could be defined as follows

$$PMGS = rPMGS_f, \qquad PF = rPF_f \tag{17}$$

where r is the exchange-rate (defined as units of domestic currency per one unit of foreign currency) and the subscript f denotes magnitudes in foreign currency. Then, the determination of the equilibrium exchange-rate – which is one of the possible simulations for which the model can be used – can be carried out by introducing an exchange-rate equilibrium equation. This will be described in detail in the following chapter.

5.3. Steady-state properties of the model

In order to find a steady-state solution, we assume that the exogenous variables increase at constant growth rates, that is

$$\begin{aligned} &PMGS = PMGS_0 e^{\lambda_1 t}, \qquad PF = PF_0 e^{\lambda_2 t}, \qquad YF = YF_0 e^{\lambda_3 t}, \\ &PROD = PROD_0 e^{\lambda_4 t}, \qquad N = N_0 e^{\lambda_6 t}, \end{aligned} \tag{18}$$

and then we use the method of undetermined coefficients, substituting in eqs. (1)–(12), in addition to (18), the trial functions

$$\begin{aligned} &C = C^* e^{\rho_1 t}, \qquad K = K^* e^{\rho_2 t}, \qquad \tilde{Y} = \tilde{Y}^* e^{\rho_3 t}, \\ &MGS = MGS^* e^{\rho_4 t}, XGS = XGS^* e^{\rho_5 t}, \\ &Y = Y^* e^{\rho_6 t}, \qquad P = P^* e^{\rho_7 t}, \qquad PXGS = PXGS^* e^{\rho_8 t}, \\ &W = W^* e^{\rho_9 t}, \qquad V = V^* e^{\rho_{10} t}, \end{aligned} \tag{19}$$

and, of course, $m = m^*$, $k = k^* = \rho_2$.

The details of the procedure are treated in Appendix I to this chapter; here we state and comment on the results.

Regarding the solution for the steady-state growth rates ρ_i, we must distinguish two cases. The first is that in which we simply solve the system obtained by the undetermined coefficients method. The second is the case in which we impose *additional* constraints, consisting of properties deriving from *a priori* information and of "desiderable" properties that in our opinion the steady-state of our model ought to satisfy. To the first category belongs the well-known standard property according to which in the steady state the rate of growth of the real wage rate should equal the rate of growth of productivity, so that the distributive shares of domestic product do not change, whence: rate of growth of money wage rate = rate of growth of domestic price level + rate of growth of productivity (see, however, what was said above, footnote 14). To the second category belongs the property that in the steady state there should be a full equilibrium in the balance of payments, meaning that exports and imports in value terms are equal (and therefore grow at the same rate) and that the credit and debit entries in the capital movements balance are also equal (so that their ratio is constant[18]). In fact, if it were not so, there would be an ever-increasing surplus (or deficit) in the current account and an ever-increasing deficit (or surplus) in the capital account. This is a situation which is hardly tenable in the long (or even in the medium) run and, therefore, it should be ruled out from the steady-state properties.

The following table summarizes the results (derived in Appendix I) in the two cases.

The real variables (including expected output[19]) grow at a rate which, given the elasticities, depends only on the rest of the world

[18]All this neglects unilateral tranfers. Since they are considered exogenous, to our purposes they can be incorporated in the capital movements, which are also exogenous. Note that full equilibrium requires not only that the value of exports grows at the same rate as the value of imports etc., but also that these values be equal (this implies that the initial values are equal). In fact, if the initial values were not equal, equal growth rates would give even so rise to increasing differences (surpluses or deficits) in absolute terms.

[19]In steady-state, expected output must grow at the same rate as actual output, but the former is *not* equal to the latter. In fact, as we show later, $\tilde{Y}^* \neq Y^*$ and, precisely, $\tilde{Y}^* = [\eta/(\rho_3 + \eta)]Y^*$. Therefore, in steady-state $\tilde{Y}$ is always smaller than

Table 3.
Steady-state growth rates of the endogenous variables.

Variable	Steady-state growth rate	
	First case	Second case
$C, K, \tilde{Y}, MGS, XGS, Y, V$	$\beta_8(\lambda_2 - \lambda_1) + \beta_9\lambda_3 + \beta_8(\delta_5/\delta_1)\lambda_6$	$\beta_8(\lambda_2 - \lambda_1) + \beta_9\lambda_3$
P	λ_1	λ_1
$PXGS$	$\lambda_1 - (\delta_5/\delta_1)\lambda_6$	λ_1
W	$\beta_{18}\lambda_1 + \lambda_5$	$\lambda_1 + \lambda_4$
m, k	0	0

variables that is, on the rate of growth of world output (term $\beta_9\lambda_3$), account being taken of the behaviour of the home country's competitiveness (term $\beta_8(\lambda_2 - \lambda_1) + \beta_8(\delta_5/\delta_1)\lambda_6$ in the first case, and term $\beta_8(\lambda_2 - \lambda_1)$ in the second case. Note that this latter term disappears if we impose the further condition that home prices and foreign competitors' prices on the world market grow at the same rate). This is consistent with the "export-led" way of looking at growth. Not surprisingly, the rate of growth of productivity does not enter directly into the determination of the rate of growth under consideration. This is due to the fact that our model lacks the standard aggregate production function (see above, footnote 3); consequently, the productivity variable (entirely exogenous) enters only into the price-determination equations.

Domestic prices grow at the same rate as foreign prices (represented by import prices), and this is a standard result. Export prices do not grow at the same rate as domestic and import prices unless we impose the additional condition of a full equilibrium in the balance of payments. Since in the model export prices are endogenously determined and are not identified with domestic prices, these variables may have different growth rates. If, however, we constrain the value of exports to grow at the same rate as the value of imports, then – since exports and imports in real terms grow at the same

Y, and this is the mechanism which engenders the growth of output. In fact, as $\tilde{Y} < Y$, expectations are continually revised upwards according to eq. (3) and, consequently, production is increased according to eq. (6). This allows output to increase to match the increase in demand.

rate – export prices must grow at the same rate as import prices and hence as domestic prices.

Finally, money wages grow at the exogenous rate λ_5 plus the rate of growth of domestic prices weighted by the elasticity β_{18}. Note that if we believe that the exogenous rate λ_5 is the same as the rate of growth of productivity (λ_4), then β_{18} must equal 1 for the second case in the table to be possible.

As we know (see ch. 2, para. 2.2.1) the solution for the steady-state usually gives restrictions on certain parameters. In the first case these restrictions turn out to be

$$\beta_5 + \beta_6 + \beta_7 = 1, \tag{20}$$

$$(\beta_{11} + \beta_{12}\beta_{18} - 1)\lambda_1 + \beta_{12}\lambda_5 - \beta_{13}\lambda_4 = 0, \tag{21}$$

$$(\beta_{14} + \beta_{16}\beta_{18} - 1)\lambda_1 + \beta_{16}\lambda_5 + \beta_{15}\lambda_2 - \beta_{17}\lambda_4 = 0. \tag{22}$$

In the second case we obtain the further restriction

$$\beta_{18} = (\lambda_1 + \lambda_4 - \lambda_5)/\lambda_1, \tag{23}$$

and so (21) and (22) become

$$(\beta_{11} + \beta_{12} - 1)\lambda_1 + (\beta_{12} - \beta_{13})\lambda_4 = 0, \tag{21$'$}$$

$$(\beta_{14} + \beta_{15} - 1)\lambda_1 + (\beta_{16} - \beta_{17})\lambda_4 + \beta_{14}\lambda_2 = 0. \tag{22$'$}$$

A further formal discussion of the restrictions is contained in Appendix I, section I.2. Here we note that restriction (20) is a well-known homogeneity condition, namely, that the import function must be homogeneous of the first degree with respect to the components of total sales (consumption, investment, exports). Eqs. (21) and (22) are cross-equation restrictions involving the various elasticities appearing in the price and wage equations of the model. A very strong restriction is eq. (23), which completely determines β_{18} in terms of the exogenous growth rates.

This is due to the fact that if we want money wages to grow at a rate equal to the sum of the growth rates of domestic prices and of productivity, then no degree of freedom is left to the elasticity β_{18}. Note that, as we observed above, if one believes that λ_5 is equal to λ_4, then obviously $\beta_{18} = 1$. But, as we remarked in the exposition of the model, the exogenous trend term in money wages need not be the same as the productivity trend. If the restriction on β_{18} is felt to be too strong, the standard assumption that distribution is constant in the long run can be dropped; in this case, β_{18} is left free and distribution will shift in favour of, or against, wage earners according to

$$\beta_{18}\lambda_1 - \lambda_1 - \lambda_4 + \lambda_5 \gtrless 0. \tag{24}$$

This completes our discussion of the steady-state growth rates. Regarding the steady-state levels (starred coefficients), their expressions are rather complicated and we refer the reader to Appendix I, section I.3. Here we limit ourselves to comment on the solution for m^*, which is

$$m^* = \delta_4(\lambda_y - \rho_6) - \delta_1 \log \gamma_9 - \delta_5 \log \gamma_{10}. \tag{25}$$

The steady-state growth rate of the money supply depends on two elements: firstly, on the fact that there is a discrepancy between the monetary authorities' target growth rate in real output and its steady-state growth rate. The attempt to eliminate this discrepancy induces a steady monetary expansion (or restriction, if $\lambda_y < \rho_6$). Secondly it depends on the fact that the target structure of the balance of payments is different from the full equilibrium one (that is, γ_9 and γ_{10} are different from 1) so that, although in full equilibrium the balance of payments has no impact on the domestic monetary base, all the same the monetary authorities modify their policy variable in relation to the desired structure.

It can be shown that γ_9 and γ_{10} cannot be entirely arbitrary. In fact, although the monetary authorities may wish to have a balance of payments structure different from the full equilibrium one, it would be unreasonable to suppose that they also wish to have an external disequilibrium (deficit or surplus) in the long run (that is, in steady-state). Therefore the structure is constrained by the fact that there must be an overall equilibrium in the balance of payments, that is – since the growth rates cancel out –

$$PXGS^*XGS^* - PMGS_0MGS^* + F_0^A - F_0^P = 0, \tag{26}$$

where F_0^A and F_0^P are the initial levels (in absolute value) of capital inflows and outflows[20] respectively. Now, if we substitute

[20] Including unilateral transfers. See above, footnote 18.

$PXGS^*XGS^* = \gamma_9 PMGS_0 MGS^*$ and $F_0^A = \gamma_{10} F_0^P$, we obtain

$$a\gamma_9 + b\gamma_{10} = 1, \qquad a + b = 1, \qquad a > 0, \quad b > 0, \qquad (26.1)$$

where $a \equiv PMGS_0 MGS^*/(PMGS_0 MGS^* + F_0^P)$, and $b \equiv F_0^P/(PMGS_0 MGS^* + F_0^P)$.

Since a negative steady-state growth rate of the money supply would imply a long-run zero money supply, which is not economically meaningful, we must assume that either $\lambda_y > \rho_6$ or $(-\delta_1 \log \gamma_9 - \delta_5 \log \gamma_{10}) > 0$ or both.

5.4. Comparative dynamics,[21] stability and sensitivity

The comparative dynamics of the steady-state growth rates is immediately obtained from the results reported in table 3. For example, a higher growth rate of import prices implies a lower growth rate of the real variables and a higher growth rate of the price and wage variables. On the contrary, higher growth rates of foreign competitors' prices and of world income imply a higher growth rate of the real variables and have no effect on the price and wage variables. These results are quite obvious and are consistent with the "export-led" nature of our model. In fact, the growth rate of domestic prices and of export prices is the same as the growth rate of import prices. An increase in the growth rate of export prices reduces the competitiveness of home products on foreign markets, hence the lower growth rate of exports and of all the other real variables. An opposite effect occurs when the growth rate of foreign competitors' prices increases; also an increase in the growth rate of world income has a favourable effect on exports.

Let us now consider the comparative dynamics of the steady state levels. The interesting thing is to examine the effects of changes in the policy parameters. The solution for the said levels obtained in Appendix I, section I.3, has been written in such a way that m^*, as

[21]As we are dealing with comparative dynamics, in what follows expressions such as "a higher value of x implies a lower value of y" or "an increase in x causes a decrease in y" etc., should be interpreted as meaning "consider a steady state in which the value of x is higher than in another steady state; then the value of y in the former steady state is lower than in the latter". For simplicity of exposition we use the first type of expressions, which are standard in the literature.

given by eq. (25), appears in all the expressions for these levels. Therefore, by the chain rule, it is easy to obtain the partial derivatives of the steady state levels with respect to the weights δ_4, δ_1, δ_5 and to the targets λ_y, γ_9, γ_{10}. Unfortunately, all the partial derivatives under consideration have ambiguous signs and, consequently, the best that we can do is to make taxonomic statements of the type "if the product of the elasticity of prices with respect to wages by the elasticity of wages with respect to prices is smaller (greater) than one, then an increase in the steady-state growth rate of the money supply implies an increase (decrease) in the steady-state levels of the price and wage variables, P^*, $PXGS^*$, W^*". We prefer not to bore the reader with a long list of similar (and of more complicated) statements, which are expressed in a formal way in Appendix I, section I.4. Rather, we would like here to make some general considerations, concerning the fact that not all the policy parameters have an influence on the steady-state levels. Actually, the weights δ_2, δ_3 and δ_6 do not appear in the expressions for these levels. This is as it should be, because, in the steady-state, the terms of the policy function to which these weights apply – see eq. (10.1) in table 1 – disappear. Thus in this function there are both terms which have only a short-run impact and terms which have a long-run, as well as short-run, impact. The latter are those concerning the discrepancy between the actual and the desired structure of the balance of payments, and the difference between the target and the actual growth rate of real output. The former are those concerning the rate of change of the said discrepancy, and the difference between the target and the actual rate of inflation (which disappear in the steady state).

Finally, as regards *stability analysis* and *sensitivity*, these require the previous linear approximation of the model about the steady state and its reduction to normal form. These are purely technical matters and are worked out in Appendix II to this chapter. Once this linear approximation has been performed, however, no purely qualitative results can be obtained from a 12×12 differential equations system. Therefore the stability and sensitivity analyses have been postponed to the following chapter, after the numerical estimates of the parameters have been obtained.

Appendix I. Derivation of the steady-state

I.1. Introduction

By substituting (18) and (19) in eqs. (1)–(12) of the text, we obtain

$$\rho_1 = \alpha_1[\log\gamma_1 + \beta_1\rho_6 + \beta_2\log P^* - \beta_2\log PMGS_0 + \beta_2(\rho_7 - \lambda_1)t + \log Y^* + \rho_6 t - \log C^* - \rho_1 t] + \alpha_2 m^*, \quad \text{(I.1)}$$

$$0 = \alpha_3[\alpha'(\gamma_2\tilde{Y}^*/K^*)e^{(\rho_3-\rho_2)t} - \alpha' - \rho_2] + \alpha_4 m^*, \quad \text{(I.2)}$$

$$\rho_3\tilde{Y}^* e^{\rho_3 t} = \eta(Y^* e^{\rho_6 t} - \tilde{Y}^* e^{\rho_3 t}), \quad \text{(I.3)}$$

$$\rho_4 = \alpha_5[\log\gamma_3 + \beta_3\log P^* - \beta_3\log PMGS_0 + \beta_3(\rho_7 - \lambda_1)t + \beta_4\log\gamma_2 + \beta_4\log Y^* - \beta_4\log K^* + \beta_4(\rho_6 - \rho_2)t + \beta_5\log C^* + \beta_5\rho_1 t + \beta_6\log\rho_2 + \beta_6\log K^* + \beta_6\rho_2 t + \beta_7\log XGS^* + \beta_7\rho_5 t - \log MGS^* - \rho_4 t] + \alpha_6[\log\gamma_4 + \log\tilde{Y}^* - \log V^* + (\rho_3 - \rho_{10})t], \quad \text{(I.4)}$$

$$\rho_5 = \alpha_7[\log\gamma_5 - \beta_8\log PXGS^* + \beta_8\log PF_0 - \beta_8(\rho_8 - \lambda_2)t + \beta_9\log YF_0 + \beta_9\lambda_3 t - \beta_{10}\log\gamma_2 - \beta_{10}\log Y^* + \beta_{10}\log K^* - \beta_{10}(\rho_6 - \rho_2)t - \log XGS^* - \rho_5 t], \quad \text{(I.5)}$$

$$\rho_6 = \alpha_8[\log\tilde{Y}^* - \log Y^* + (\rho_3 - \rho_6)t] + \alpha_9[\log\gamma_4 + \log\tilde{Y}^* - \log V^* + (\rho_3 - \rho_{10})t], \quad \text{(I.6)}$$

$$\rho_7 = \alpha_{10}(\log\gamma_6 + \beta_{11}\log PMGS_0 + \beta_{11}\lambda_1 t + \beta_{12}\log W^* + \beta_{12}\rho_9 t - \beta_{13}\log PROD_0 - \beta_{13}\lambda_4 t - \log P^* - \rho_7 t) + \alpha_{11}m^*, \quad \text{(I.7)}$$

$$\rho_8 = \alpha_{12}(\log\gamma_7 + \beta_{14}\log P^* + \beta_{14}\rho_7 t + \beta_{15}\log PF_0 + \beta_{15}\lambda_2 t + \beta_{16}\log W^* + \beta_{16}\rho_9 t - \beta_{17}\log PROD_0 - \beta_{17}\lambda_4 t - \log PXGS^* - \rho_8 t), \quad \text{(I.8)}$$

$$\rho_9 = \alpha_{13}(\log \gamma_8 + \beta_{18}\log P^* + \beta_{18}\rho_7 t + \lambda_5 t - \log W^* - \rho_9 t), \tag{I.9}$$

$$\begin{aligned} 0 = \alpha_{14}[& \delta_1 \log PXGS^* + \delta_1 \log XGS^* \\ & - \delta_1 \log \gamma_9 - \delta_1 \log PMGS_0 \\ & - \delta_1 \log MGS^* + \delta_1(\rho_8 + \rho_5 - \lambda_1 - \rho_4)t + \delta_2(\rho_8 + \rho_5 \\ & - \lambda_1 - \rho_4) - \delta_3(\rho_7 - \lambda_1) + \delta_4(\lambda_y - \rho_6) - \delta_5 \log \gamma_{10} \\ & + \delta_5 \log N_0 + \delta_5\lambda_6 t + \delta_6\lambda_6 - m^*], \end{aligned} \tag{I.10}$$

$$\rho_2 = k^*, \tag{I.11}$$

$$\begin{aligned} \rho_{10} V^* e^{\rho_{10} t} = & Y^* e^{\rho_6 t} + MGS^* e^{\rho_4 t} - C^* e^{\rho_1 t} - \rho_2 K^* e^{\rho_2 t} \\ & - XGS^* e^{\rho_5 t}. \end{aligned} \tag{I.12}$$

The above system will be identically satisfied if, and only if, the two following sets of equations are satisfied:

Set 1

$$\beta_2(\rho_7 - \lambda_1) + \rho_6 - \rho_1 = 0, \tag{I.1'}$$

$$\rho_3 = \rho_2, \tag{I.2'}$$

$$\rho_6 = \rho_3, \tag{I.3'}$$

$$\begin{aligned} \alpha_5[& \beta_3(\rho_7 - \lambda_1) + \beta_4(\rho_6 - \rho_2) + \beta_5\rho_1 + \beta_6\rho_2 + \beta_7\rho_5 - \rho_4] \\ & + \alpha_6(\rho_3 - \rho_{10}) = 0, \end{aligned} \tag{I.4'}$$

$$\beta_8(\lambda_2 - \rho_8) + \beta_9\lambda_3 + \beta_{10}(\rho_2 - \rho_6) - \rho_5 = 0, \tag{I.5'}$$

$$\alpha_8(\rho_3 - \rho_6) + \alpha_9(\rho_3 - \rho_{10}) = 0, \tag{I.6'}$$

$$\beta_{11}\lambda_1 + \beta_{12}\rho_9 - \beta_{13}\lambda_4 - \rho_7 = 0, \tag{I.7'}$$

$$\beta_{14}\rho_7 + \beta_{15}\lambda_2 + \beta_{16}\rho_9 - \beta_{17}\lambda_4 - \rho_8 = 0, \tag{I.8'}$$

$$\beta_{18}\rho_7 + \lambda_5 - \rho_9 = 0, \tag{I.9'}$$

$$\delta_1(\rho_8 + \rho_5 - \lambda_1 - \rho_4) + \delta_5\lambda_6 = 0, \tag{I.10'}$$

$$\rho_2 = k^* \text{ (for record)}, \tag{I.11'}$$

$$\rho_{10} = \rho_6 = \rho_4 = \rho_1 = \rho_2 = \rho_5. \tag{I.12'}$$

Set 2

$$\log C^* - \log Y^* - \beta_2 \log P^* = \log\gamma_1 + \beta_1\rho_6 - \beta_2 \log PMGS_0 - \rho_1/\alpha_1 + (\alpha_2/\alpha_1)m^*, \quad (I.1'')$$

$$\tilde{Y}^*/K^* = (\alpha' + \rho_2)/\alpha'\gamma_2 - (\alpha_4/\alpha_3\alpha'\gamma_2)m^*, \quad (I.2'')$$

$$\tilde{Y}^* - [\eta/(\rho_3 + \eta)]Y^* = 0, \quad (I.3'')$$

$$\beta_5 \log C^* + \beta_6 \log K^* - \log MGS^* - \beta_4 \log(K^*/Y^*) - (\alpha_6/\alpha_5)\log(V^*/\tilde{Y}^*) + \beta_7 \log XGS^* + \beta_3 \log P^* = \rho_4/\alpha_5 - \log\gamma_3 + \beta_3 \log PMGS_0 - \beta_4 \log\gamma_2 - \beta_6 \log\rho_2 - (\alpha_6/\alpha_5)\log\gamma_4, \quad (I.4'')$$

$$\log XGS^* - \beta_{10} \log(K^*/Y^*) + \beta_8 \log PXGS^* = -\rho_5/\alpha_7 + \log\gamma_5 + \beta_8 \log PF_0 + \beta_9 \log YF_0 - \beta_{10} \log\gamma_2, \quad (I.5'')$$

$$\log V^* - \log\tilde{Y}^* + (\alpha_8/\alpha_9)\log(Y^*/\tilde{Y}^*) = -\rho_6/\alpha_9 + \log\gamma_4, \quad (I.6'')$$

$$\beta_{12} \log W^* - \log P^* = \rho_7/\alpha_{10} - \log\gamma_6 - \beta_{11} \log PMGS_0 + \beta_{13} \log PROD_0 - (\alpha_{11}/\alpha_{10})m^*, \quad (I.7'')$$

$$\beta_{16} \log W^* + \beta_{14} \log P^* - \log PXGS^* = \rho_8/\alpha_{12} - \log\gamma_7 - \beta_{15} \log PF_0 + \beta_{17} \log PROD_0, \quad (I.8'')$$

$$-\log W^* + \beta_{18} \log P^* = \rho_9/\alpha_{13} - \log\gamma_8, \quad (I.9'')$$

$$m^* - \delta_1 \log(PXGS^*XGS^*/PMGS_0 MGS^*) = -\delta_1 \log\gamma_9 - \delta_5 \log\gamma_{10} + \delta_2(\rho_8 + \rho_5 - \lambda_1 - \rho_4) - \delta_3(\rho_7 - \lambda_1) + \delta_4(\lambda_y - \rho_6) + \delta_5 \log N_0 + \delta_6\lambda_6, \quad (I.10'')$$

$$\rho_2 = k^*, \quad (I.11'')$$

$$\rho_{10}V^* = Y^* + MGS^* - C^* - \rho_2 K^* - XGS^*. \quad (I.12'')$$

We now solve set 1 and then set 2. It is convenient to follow this order because the growth rates ρ_i also appear in set 2, whereas the initial levels do not appear in set 1, in which the only unknowns are the ρ_i.

I.2. Solution for the steady-state growth rates

Although set 1 is a simultaneous system, not all the unknowns appear in each equation. Therefore a step by step procedure is more convenient than a simultaneous approach.

Equations (I.2′), (I.3′), (I.12′) state that all the "real" variables must grow at the same rate (incidentally, note that eq. (I.6′) is then identically satisfied). Eq. (I.10′) gives $\rho_8 = \lambda_1 - (\delta_5/\delta_1)\lambda_6$; by substituting in eq. (I.5′) and solving for ρ_5 we find that the common rate of growth of the variables is $\beta_8(\lambda_2 - \lambda_1) + \beta_9\lambda_3 + \beta_8(\delta_5/\delta_1)\lambda_6$.

Equation (I.1′), as $\rho_6 = \rho_1$, yields $\rho_7 = \lambda_1$. Then eq. (I.4′), taking account of the results so far obtained, gives a constraint on some elasticities appearing in the import function, that is $\beta_5 + \beta_6 + \beta_7 = 1$. From eq. (I.9′) we obtain $\rho_9 = \beta_{18}\lambda_1 + \lambda_5$.

The growth rates are completely determined; therefore, eqs. (I.7′) and (I.8′) yield constraints on the elasticities appearing in them, that is

$$(\beta_{11} + \beta_{12}\beta_{18} - 1)\lambda_1 + \beta_{12}\lambda_5 - \beta_{13}\lambda_4 = 0,$$

$$(\beta_{14} + \beta_{16}\beta_{18} - 1)\lambda_1 + \beta_{16}\lambda_5 + \beta_{15}\lambda_2 - \beta_{17}\lambda_4 = 0.$$

We shall now consider the consequences of imposing the additional constraints from outside the model. The first is $\rho_9 = \lambda_1 + \lambda_4$: it follows that β_{18} is completely constrained, i.e. $\beta_{18} = (\lambda_1 + \lambda_4 - \lambda_5)/\lambda_1$; substitution in the above two constraints gives

$$(\beta_{11} + \beta_{12} - 1)\lambda_1 + (\beta_{12} - \beta_{13})\lambda_4 = 0,$$

$$(\beta_{14} + \beta_{16} - 1)\lambda_1 + (\beta_{16} - \beta_{17})\lambda_4 + \beta_{15}\lambda_2 = 0.$$

Note that the same result would be obtained if we assumed $\lambda_5 = \lambda_4$ (whence $\beta_{18} = 1$, etc.).

The second outside constraint implies $\lambda_6 = 0$; therefore the common rate of growth of the real variables reduces to $\beta_8(\lambda_2 - \lambda_1) + \beta_9\lambda_3$, and the rate of growth of export prices becomes λ_1.

Further additional constraints might be introduced: for example, that home prices grow at the same rate as foreign competitors' prices on world markets (whence $\lambda_1 = \lambda_2$, and the common rate of growth of the real variables becomes $\beta_9\lambda_3$); that domestic output grows at the same rate as world output ($\beta_9\lambda_3 = \lambda_3$, whence $\beta_9 = 1$); that W and $PROD$ do not enter separately in eqs. (7.1) and (8.1) of the text, but only their ratio $W/PROD$ does (whence $\beta_{12} = \beta_{13}$, $\beta_{16} = \beta_{17}$, and so $\beta_{11} + \beta_{12} = 1$, $\beta_{14} + \beta_{15} + \beta_{16} = 1$); etc. But we do not think it fruitful to pursue this line any further.

I.3. Solution for the steady-state initial levels

The same remark applies to set 2 as to set 1. For simplicity's sake we consider only the situation in which the additional condition of a full equilibrium in the balance of payments is imposed. This implies

$$PXGS^*XGS^* = PMGS_0 MGS^*, \qquad N_0 = 1, \quad \lambda_6 = 0. \tag{I.13}$$

Taking account of the results concerning the steady-state growth rates, eq. (I.10″) gives

$$m^* = -\delta_1 \log \gamma_9 - \delta_5 \log \gamma_{10} + \delta_4(\lambda_y - \rho_6). \tag{I.14}$$

Therefore in the equations that follow m^* is to be considered as given by eq. (I.14). The various ρ_i are, of course, given by the solution of set 1. We now observe that eqs. (I.7″) and (I.9″) form a subset which determines $\log W^*$ and $\log P^*$. Letting

$$\begin{aligned} a_1 &\equiv \rho_7/\alpha_{10} - \log \gamma_6 - \beta_{11} \log PMGS_0 + \beta_{13} \log PROD_0 \\ &\quad - (\alpha_{11}/\alpha_{10})m^*, \\ a_2 &\equiv \rho_9/\alpha_{13} - \log \gamma_8, \end{aligned} \tag{I.15}$$

we obtain

$$\begin{aligned} \log W^* &= (a_1\beta_{18} + a_2)/(\beta_{12}\beta_{18} - 1), \\ \log P^* &= (a_2\beta_{12} + a_1)/(\beta_{12}\beta_{18} - 1). \end{aligned} \tag{I.16}$$

From eq. (I.8″) we then have

$$\begin{aligned} \log PXGS^* = &-\rho_8/\alpha_{12} + \log \gamma_7 \\ &+ \beta_{15} \log PF_0 - \beta_{17} \log PROD_0 \\ &+ \beta_{16}(a_1\beta_{18} + a_2)/(\beta_{12}\beta_{18} - 1) \\ &+ \beta_{14}(a_2\beta_{12} + a_1)/(\beta_{12}\beta_{18} - 1). \end{aligned} \tag{I.17}$$

Since $\tilde{Y}^* = [\eta/(\rho_3+\eta)]Y^*$ from eq. (I.3″), substitution in eq. (I.2″) yields

$$Y^*/K^* = \frac{(\alpha' + \rho_2)(\rho_3+\eta)}{\alpha'\gamma_2\eta} - \frac{\alpha_4(\rho_3+\eta)}{\alpha_3\alpha'\gamma_2\eta} m^*, \tag{I.18}$$

whence

$$K^*/Y^* = \frac{\alpha_3\alpha'\gamma_2\eta}{\alpha_3(\alpha'+\rho_2)(\rho_3+\eta) - \alpha_4(\rho_3+\eta)m^*}. \tag{I.18.1}$$

It can now be seen that eq. (I.5″) immediately determines $\log XGS^*$, because K^*/Y^* and $PXGS^*$ are known from eqs. (I.18.1) and (I.17) respectively. Therefore

$$\begin{aligned}\log XGS^* = & -\rho_5/\alpha_7 + \log\gamma_5 + \beta_8(1-\beta_{15})\log PF_0 \\ & + \beta_9 \log YF_0 + \beta_8\rho_8/\alpha_{12} \\ & - \beta_8 \log\gamma_7 + \beta_8\beta_{17}\log PROD_0 \\ & - \beta_8\beta_{16}(a_1\beta_{18}+a_2)/(\beta_{12}\beta_{18}-1) \\ & - \beta_8\beta_{14}(a_2\beta_{12}+a_1)/(\beta_{12}\beta_{18}-1) \\ & + \beta_{10}\log\{\alpha_3\alpha'\eta/[\alpha_3(\alpha'+\rho_2)(\rho_3+\eta) \\ & - \alpha_4(\rho_3+\eta)m^*]\}. \end{aligned} \tag{I.19}$$

From eq. (1.6″) we obtain, by using eq. (I.3″),

$$\log(V^*/Y^*) = -\rho_6/\alpha_9 + \log\gamma_4 + \frac{\alpha_8+\alpha_9}{\alpha_9}\log[\eta/(\rho_3+\eta)]. \tag{I.20}$$

Since $\log P^*$ is known from eqs. (I.16), eq. (I.1″) yields

$$\begin{aligned}\log(C^*/Y^*) = & \log\gamma_1 + \beta_1\rho_6 - \beta_2\log PMGS_0 - \rho_1/\alpha_1 \\ & + (\alpha_2/\alpha_1)m^* + \beta_2(a_2\beta_{12}+a_1)/(\beta_{12}\beta_{18}-1). \end{aligned} \tag{I.21}$$

Consider now eq. (I.4″): by adding and subtracting $(\beta_5 + \beta_6)\log Y^*$ one obtains

$$\begin{aligned}(\beta_5+\beta_6)\log Y^* = & \rho_4/\alpha_5 - \log\gamma_3 + \beta_3\log PMGS_0 \\ & - \beta_4\log\gamma_2 - \beta_6\log\rho_2 \\ & - (\alpha_6/\alpha_5)\log\gamma_4 - (\alpha_6/\alpha_5)\log[\eta/(\rho_3+\eta)] \\ & - \beta_5\log(C^*/Y^*) + (\beta_4-\beta_6)\log(K^*/Y^*) \\ & + (\alpha_6/\alpha_5)\log(V^*/Y^*) - \beta_7\log XGS^* \\ & + \log MGS^* - \beta_3\log P^*. \end{aligned} \tag{I.22}$$

Note that $\log(C^*/Y^*)$, $\log(K^*/Y^*)$, $\log(V^*/Y^*)$, $\log XGS^*$, $\log P^*$ are known from eqs. (I.21), (I.18.1), (I.20), (I.19), (I.16) respectively. Furthermore, MGS^* is also known, because from eq. (I.13) we obtain

$$MGS^* = PXGS^*XGS^*/PMGS_0, \tag{I.13.1}$$

and $PXGS^*$, XGS^* are given by eqs. (I.17) and (I.19) respectively. Thus the right-hand side of eq. (I.22) is a known constant, henceforth called A. Therefore we have

$$\log Y^* = A/(\beta_5 + \beta_6), \tag{I.23}$$

which yields a unique positive value for Y^*:

$$Y^* = \exp[A/(\beta_5 + \beta_6)]. \tag{I.23.1}$$

Considering eqs. (I.3″), (I.18.1), (I.20), (I.21) we obtain

$$\tilde{Y}^* = [\eta/(\rho_3 + \eta)]\exp[A/(\beta_5 + \beta_6)], \tag{I.3″.1}$$

$$K^* = \frac{\alpha_3\alpha'\eta}{\alpha_3(\alpha' + \rho_2)(\rho_3 + \eta) - \alpha_4(\rho_3 + \eta)m^*} \times \exp[A/(\beta_5 + \beta_6)], \tag{I.18.2}$$

$$\log V^* = A/(\beta_5 + \beta_6) + \text{r.h.s. of eq. (I.20)}, \tag{I.20.1}$$

$$\log C^* = A/(\beta_5 + \beta_6) + \text{r.h.s. of eq. (I.21)}, \tag{I.21.1}$$

This completes the solution for the steady-state levels. As we know, this solution usually gives restrictions on certain parameters. In our case, the restriction comes from eq. (I.12″): in fact, if in this equation we substitute the values found above for V^*, Y^*, etc., we obtain a relation which must be satisfied by the parameters. However, since this relation involves practically all the parameters of the model, it does not seem possible to derive any economically meaningful restriction from it. From the formal point of view, the fact that we obtain a restriction is due to the fact that system (I.1″)–(I.12″), which is determined, becomes overdetermined once we impose the additional condition (I.13); therefore, one of the equations of the system must be functionally dependent on all the others.

The solution that we have found can be simplified if we assume that λ_y, the authorities' target rate of growth of output, coincides with the steady-state growth rate, that is $\lambda_y = \rho_6$, or if we assume that they wish to have a fully balanced external equilibrium (that is, $\gamma_9 = \gamma_{10} = 1$). In the first case the steady-state rate of growth of the money supply becomes

$$m^* = -\delta_1 \log \gamma_9 - \delta_5 \log \gamma_{10}, \tag{I.14.1}$$

and, if we further assume that in the steady-state the rate of growth of the money supply must equal the rate of growth of nominal income (that is, $m^* = \rho_7 + \rho_6$) we obtain the following restriction

$$-\delta_1 \log \gamma_9 - \delta_5 \log \gamma_{10} = (1 - \beta_8)\lambda_1 + \beta_8\lambda_2 + \beta_9\lambda_3. \tag{I.14.2}$$

Note, however, that the condition that the rate of growth of the money supply equals the rate of growth of nominal income is *not* a result of the model (in the sense that it derives from the steady-state solution or must be imposed in order to obtain this solution), but belongs to the category of additional conditions discussed in the text. Then, since our model does not require this condition for its consistency, and since we have already imposed other additional conditions, we can dispense with the condition under consideration. Also note that the model only determines the rate of growth of the money supply, but not its level. From the formal point of view, these results are due to the fact that money supply and demand nowhere appear[22] in the model. From the economic point of view they reflect our opinion, already discussed in the text, that what is important is not the *level* of the money supply and its changes, but its proportional *rate of change* (and changes in this rate).

In the second case, the steady-state rate of growth of the money supply becomes

$$m^* = \delta_4(\lambda_y - \rho_6), \tag{I.14.3}$$

and if we further assume $m^* = \rho_7 + \rho_6$, we obtain the following restriction

$$\delta_4\lambda_y = \delta_4[\beta_8(\lambda_2 - \lambda_1) + \beta_9\lambda_3] + (1 - \beta_8)\lambda_1 + \beta_8\lambda_2 + \beta_9\lambda_3, \tag{I.14.4}$$

to which the same comments apply as to eq. (I.14.2). Furthermore, if

[22] If one considers a traditional money supply = money demand equation (the latter depending on the rate of interest and on money income with the usual homogeneity property) then – as the rate of interest is constant in the steady state – the condition that nominal income must grow at the same rate as money supply follows.

we accepted the condition $m^* = \rho_7 + \rho_6$, then m^* would lose its role as policy variable. In other words, in steady-state no monetary policy would be possible.

I.4. Comparative dynamics results

The comparative dynamics of steady-state growth rates is immediate and has already been expounded in the text. Let us now consider the comparative dynamics of the steady-state levels.

We have to compute the partial derivatives of these levels with respect to the parameters appearing in the monetary function. These parameters are present in the expressions for the levels only through the presence of m^* as given by eq. (I.14), and, therefore, only $\delta_1, \delta_4, \delta_5, \gamma_9, \gamma_{10}, \lambda_y$ influence the steady-state levels. By the chain rule, we have $\partial(\text{level})/\partial(\text{parameter}) = [\partial(\text{level})/\partial m^*]\cdot[\partial m^*/\partial(\text{parameter})]$.

Since the partial derivatives $\partial m^*/\partial(\text{parameter})$ are quite easily computed from eq. (I.14), the only problem is to compute the partial derivatives $\partial(\text{level})/\partial m^*$. The result is

$$\frac{\partial \log C^*}{\partial m^*} = \frac{\partial \log Y^*}{\partial m^*} + \alpha_2/\alpha_1 + (\alpha_{11}/\alpha_{10})\beta_2/(1-\beta_{12}\beta_{18}), \tag{I.24}$$

$$\frac{\partial \log K^*}{\partial m^*} = \frac{\partial \log Y^*}{\partial m^*} + q, \tag{I.25}$$

$$\frac{\partial \log \tilde{Y}^*}{\partial m^*} = \frac{\partial \log Y^*}{\partial m^*}, \tag{I.26}$$

$$\frac{\partial \log MGS^*}{\partial m^*} = (1-\beta_8)s + \beta_{10}q, \tag{I.27}$$

$$\frac{\partial \log XGS^*}{\partial m^*} = -\beta_8 s + \beta_{10}q, \tag{I.28}$$

$$\begin{aligned}\frac{\partial \log Y^*}{\partial m^*} = (\beta_5+\beta_6)^{-1}\{&-\beta_5(\alpha_2/\alpha_1)\\ &-(\beta_5\beta_2+\beta_3)(\alpha_{11}/\alpha_{10})/(1-\beta_{12}\beta_{18})\\ &+[\beta_4-\beta_6+\beta_{10}(1-\beta_7)]q\\ &+[1-(1-\beta_7)\beta_8]s\},\end{aligned} \tag{I.29}$$

$$\frac{\partial \log P^*}{\partial m^*} = (\alpha_{11}/\alpha_{10})/(1 - \beta_{12}\beta_{18}), \tag{I.30}$$

$$\frac{\partial \log PXGS^*}{\partial m^*} = \acute{s}, \tag{I.31}$$

$$\frac{\partial \log W^*}{\partial m^*} = (\alpha_{11}/\alpha_{10})\beta_{18}/(1 - \beta_{12}\beta_{18}), \tag{I.32}$$

$$\frac{\partial \log V^*}{\partial m^*} = \frac{\partial \log Y^*}{\partial m^*}, \tag{I.33}$$

where

$$q \equiv \alpha_4(\rho_3 + \eta)/[\alpha_3(\alpha' + \rho_2)(\rho_3 + \eta) - \alpha_4(\rho_3 + \eta)m^*],$$

$$s \equiv (\beta_{16}\beta_{18} + \beta_{14})[(\alpha_{11}/\alpha_{10})/(1 - \beta_{12}\beta_{18})]. \tag{I.34}$$

Since the denominator of q is the same as the denominator of eq. (I.18.1) above, it must be positive, because K^*/Y^* must be positive for the model to have an economically meaningful solution. Therefore we assume $q > 0$. The sign of s depends on the sign of $(1 - \beta_{12}\beta_{18})$. Now, stability considerations, although of a partial nature only, seem to require that $\beta_{12}\beta_{18} < 1$. In fact, if the product of the elasticity of prices with respect to wages by the elasticity of wages with respect to prices were greater than one, then, *ceteris paribus*, an explosive wage–price spiral would occur.[23] In any case if we do not wish to make the assumption $s > 0$, we can always make conditional statements of the type given in the text.

The assumptions $q > 0$, $s > 0$, are not enough, however, to enable us to derive unambiguous comparative dynamics results. In fact, they allow us to determine the effects of a change in m^* on the steady-state levels of the price and wage variables ($\partial \log P^*/\partial m^*$, $\partial \log PXGS^*/\partial m^*$, $\partial \log W^*/\partial m^*$ are all positive, and this is a sensible result), but they are not sufficient to determine the signs of the other partial derivatives. It is likely that if we examined the

[23] Formally, consider the subsystem

$$\mathrm{D}\log P = \alpha_{10}[\log W^{\beta_{12}} - \log P],$$

$$\mathrm{D}\log W = \alpha_{13}[\log P^{\beta_{18}} - \log W],$$

which has the characteristic equation $\mu^2 + (\alpha_{10} + \alpha_{13})\mu + \alpha_{10}\alpha_{13}(1 - \beta_{12}\beta_{18}) = 0$. The necessary and sufficient condition for this subsystem to be stable is $1 - \beta_{12}\beta_{18} > 0$.

stability conditions of the linearized system (see Appendix II to this chapter) we could obtain restrictions useful for the determination of the ambiguous partial derivatives. But the tremendous task of examining the stability conditions in algebraic terms for a 12×12 differential system is not worth pursuing, because we can obtain the necessary information by the empirical analysis carried out in the next chapter.

Appendix II. Linearization about the steady-state

The first step is to write the model in terms of the logarithmic deviations of the original variables from their respective steady-state paths. In fact, a convenient property of our model is that the logarithms of the ratios of the variables to their steady-state paths satisfy a non-linear *autonomous* differential system (see ch. 2, para. 2.2.3). To this purpose we define new variables x_i as follows:

$$
\begin{aligned}
x_1 &= \log(C/C^* e^{\rho_1 t}),\\
x_2 &= k - k^*,\\
x_3 &= \log(\tilde{Y}/\tilde{Y}^* e^{\rho_3 t}),\\
x_4 &= \log(MGS/MGS^* e^{\rho_4 t}),\\
x_5 &= \log(XGS/XGS^* e^{\rho_5 t}),\\
x_6 &= \log(Y/Y^* e^{\rho_6 t}),\\
x_7 &= \log(P/P^* e^{\rho_7 t}),\\
x_8 &= \log(PXGS/PXGS^* e^{\rho_8 t}),\\
x_9 &= \log(W/W^* e^{\rho_9 t}),\\
x_{10} &= m - m^*,\\
x_{11} &= \log(K/K^* e^{\rho_2 t}),\\
x_{12} &= \log(V/V^* e^{\rho_{12} t}).
\end{aligned}
$$

It is then easy to transform the original system into an autonomous system in terms of the variables x_i. Consider, for example, eq.

(1) of the model

$$\mathrm{D}\log C = \alpha_1 \log\left[\gamma_1 \exp[\beta_1 \mathrm{D}\log Y]\left(\frac{P}{PMGS}\right)^{\beta_2} Y\right] - \alpha_1 \log C + \alpha_2 m.$$

Since, by definition, it is also satisfied by the steady-state paths, we can write

$$\mathrm{D}\log C^* \mathrm{e}^{\rho_1 t} = \alpha_1 \log\left[\gamma_1 \exp[\beta_1 \mathrm{D}\log Y^* \mathrm{e}^{\rho_6 t}]\left(\frac{P^* \mathrm{e}^{\rho_7 t}}{PMGS}\right)^{\beta_2} Y^* \mathrm{e}^{\rho_6 t}\right] - \alpha_1 \log C^* \mathrm{e}^{\rho_1 t} + \alpha_2 m^*.$$

Subtracting this equation from the previous one, noting that the known function of time *PMGS* is the same in the two equations (so that it cancels out: this is true for all the exogenous variables), and using the x_i variables defined above, we obtain

$$\mathrm{D}x_1 = \alpha_1(\beta_1 \mathrm{D}x_6 + \beta_2 x_7 + x_6 - x_1) + \alpha_2 x_{10}. \tag{II.1}$$

In a similar way we get (eqs. (II.2), (II.3) and (II.12) require a few elementary manipulations):

$$\mathrm{D}x_2 = \alpha_3\left[\alpha' \gamma_2(\tilde{Y}^*/K^*)(\mathrm{e}^{x_3 - x_{11}} - 1) - x_2\right] + \alpha_4 x_{10}, \tag{II.2}$$

$$\mathrm{D}x_3 = (\rho_3 + \eta)(\mathrm{e}^{x_6 - x_3} - 1), \tag{II.3}$$

$$\mathrm{D}x_4 = \alpha_5(\beta_3 x_7 + \beta_4 x_6 - \beta_4 x_{11} + \beta_5 x_1 + \beta_6 x_{11} + \beta_7 x_5 - x_4) + \alpha_6(x_3 - x_{12}), \tag{II.4}$$

$$\mathrm{D}x_5 = \alpha_7(-\beta_8 x_8 - \beta_{10} x_6 + \beta_{10} x_{11} - x_5), \tag{II.5}$$

$$\mathrm{D}x_6 = \alpha_8(x_3 - x_6) + \alpha_9(x_3 - x_{12}), \tag{II.6}$$

$$\mathrm{D}x_7 = \alpha_{10}(\beta_{12} x_9 - x_7) + \alpha_{11} x_{10}, \tag{II.7}$$

$$\mathrm{D}x_8 = \alpha_{12}(\beta_{14} x_7 + \beta_{16} x_9 - x_8), \tag{II.8}$$

$$\mathrm{D}x_9 = \alpha_{13}(\beta_{18} x_7 - x_9), \tag{II.9}$$

$$\mathrm{D}x_{10} = \alpha_{14}\left[\delta_1(x_8 + x_5 - x_4) + \delta_2(\mathrm{D}x_8 + \mathrm{D}x_5 - \mathrm{D}x_4) - \delta_3 \mathrm{D}x_7 - \delta_4 \mathrm{D}x_6 - x_{10}\right], \tag{II.10}$$

$$\mathrm{D}x_{11} = x_2, \tag{II.11}$$

$$\begin{aligned}\mathrm{D}x_{12} = {} & (Y^*/V^*)(\mathrm{e}^{x_6 - x_{12}} - 1) + (MGS^*/V^*)(\mathrm{e}^{x_4 - x_{12}} - 1) \\ & - (C^*/V^*)(\mathrm{e}^{x_1 - x_{12}} - 1) - (K^*/V^*)x_2 \mathrm{e}^{x_{11} - x_{12}} \\ & - k^*(K^*/V^*)(\mathrm{e}^{x_{11} - x_{12}} - 1) - (XGS^*/V^*)(\mathrm{e}^{x_5 - x_{12}} - 1).\end{aligned} \tag{II.12}$$

The second step is to linearize the transformed system. Most equations are already linear: only eqs. (II.2), (II.3), (II.12) need linearization. This can be easily performed by using the formulae contained in section I.1 of Appendix I to ch. 3. The result is

$$\mathrm{D}x_2 = \alpha_3\alpha'\gamma_2(\tilde{Y}^*/K^*)(x_3 - x_{11}) - \alpha_3 x_2 + \alpha_4 x_{10}, \qquad \text{(II.2.1)}$$

$$\mathrm{D}x_3 = (\rho_3 + \eta)(x_6 - x_3), \qquad \text{(II.3.1)}$$

$$\begin{aligned}\mathrm{D}x_{12} = & -(C^*/V^*)x_1 - (K^*/V^*)x_2 + (MGS^*/V^*)x_4 \\ & -(XGS^*/V^*)x_5 \\ & +(Y^*/V^*)x_6 - k^*(K^*/V^*)x_{11} + [(C^*/V^*) \\ & -(MGS^*/V^*) \\ & +(XGS^*/V^*) - (Y^*/V^*) + k^*(K^*/V^*)]x_{12}.\end{aligned} \qquad \text{(II.12.1)}$$

The system consisting of eqs. (II.1), (II.2.1), (II.3.1), (II.4)–(II.11), (II.12.1) is a linear first-order differential system with constant coefficients, but it is not in normal form. Therefore the third, and last, step is to transform this system into a first-order system in normal form (see Gandolfo, 1980, Part II, ch. 8). This can be done quite easily by means of suitable substitutions from the remaining equations of the system in eqs. (II.1) and (II.10), which are the only ones not in normal form. The result is

$$\begin{aligned}\mathrm{D}x_1 = & -\alpha_1 x_1 + \alpha_1\beta_1(\alpha_8 + \alpha_9)x_3 + \alpha_1(1 - \alpha_8\beta_1)x_6 + \alpha_1\beta_2 x_7 \\ & + \alpha_2 x_{10} - \alpha_1\alpha_9\beta_1 x_{12},\end{aligned} \qquad \text{(II.1.1)}$$

$$\begin{aligned}\mathrm{D}x_{10} = & -\alpha_{14}\alpha_5\delta_2\beta_5 x_1 \\ & -\alpha_{14}[\alpha_6\delta_2 + (\alpha_8 + \alpha_9)\delta_4]x_3 + \alpha_{14}(\alpha_5\delta_2 - \delta_1)x_4 \\ & +\alpha_{14}[\delta_1 - (\alpha_7 + \alpha_5\beta_7)\delta_2]x_5 - \alpha_{14}[\delta_2(\alpha_7\beta_{10} + \alpha_5\beta_4) \\ & -\alpha_8\delta_4]x_6 + \alpha_{14}[(\alpha_{12}\beta_{14} - \alpha_5\beta_3)\delta_2 + \alpha_{10}\delta_3]x_7 \\ & +\alpha_{14}[\delta_1 - (\alpha_{12} + \alpha_7\beta_8)\delta_2]x_8 \\ & +\alpha_{14}(\alpha_{12}\delta_2\beta_{16} - \alpha_{10}\delta_3\beta_{12})x_9 \\ & -\alpha_{14}(1 + \alpha_{11}\delta_3)x_{10} + \alpha_{14}[\delta_2\alpha_7\beta_{10} \\ & +\alpha_5\delta_2(\beta_4 - \beta_6)]x_{11} \\ & +\alpha_{14}(\alpha_6\delta_2 + \alpha_9\delta_4)x_{12}.\end{aligned} \qquad \text{(II.10.1)}$$

This completes the finding of the linearization, which will be used for the stability and sensitivity analyses in the next chapter.

References

Allen, K. and Stevenson, A., 1974, *An Introduction to Italian Economy* (Martin Robertson & Co., London)

Baffi, P., 1971, Ways and Programmes of Monetary Action in Italy: A Glance at Two Decades, in: *Verstehen und Gestalten der Wirtschaft* (Mohr, Tübingen), 237–53.

Bergstrom, A. R. and Wymer, C. R., 1976, A Model of Disequilibrium Neoclassical Growth and its Application to the United Kingdom, in: Bergstrom, A. R., ed., 1976, *Statistical Inference in Continuous Time Economic Models* (North-Holland, Amsterdam), 267–327.

Borts, G. H. and Kopecky, K. J., 1972, Capital Movements and Economic Growth in Developed Countries, in: Machlup, F., Salant, W. S. and Tarshis, L., eds., 1972, *International Mobility and Movement of Capital* (Columbia University Press for the National Bureau of Economic Research, New York), 563–92.

Deardoff, A. V. and Stern, R. M., 1978, The Terms-of-Trade Effect on Expenditure: Some Evidence from Econometric Models, *Journal of International Economics* **8**, 409–14.

Fazio, A., 1979, La politica monetaria in Italia dal 1947 al 1978, *Moneta e Credito* **32**, 269–319 (abridged English version: Monetary Policy in Italy from 1970 to 1978, *Kredit und Kapital* **12**, 1979, 145–80).

Friedman, B. M., 1979, Optimal Expectations and the Extreme Information Assumption of 'Rational Expectations' Models, *Journal of Monetary Economics* **5**, 23–41.

Gandolfo, G. *et al*., 1976, *Il tasso di cambio di equilibrio: aspetti teorici e risultati empirici* (Isedi, Milano).

Gandolfo, G., 1979, The Equilibrium Exchange Rate: Theory and Empirical Evidence, in: Sarnat, M. and Szegö, G. P., eds., 1979, *International Finance and Trade* (Ballinger, Cambridge, Mass.), Vol. I, 99–130.

Gandolfo, G., 1980, *Economic Dynamics: Methods and Models* (North-Holland, Amsterdam).

Garegnani, P., 1970, Heterogeneous Capital, the Production Function and the Theory of Distribution, *Review of Economic Studies* **37**, 407–36.

Gordon, R. J., 1976, Recent Developments in the Theory of Inflation and Unemployment, *Journal of Monetary Economics* **2**, 185–219.

Granger, C. W. J. and Newbold, P., 1977, *Forecasting Economic Time Series* (Academic Press, New York).

Hicks, J. R., 1974, *The Crisis in Keynesian Economics* (Blackwell, Oxford).

Hodgman, D. R., 1974, *National Monetary Policies and International Monetary Cooperation* (Little, Brown & Co., Boston).

Kalecki, M., 1933, Outline of a Theory of the Business Cycle, in: Kalecki, M., 1969, *Studies in the Theory of Business Cycles, 1933–39* (Basil Blackwell), 3–15, and in: Kalecki, M., 1970, *Selected Essays on the Dynamics of the Capitalist Economy, 1933–70* (Cambridge University Press), 1–14.

Knight, M., 1976, Output, Prices and the Floating Exchange Rate in Canada: A Monetary Approach, International Monetary Fund Research Department DM/77/1, mimeo.

Knight, M. D. and Wymer, C. R., 1978, A Macroeconomic Model of the United Kingdom, *IMF Staff Papers* **25**, 742–78.

Laursen, S. and Metzler, L. A., 1950, Flexible Exchange Rates and the Theory of Employment, *Review of Economics and Statistics* **32**, 281–99. Reprinted in: Metzler, L. A., 1973, *Collected Papers* (Harvard University Press), 275–307. Pages refer to the original.

Lindbeck, A., ed., 1979, *Inflation and Employment in Open Economies* (North-Holland, Amsterdam).

Mussa, M., 1978, On the Inherent Stability of Rationally Adaptive Expectations, *Journal of Monetary Economics* **4**, 307–13.

Muth, J. F., 1960, Optimal Properties of Exponentially Weighted Forecasts, *Journal of the American Statistical Association* **55**, 299–306.

Muth, J. F., 1961, Rational Expectations and the Theory of Price Movements, *Econometrica* **29**, 315–35.

OECD, 1973, *Monetary Policy in Italy* (OECD, Paris).

Pasinetti, L. L., 1977, *Lectures on the Theory of Production* (Columbia University Press, New York).

Petit, M. L., 1979, Modelli di squilibrio e metodi di stima: un'applicazione al mercato delle esportazioni italiane, unpublished manuscript.

Phillips, A. W., 1954, Stabilisation Policy in a Closed Economy, *Economic Journal* **64**, 290–323.

Robinson, J., 1953, The Production Function and the Theory of Capital, *Review of Economic Studies* **21**, 81–106.

Sargent, T. and Wallace, N., 1973, Rational Expectations and the Dynamics of Hyperinflation, *International Economic Review* **14**, 328–50.

Sraffa, P., 1960, *Production of Commodities by Means of Commodities* (Cambridge University Press).

Sylos-Labini, P., 1979, Prices and Income Distribution in Manufacturing Industry, *Journal of Post Keynesian Economics* **2**, 3–25.

Wymer, C. R., 1979, The Use of Continuous Time Models in Economics, unpublished manuscript.

CHAPTER 6

A minimal model: Empirical results*

6.1. Introduction

In this chapter we present the estimates of the parameters of the theoretical model described in chapter 5. Besides results of the two estimated versions of the model, stability and sensitivity results are discussed as well as simulations for the equilibrium exchange rate over the sample period. In what follows, the equations of the model are referred to by the number given to them in ch. 5, table 1.

It should be pointed out at the outset that eq. (3), relating to the behaviour of expected output, has not been included in the estimation. The reason for this omission is self-evident. In order to estimate eq. (3), expected output observations are needed. These in turn cannot be discovered without knowing *a priori* the appropriate value of η, the expectations coefficient, which makes it impossible to estimate η together with the remaining parameters. Our solution – which follows Knight and Mathieson (1979) – was to produce time-series for $\tilde{Y}$ by solving eq. (3), using different values of η. We then estimated the model with each of these series in turn and chose the η that yielded the "best" results.[1]

Some of the parameters included in the model were restricted during estimation. Constraints were imposed according to steady-state analysis results or to *a priori* information and, in one case,

*By Pietro Carlo Padoan

[1] The values of η considered were 0.2, 0.5, 0.8, 1.0, 1.4, 1.7, 2.0, 2.5. The "best" results (both in terms of the maximum of the likelihood function and of the number of significant parameters) were obtained for $\eta = 0.5$. An alternative (and perhaps more satisfactory) procedure would have been the elimination of $\tilde{Y}$ by means of suitable manipulations, thus allowing a simultaneous estimation of η. This procedure, however, would have raised the order of all equations where expectations appear. Therefore, for convenience, we preferred the simpler procedure described in the text.

because the value of the parameter obtained in earlier stages of estimation did not differ significantly from the value to which it was eventually constrained. All parameter restrictions increased the efficiency of the estimates.

The model was linearized in the logarithms about sample means in its non-linear parts (pertaining to eqs. (2), (4), and (12); details of linearization procedures are given in Appendix I to this chapter). The continuous log-linear model was then reduced to the approximate discrete analogue; full details of the discrete version of the model are also given in Appendix I. As explained in ch. 5, this is not the definitive version of the model. Therefore – in accordance with the suggestions contained in ch. 3, para. 3.3.2 – we limited ourselves to the estimation of the approximate discrete analogue, deferring the extremely costly estimation of the exact discrete analogue to a later stage of research work.

On the whole, estimation results are satisfactory and they stand above the average results so far obtained in the estimations of continuous macrodynamic models.[2]

[2]It might be interesting to supply some information on the average results obtained by such of the estimated continuous time economy-wide macroeconometric models as are known to us (Bergstrom and Wymer, 1976; Jonson, 1976; Knight, 1976; Sassanpour and Sheen, 1976; Reserve Bank of Australia, 1977; Knight and Wymer, 1978; Knight and Mathieson, 1979; at the time of writing, the empirical results of Bailey, Hall and Phillips, 1979, are not available to us). On the average, 9.3 per cent of parameters included in the above models were constrained to a given value (the range is from 5.6 to 26.8 per cent); 91.9 per cent of the estimated parameters have the correct sign (the range is from 89.7 to 100.0 per cent), while on the average 66.6 per cent of the estimated parameters are significantly different from zero (range from 54.5 to 88.7 per cent). Finally, let us note that it is not possible to make a comparison with regard to the overall goodness of fit and to the over-identifying restrictions, because no statistics to this purpose are reported in the above mentioned models. The only exception is the RBA model, where the likelihood ratio test is reported in the commentaries on the model (Reserve Bank of Australia, 1977, p. 220 and p. 238). This test always leads to the rejection of the restrictions by a large margin; these, however, are retained in the model. As far as our model is concerned, the Carter-Nagar R^2_w statistic (Carter and Nagar, 1977; see also ch. 3, section 3.4) is 0.4562, and the associated χ^2 value is 453 with 46 d.f.; therefore, the hypothesis that the model as a whole is not consistent with the data is rejected. The log-likelihood ratio test (see ch. 3, section 3.4) gives a χ^2 of 821 with 206 d.f.; this should lead to reject the hypothesis that the over-identifying restrictions are consistent with the sample: as, however, this asymptotic test may be invalid even for samples of 100 observations (and, *a fortiori*, for smaller samples such as ours), we decided to retain the restrictions.

Of 49 estimated parameters, 36 (i.e. 73.5%) are significantly different from zero at least at the 5% level on asymptotic tests;[3] only two (4.1%) have an incorrect sign but they are not significantly different from zero. It is also noteworthy that these results were obtained by constraining only two out of fifty-one (4.1%) parameters to a given value.

6.2. Estimation results

Let us now examine the estimation results in detail. We shall begin by looking at the estimated adjustment parameters (see table 1). All of these, except α_2, α_4, α_6, α_9 and α_{11}, show the speed at which the relevant variable adjusts to its partial equilibrium (target or desired) level. As is shown in ch. 1 above, section 1.2 (see also ch. 2, para. 2.1.1), in this case the reciprocal of the adjustment speed can be interpreted as the mean time lag, i.e. the time needed to eliminate about 63 per cent of the divergence between actual and partial equilibrium values; mean time lags and their standard errors are also shown in table 1. Of the fifteen adjustment parameters all but two (α_2 and α_{13}) are significant at least at the 5 per cent level.

The highest adjustment speed (i.e. the lowest mean time lag) is α_{14}, the monetary authorities' adjustment speed to the desired value of m, the proportional rate of change of money-stock. This result is not surprising since it is reasonable to expect that monetary authorities are able to achieve their target in quite a short time. In this case just over a month is necessary to eliminate 63 per cent of the divergence between the actual and target values of m.

Estimates show that producers are able to adjust existing output to its expected value with a mean time lag ($1/\alpha_8$) of just over one and a half months. As we said above, the expected output used in estimation is associated with a value of the expectations coefficient (η) of 0.5. This means that producers are rather cautious in revising

[3]The t-value here should be interpreted merely as the ratio of the parameter estimate to its asymptotic standard error, and does not imply that it follows a Student's t distribution. With sufficiently large samples, this ratio tends to be normally distributed and therefore it is significantly different from zero at the five per cent level ("significant") if it lies outside the interval ± 1.96 and significantly different from zero at the one per cent level ("highly significant") if it lies outside the interval ± 2.58.

Table 1.
Estimated adjustment parameters.

Parameter	Entering equation number	Point estimate	Asymptotic standard error	Mean time lag	Standard error of mean time lag
α_1	(1)	0.512	0.186	1.95	0.71
α_2	(1)	– 0.311	0.270		
α_3	(2)	0.328	0.125	3.05	1.16
α_4	(2)	0.193	0.039		
α_5	(4)	0.449	0.166	2.23	0.82
α_6	(4)	0.432	0.166		
α_7	(5)	1.136	0.247	0.88	0.19
α_8	(6)	1.898	0.579	0.53	0.16
α_9	(6)	0.062	0.019		
α_{10}	(7)	0.749	0.175	1.34	0.31
α_{11}	(7)	0.764	0.250		
α_{12}	(8)	0.857	0.259	1.17	0.35
α_{13}	(9)	0.768	0.442	1.30	0.75
α_{14}	(10)	2.414	0.532	0.41	0.09
α'	(2)	0.058	0.008	17.24	2.40

their expectations, but once this revision has been performed, they are quite fast in adjusting actual values to the new expected ones. On the contrary, producers' reaction coefficient to a discrepancy between the desired and actual stock of inventories is very low ($\alpha_9 = 0.062$) though highly significant.

Exports of goods and services are adjusted with a mean time lag ($1/\alpha_7$) of about two and a half months, which is a rather short time. If we consider also the speed at which export prices are moved towards their target level ($\alpha_{12} = 0.857$ corresponding to a mean time lag of about three and a half months) we gain the impression that exporting firms are able (or forced) to keep both price and quantity at all times very close to their respective partial equilibrium values. This impression is further reinforced if we notice that the adjustment speeds of the remaining price and quantity variables are all rather low (although all highly significant).

Real consumption shows a mean time lag of almost six months. Real imports have very similar adjustment speeds in their two components (MGS and V). This latter result suggests that importing firms regard imports as aimed at meeting internal demand or at adjusting inventories on the same ground. In the previous chapter it was suggested that the two determinants of the behaviour of imports might show different adjustment speeds also because of a possible "speculative" behaviour of importing firms relative to changes in inventories; but estimation results do not support this hypothesis.

In the investment function two adjustment speeds, α' and α_3, are involved. The first one – which implies a mean time lag of over four years – indicates that the speed at which firms would like to adjust the existing capital stock to its desired value is very low (but highly significant); this, however, is not surprising if we consider that the accumulation process in capitalist economies is typically a long-run phenomenon. The mean time lag associated with α_3, on the contrary, is just about nine months. This means that entrepreneurs are much faster in adjusting the proportional rate of change of capital stock to its desired value. In other words, if firms take quite a long time in changing the fixed capital stock of the economy, they take a much shorter time in changing the speed at which accumulation proceeds.

Let us now discuss the estimated values of α_{10} and α_{13}; they are conveniently considered jointly since this can give an idea of the wage–price spiral in the Italian economy. It is interesting to note that they have an approximately equal value (associated with a mean time lag of about four months) suggesting that the two variables have kept chasing each other at a fairly constant pace, a result which fits well with wage–price behaviour of the Italian economy.[4] Unfortunately the wage-equation adjustment speed is significant only at the 10% level displaying a t-value of about 1.74.

The remaining adjustment parameters, α_2, α_4 and α_{11} indicate the effect of the rate of growth of money stock on the adjustment speeds of real aggregate consumption, the proportional rate of growth of capital stock, and the price level (respectively).

The effect of monetary expansion in the real consumption equation is negative. One explanation could be that money stock growth enhances wealth accumulation and thus depresses the speed at which consumption expenditure is adjusted to its target level. Therefore (in partial modification of the assumptions made in ch. 5,

[4] In 1975 a fuller indexation of wages through escalator clauses was introduced into the Italian economy. This has produced a much closer relationship between wage and price behaviour. Since our sample does not cover the period following 1975, this effect has not been included in the model.

section 5.2), we did not count $\alpha_2 < 0$ as a "wrong" sign. However, since the estimated value of α_2 is not significantly different from zero, the above interpretation is not fully warranted.

Monetary expansion does seem to have a positive effect on investment decisions, as theoretical considerations suggest. The value of α_4 is not very high but is highly significant. This indicates that general monetary and credit conditions (which the presence of our only endogenous monetary variable aimed to represent) positively influence the speed at which firms adjust the proportional rate of growth of capital stock to its target level.

Monetary expansion also has a positive and highly significant effect on domestic inflation, and the higher value of α_{11} with respect to α_4 suggests that the effect on prices is somewhat greater than the effect on quantities.

Let us now discuss the remaining estimated parameters (table 2) by examining each equation separately.

The long-run propensity to consume shows a very reasonable value ($\gamma_1 = 0.867$) and is significant. The hypothesis that the propensity to consume varies over the trade cycle can be accepted: β_1 is highly significant and positive. This indicates that aggregate consumption behaviour is "pro-cyclically oriented". Since aggregate consumption includes government consumption, our results are consistent with the widely-held opinion that Italian public expenditure is largely unable to provide a cycle-stabilization effect due to the highly inelastic nature of its composition (mostly public employees' salaries and net transfers to the private sector). The elasticity associated with the Laursen and Metzler effect (β_2) was eventually constrained to be zero since earlier stages of estimation showed that this parameter did not significantly differ from that value; in addition, this constraint helped to increase the general efficiency of the estimates. The theoretical ambiguity concerning the expected sign (discussed in ch. 5, section 5.1) has not therefore been eliminated by our empirical results.

Of the four parameters included in the equation explaining the change in the proportional rate of change of the capital stock, three ($\alpha', \alpha_3, \alpha_4$) have already been discussed above. The fourth, γ_2, was given an *a priori* value of 5.0 (and thus $\log \gamma_2 = 1.609$ in eqs. (4) and (5)). As explained in the previous chapter, γ_2 is actually the product

Table 2.
Estimated elasticities, proportions, and growth rates.

Parameter	Entering equation number	Point estimate	Asymptotic standard error
β_1	(1)	1.338	0.471
β_2	(1)	0.000†	
β_3	(4)	− 0.196	0.299
β_4	(4)	− 2.681	1.146
β_5	(4)	1.255	0.489
β_6	(4)	0.794	0.236
β_7	(4)	− 1.049	0.575
β_8	(5)	0.631	0.299
β_9	(5)	2.064	0.217
β_{10}	(5)	0.065	0.143
β_{11}	(7)	0.156	0.027
β_{12}	(7)	0.595	0.036
β_{13}	(7)	0.321	0.059
β_{14}	(8)	− 1.302	0.536
β_{15}	(8)	1.001	0.113
β_{16}	(8)	0.935	0.318
β_{17}	(8)	0.659	0.195
β_{18}	(9)	0.544	0.222
δ_1	(10)	0.038	0.026
δ_2	(10)	0.062	0.058
δ_3	(10)	− 0.108	0.079
δ_4	(10)	0.288	0.140
δ_5	(10)	− 0.011	0.007
δ_6	(10)	0.003	0.006
$\log \gamma_1$	(1)	− 0.143	0.064
$\gamma_2, \log \gamma_2$	(2), (4), (5)	5.0†, 1.609†	
$\log \gamma_3$	(4)	− 2.725	1.288
$\log \gamma_4$	(4), (6)	− 0.570	0.587
$\log \gamma_5$	(5)	− 13.598	2.216
$\log \gamma_6$	(7)	0.277	0.047
$\log \gamma_7$	(8)	0.419	0.170
$\log \gamma_8$	(9)	− 0.753	0.025
$\log \gamma_9$	(10)	− 0.359	0.592
$\log \gamma_{10}$	(10)	0.781	1.287
λ_5	(9)	0.020	0.003
λ_y	(10)	0.023	0.002

†Value imposed.

of the capital/output ratio and the reciprocal of the desired degree of capacity utilization. Since in the specification of the model it was assumed that γ_2 was constant over the sample period, we decided to give γ_2 an *a priori* value because this greatly increased the efficiency of the estimates. The value imposed was obtained by applying a desired degree of capacity utilization of 0.90 to the average capital/output ratio displayed by sample observations of about 4.5.

Let us now discuss the results concerning the import and export functions.

The marginal propensity to import out of total sales was supposed to vary according to relative prices and to a capacity effect. The elasticity with respect to relative prices was found neither to have the correct sign nor to be significantly different from zero. This result is a not infrequent finding in general, and almost the rule as far as Italy is concerned (see, for example, Houthakker and Magee, 1969; Drollas, 1976; Goldstein and Khan, 1976; in Gandolfo *et al.*, 1976, this effect was significant but with the "wrong" sign). However not too much weight should be attached to this result, because the microeconomic reasoning underlying the effect under consideration might no longer be valid at such a high level of aggregation as is implied by considering total imports, owing to well-known index-numbers problems (see appendix to ch. 2 in Leamer and Stern, 1970, and appendix 3 in Gandolfo *et al.*, 1976).

Our results suggest that the marginal propensity of Italian imports seems fundamentally determined by quantity rather than by price factors. The parameter (β_4) associated with the capacity effect is significant and negative. This means that as the degree of domestic capacity utilization rises, demand is satisfied by domestic rather than by foreign output and therefore imports decrease (see above, ch. 5, section 5.2; such a result was already obtained in Gandolfo *et al.*, 1976).

Different elasticities were estimated for the components of total sales (as discussed in ch. 5, section 5.2). The elasticities with respect to consumption expenditure and to net investment expenditure are positive and significant; the former is greater than one (but not significantly so) while the latter is smaller than one (though not significantly so). The surprising, but by us expected, result is that the elasticity with respect to exports is not significantly different from zero (and has the "wrong" sign).[5] This suggests that at the aggregate level exports do not seem directly to create a demand for imports of their own, a result that we found constantly in our work (see Gandolfo *et al.*, 1976, and appendix 4 therein for references to similar results by other researchers).

Although the adjustment speed of the inventory component of the import function has a significant value, the estimated value of $\log \gamma_4$ (γ_4 is the ratio of desired inventories to expected output) is not significant.

The theoretical specification of the export function includes both demand and supply effects and in this sense is not entirely satisfactory. The estimation results confirm the necessity to improve this specification by introducing a fully-fledged supply and demand export sector in our model (this we intend to do in future versions of the model). In fact, the elasticity associated with the supply constraint effect has the correct sign but is not significant; the high significance of the constant term also suggests the need for a better specification of the export function. The price elasticity is significant and has the correct sign. The elasticity associated with world demand (as defined in Appendix II) is highly significant and has a value of about 2. This suggests that Italian exports have grown faster than world demand over the sample period, i.e. they have increased their share in the world market, a result which is also quite realistic.

Parameter estimates of equation (6) have already been discussed (results concerning α_8 and α_9 at the beginning of section 6.2, and those concerning γ_4 where the import function was considered), so we shall now discuss the price-sector estimates.

Our price equations behave in a fairly satisfactory manner. All parameters and elasticities have the correct sign and are in most cases highly significant and, as expected, show a highly interconnected behaviour. The elasticity of domestic price with respect to

[5] In order to increase the efficiency of the estimates we imposed the constraint $\beta_5 + \beta_6 + \beta_7 = 1$, derived from steady-state analysis (see eq. (20) of ch. 5, section 5.2). As this gave rise to the unsatisfactory result concerning β_7, we also estimated the model with the additional constraints $0 < \beta_5 < 1$, $0 < \beta_6 < 1$, $0 < \beta_7 < 1$. But even so, estimates of β_7 were not significant while other parameter estimates lost significance; therefore we decided to report the original estimated value.

wages (β_{12}) is about one-half of the corresponding elasticity of the export price (β_{16}), confirming the higher sensitivity of the export sector to cost behaviour. This result is confirmed by estimates of productivity elasticities in the two equations: also in this case the export price elasticity ($-\beta_{17}$) is about twice as great in absolute value as the corresponding elasticity in the domestic price equation ($-\beta_{13}$).

Both the elasticity of *PXGS* with respect to wages and the elasticity with respect to foreign prices are close to unity and highly significant. This suggests that exporting firms tend, *ceteris paribus*, to transfer fully to prices any increase in wages, and that they also tend, *ceteris paribus*, to take full advantage of any opportunity offered by foreign competition to increase prices in order to increase profits in domestic currency (or to keep them unchanged if costs have also risen) while leaving their competitive position unaltered.

As far as the remaining two elasticities are concerned, import prices do have a significant effect on the domestic price level, suggesting that a 1 per cent increase in import prices gives rise to a 0.15 per cent increase in domestic prices (β_{11}). The negative (greater than one in absolute value) elasticity of export prices with respect to domestic prices (β_{14}) is consistent with the hypothesis that exporting firms tend to decrease export prices whenever a rise in domestic prices increases profits from sales on the domestic market (at given costs levels) in order to increase competitiveness on foreign markets, while maintaining a fairly stable overall profit flow (i.e. profits coming from the sum of domestic and foreign sales).

Estimates of the wage equation parameters are also satisfactory. Wage elasticity with respect to domestic prices (β_{18}) is about 0.5 and is significant. This, coupled with an elasticity of domestic prices with respect to wages of about 0.6, allows us to conclude that the wage–price spiral by itself and *ceteris paribus*, is not explosive (see ch. 5, Appendix I, section I.4, fn. 23). The time trend gives a growth rate of 2 per cent per quarter and is also highly significant, showing a constant pressure of institutional factors (as discussed in ch. 5, section 5.2) on wage behaviour in the sample period.

Let us now discuss the estimates of the monetary authorities' reaction function. The theoretical problems implicit in the specification of this function discussed in ch. 5, section 5.2, were reflected in the estimation problems that we encountered. The very high number of parameters involved in the equation led us to impose constraints (but not *a priori* values) on some of them in order to avoid identification problems. The constraints are relative to γ_9, γ_{10} and to λ_y and come from the steady-state analysis of the model carried out in ch. 5. More precisely, the constraints used were eq. (26.1) of ch. 5, section 5.3, as far as γ_9 and γ_{10} are concerned, and the (additional) assumption that the monetary authorities' target growth rate of real output coincides with the steady-state growth rate, i.e. $\lambda_y = \beta_8(\lambda_2 - \lambda_1) + \beta_9\lambda_3$ (see ch. 5, section 5.3, table 3).[6] This allowed us to obtain a reasonable and highly significant value for λ_y (which is about two per cent per quarter), and also a significant value of the associated coefficient (δ_4). The remaining δ's are not significant.

The rather unsatisfactory results concerning the estimation of the policy reaction function are probably due to the large number of variables which were included in this function for the theoretical reasons explained in ch. 5, section 5.2. Now, considering the fact – already remarked there – that not all the terms of the function under consideration are always present in it throughout the sample period, we decided to use *a priori* information in order to increase the efficiency of the estimates. This information derives from the fact that in the period from 1966-II to 1969-II the Banca d'Italia pegged the long-term bond rate, and consequently followed a policy which insulated the Italian economy, at least to some degree, from foreign monetary conditions, fully sterilizing the impact of balance of payments flows on money supply. Therefore the first two and the last two terms in $\hat{m}$ must be zero in that period. This can be obtained by introducing a multiplicative dummy variable on the parameters δ_1, δ_2, δ_5 and δ_6, which takes on the value one outside the pegging period and the value zero within it. The modified monetary policy function is as follows:

[6] As regards λ_1, λ_2 and λ_3 (that is, the exogenous growth rates of *PMGS*, *PF* and *YF* respectively), attempts to determine these simultaneously with the other parameters of the model during estimation were not successful, and so we obtained the values of these λ's interpolating the time series concerning the afore-mentioned exogenous variables with an exponential equation of the type $ae^{\lambda_i t}$. As regards MGS^* in eq. (26.1), for simplicity's sake this was set equal to MGS_0.

$$\begin{aligned} \mathrm{D}m = \alpha_{14}\Bigg[& Z\delta_1 \log \frac{PXGS \cdot XGS}{\gamma_9 PMGS \cdot MGS} \\ & + Z\delta_2 \,\mathrm{D}\log \frac{PXGS \cdot XGS}{\gamma_9 PMGS \cdot MGS} - \delta_3 \,\mathrm{D}\log \frac{P}{PMGS} \\ & + \delta_4(\lambda_y - \mathrm{D}\log Y) + Z\delta_5 \log \frac{1}{\gamma_{10}} N \\ & + Z\delta_6 \,\mathrm{D}\log \frac{1}{\gamma_{10}} N - m \Bigg], \end{aligned} \tag{10'}$$

where Z is the dummy variable. This introduces a non-linearity in the variables in eq. (10′) which, therefore, has to be linearized for estimation purposes (see Appendix I).

The overall estimation results obtained with the introduction of eq. (10′) in the place of eq. (10) were not entirely satisfactory. Although some of the parameters involved in the monetary authorities' reaction function did assume significant values, the estimates of other important parameters fell below acceptable standards. On the whole, the benefits relative to improvements in some of the parameters of eq. (10′) were more than offset by additional disadvantages due to unsatisfactory results in the estimation of parameters entering other equations. Therefore, we decided to retain the original model for the subsequent analysis. However, as it might be interesting to know the main results of the modified model, these are given below.

The adjustment speed of the actual to the target value of the proportional rate of growth of money stock (α_{14}) almost doubled its value – up to 4.428 – (and thus the mean time lag fell to less than three weeks), thus further stressing the ability of the monetary authorities to keep the proportional rate of the money growth on its target value by almost instantly effective action.

Only two of the δ's associated with the determinants of $\hat{m}$ in eq. (10′) were significant. They are δ_2 and δ_5, pertaining respectively to the rate of change of the balance on current account and to the level of the ratio of capital inflows to capital outflows. Both are negative ($\delta_2 = -0.101$, A.S.E. = 0.043; $\delta_5 = -0.016$, A.S.E. =

0.007); as δ_2 is greater than δ_5 in absolute value, this suggests that the rate of change of the balance on current account has a greater weight in the central banker's policy function.

Contrary to the previous results, δ_4, the parameter associated with the divergence between the actual and target rate of growth of output, was not found to be significant. It should be pointed out that in the estimation of (10′) the constraint on λ_y imposed in the earlier version was removed, because this parameter was now identified.

The new version of the equation explaining the change in *m* produced some effects on two of the parameters associated with *m* in other equations. The value of α_2, the adjustment coefficient in the consumption function, increased in value in absolute terms although remaining negative and became significant ($\alpha_2 = -1.090$, A.S.E. = 0.437) thus supporting the theoretical explanation of the negativity outlined above. The value of α_4, the adjustment coefficient of *m* in the investment function, did not change much but its significance fell just below the 5% level ($\alpha_4 = 0.127$, A.S.E. = 0.066).

The value and A.S.E. of α_{11}, the coefficient of *m* in the price equation, were practically untouched.

The parameters most affected by the introduction of the multiplicative dummy variable in eq. (10) were those associated with the import and export equations[7] (4) and (5). In particular, the elasticity of exports with respect to relative prices, β_8, did not turn out to be significant.

Let us consider, finally, the *in-sample predictive performance* of the model by analyzing the mean square errors of the endogenous variables in the estimated model.

[7]These results led us to try to improve the import and export equations performance by introducing additional dummy variables in both of them. In particular, a dummy variable (which assumed the value one from 1969-IV to 1973-II and zero elsewhere) was introduced into both equations in order to take account of the depressing effects on exported and imported quantities of general strikes in manufacturing industry. In addition, a dummy variable (assuming the value one from 1972-II to 1973-III and zero elsewhere) was introduced in the import function, in order to take account of the depressing effects on imported quantities of strikes by Italian customs personnel. The introduction of these dummies, alone or in combination, did not lead to satisfactory results.

Two sets of mean square errors are given in table 3. In the second column we give the mean squares of the residuals calculated from the restricted reduced form for the sample period. This is equivalent to calculating "forecasts" of the endogenous variables for each observation in the sample period by letting the predetermined variables take on their actual values.

In the third column we give the mean square errors of "dynamic forecasts", that is, when the lagged endogenous variables take on the values forecast by the model for the previous period (for the first period the observed values are of course used). These errors, therefore, are generally larger than the ones in the second column.

It should be remembered that the variables are expressed in logarithms; consequently, the root-mean-square error gives the average error as a *proportion* of the actual level of the endogenous variable.

The errors in the single period forecasts are below 10 per cent for 8 out of 11 endogenous variables, six of which are also below 5 per cent. As expected, the errors of dynamic forecasts are larger. The largest of all are displayed by imports, exports, and inventories. There are good economic and statistical reasons for accepting this result as unsurprising.

As far as the behaviour of inventories is concerned (which have the largest error of all), it should be remembered that changes in

Table 3.
Ex-post root-mean-square errors
(first quarter 1960–fourth quarter 1975).

Variable	Root-mean-square error of single-period forecasts	Root-mean-square error of dynamic forecasts
C	0.037	0.232
k	0.003	0.014
MGS	0.117	0.336
XGS	0.215	0.287
Y	0.075	0.184
P	0.016	0.041
W	0.095	0.189
$PXGS$	0.034	0.042
m	0.031	0.023
K	0.001	0.202
V	0.385	0.542

inventories generally display a highly volatile behaviour in advanced economies. In addition, data for changes in inventories in Italy are defined as a residual after the main components of national accounting have been computed, given the overall balance constraint. This means that data for DV contain "errors and omissions" components of national accounts as well as actual changes in inventories. Note that although the equation for DV does define the change in inventories as a residual, V also appears in other equations of the model as explained in ch. 5.

As far as the behaviour of XGS is concerned, an explanation for the unsatisfactory results can be found in the hybrid nature of the export function already discussed. The mediocre results concerning MGS might be due to the problems concerning the relative price effect discussed above.

6.3. Stability and sensitivity analyses

The (local) stability of the model, given the parameter estimates, can be examined according to the procedures expounded in ch. 2, para. 2.2.3 and ch. 3, section 3.4. As explained there, we shall use the model expressed in terms of the logarithmic deviations of the variables about their steady state (see Appendix II to ch. 5).

The estimates of the characteristic roots of the model, together with their asymptotic standard errors, are given in table 4. The damping period is the time required for about 63 per cent of the initial deviation to be eliminated (of course the damping period is defined only for stable roots). The period of the cycle corresponding to the complex roots is defined in the usual way.

All the real characteristic roots are negative, and all the complex roots have negative real parts. The steady-state path is locally asymptotically stable; the convergence, however, will not be monotonic since cycles will occur. Therefore our model gives rise to a stable cyclical growth behaviour, which is certainly the type of movement which most developed countries experienced in the period under consideration. It should be noted, however, that only the short cycle (with a period of about one and a half years) is significant, whereas the other two longer cycles (with a period of about 6 and 13 years respectively) are not significant.

Table 4.
Characteristic roots of the model.

Root	Asymptotic standard error	Damping period (quarters)	Period of cycle (quarters)
− 2.794	0.753	0.358	
− 1.583	0.491	0.632	
− 0.990	0.267	1.011	
− 0.067	0.011	14.917	
− 0.333	0.083	3.000	
− 0.832 ± 0.993i	0.291, 0.329	1.203	6.330
− 0.792 ± 0.271i	0.421, 0.262	1.262	23.218
− 0.439 ± 0.123i	0.264, 0.347	2.275	51.217

The *sensitivity analysis* can be carried out along the lines laid down in ch. 2, para. 2.2.4.1. Since there are 11 characteristic roots and 49 estimated parameters, the complete sensitivity matrix, which contains the partial derivatives of each characteristic root with respect to each parameter, is an 11 × 49 matrix. We therefore decided to limit ourselves to a presentation of only the most important results, which are:

(a) the partial derivatives of the characteristic roots with respect to the relevant policy parameters;
(b) some particularly large partial derivatives, which imply that the parameter concerned crucially affects stability.

As regards point (a), the parameters that can be considered as policy parameters are those present in the policy reaction function of the monetary authorities, i.e. α_{14}, γ_9, γ_{10}, and the δ's. However, γ_9, γ_{10}, δ_3, δ_4, δ_5 and δ_6 are not included in the matrix of the system that we are examining, because the corresponding terms disappear when we consider the logarithmic deviations of the variables about the steady state (see Appendix II to ch. 5). Therefore only α_{14}, δ_1, and δ_2 remain. The partial derivatives of the characteristic roots with respect to these parameters are reported in the second, third, and fourth columns of table 5.

An increase in α_{14} appears to be generally stabilizing: in fact, although some partial derivatives are positive, the only root on

Table 5.
Sensitivity analysis with respect to selected parameters.

Characteristic root (μ)	Partial derivative with respect to α_{14} $\left(\frac{\partial\mu}{\partial\alpha_{14}}\right)$	Partial derivative with respect to δ_1 $\left(\frac{\partial\mu}{\partial\delta_1}\right)$	Partial derivative with respect to δ_2 $\left(\frac{\partial\mu}{\partial\delta_2}\right)$	Partial derivative with respect to α_9 $\left(\frac{\partial\mu}{\partial\alpha_9}\right)$
-2.794	-1.101	-0.671	1.874	2.049
-1.583	0.132	2.853	-4.517	2.934
-0.990	-0.003	0.016	-0.016	-0.804
-0.067	-0.002	0.268	-0.018	0.073
-0.333	0.004	0.745	-0.248	0.411
$-0.832 \pm 0.993i$	$0.038 \pm 0.072i$	$-0.291 \mp 1.599i$	$1.830 \pm 1.041i$	$-11.172 \pm 6.073i$
$-0.792 \pm 0.271i$	$-0.064 \mp 0.051i$	$1.801 \mp 1.719i$	$-0.962 \pm 1.849i$	$9.690 \mp 1.020i$
$-0.439 \pm 0.123i$	$0.010 \mp 0.019i$	$-3.115 \pm 6.302i$	$0.594 \mp 3.153i$	$-0.851 \pm 3.162i$

which this parameter has an appreciable effect is the first real root (−2.794), and the relevant partial derivative is negative (−1.101). Conversely, an increase in δ_1 tends to be destabilizing: although some roots are stabilized, the relatively large positive partial derivatives of the second real root and of the real part of the second pair of complex conjugate roots with respect to this parameter imply a destabilizing effect. A similar result holds with reference to δ_2, given the relatively large positive partial derivatives of the first real root and of the real part of the first pair of complex conjugate roots with respect to this parameter.

All this means that too much weight assigned to the balance of goods and services (and to its rate of change) in the policy reaction function of the monetary authorities may cause instability, which will be both of a monotonic and cyclical nature. Conversely, an increase in the speed of adjustment of actual to target values of the policy variable (the rate of growth of the money supply) tends to be stabilizing, provided that this increase is not exceptionally great.

As regards point (b), the only parameter which appears to have a crucial effect upon stability is α_9, which indicates the "spillover effect" of a discrepancy between the desired and actual level of inventories on the output adjustment equation. The partial derivatives with respect to this parameter are given in the last column of table 5.

An increase in α_9 has a destabilizing effect on the first and second real root and on the real part of the second pair of complex conjugate roots. The latter effect is comparatively greater: for example, to a first approximation, an increase of α_9 from 0.062 to 0.144 is sufficient to change the real part of the complex roots considered from negative to positive, whereas a much greater increase in α_9 is required to bring the first and second real root into the positive range. This means that as α_9 increases, an unstable cyclical motion will take place long before the occurrence of monotonically divergent movements. In conclusion, if the reaction of producers to a discrepancy between the desired and actual level of inventories is too great, an unstable inventory cycle will occur; this cycle will also have a longer period than the corresponding stable cycle observed when α_9 is below its critical value.

6.4. The equilibrium exchange rate

As already mentioned in the previous chapter (see at the end of section 5.2), the model includes the exchange rate only implicitly. As a matter of fact, both *PMGS* and *PF* can be defined as follows

$$PMGS = rPMGS_f, \qquad PF = rPF_f,$$

where r is the exchange rate (defined as units of domestic currency per one unit of foreign currency), and $PMGS_f$ and PF_f are magnitudes in foreign currency.

Therefore, in order to simulate the model to obtain an equilibrium exchange rate, the first step is to substitute the expressions above in place of *PMGS* and *PF*, respectively, wherever they appear in the original non-linear model. In particular *PMGS* will be replaced by $rPMGS_f$ in eqs. (1), (4), (7) and (10) of the model and *PF* will be replaced by rPF_f in eqs. (5) and (8).

The second step is to impose the condition that the exchange rate adjusts to its equilibrium value, i.e. to that value which would equilibrate the balance of payments.[8]

In our case the equilibrium exchange rate refers to the balance of goods and services. Although capital movements are also present in the model, they are treated as exogenous and so their level is not influenced by the behaviour of the exchange rate. This limitation is a consequence of the general limitation imposed to the financial sector of the model, already discussed in section 2. Future versions of the model will endogenize capital movements and so will allow us to obtain results for the equilibrium exchange rate related to the overall balance of payments as well.

Now, by its very definition, we can say that the equilibrium exchange rate $\hat{r}$ is such that

$$\frac{\hat{r}}{r_\omega} = f(B), \qquad f(B) \gtreqless 1 \quad \text{when } B \lesseqgtr 1,$$

where r_ω is the *observed* exchange rate and $B \equiv PXGS \cdot XGS/$

[8]Alternatively, we could impose the condition that the exchange rate equals its equilibrium value at each instant; but this seems too strong a requirement. Therefore we preferred the less stringent assumption of a partial adjustment, as formalized below.

Table 6.
Equilibrium exchange rates, 1962–74.

Year	Actual exchange rate	Simulated eq. exchange rate	Eq. exchange rate (Gandolfo, 1979)
1962	620.746	621	670
1963	621.537	612	681
1964	624.357	611	645
1965	624.788	610	607
1966	624.410	609	617
1967	624.066	610	625
1968	623.339	608	603
1969	627.277	610	617
1970	627.270	615	632
1971	618.319	606	617
1972	583.412	571	583
1973	582.584	575	610
1974	650.309	647	682

$PMGS \cdot MGS$; a suitable functional form for $f(B)$ is

$$f(B) = (PXGS \cdot XGS / PMGS \cdot MGS)^{-\beta_{19}}, \qquad \beta_{19} > 0.$$

Then, in order to simulate the model over the sample period, we have to add the following partial adjustment equation for the exchange rate

$$\mathrm{D} \log(r/r_\omega) = \alpha_{15} \log \frac{\hat{r}/r_\omega}{r/r_\omega}, \qquad \alpha_{15} > 0,$$

where the values of α_{15} and β_{19} are given *a priori*.

The last step is to solve the differential equation system resulting from the substitutions and additions described above in the original non linear model (see Part I, ch. 3, para. 3.4.2), where the estimated values of the parameters have also been substituted.[9]

The results for the exchange rate are contained in table 6. They are given on a yearly basis (period averages) with reference to the lira/U.S. dollar exchange rate in order to allow a comparison with previous results obtained by Gandolfo (1979). Since the latter (which are listed in the last column of table 6) were obtained in a static

[9]These additions and substitutions can easily be carried out thanks to facilities built in the computer programs. See Wymer, RESIMUL and APREDIC Manuals and Supplement No. 3. The values given to α_{15} and β_{19} respectively were 2.5 and 0.1. Experimentation with other values did not yield substantially different results.

partial equilibrium framework (all the caveats of the case were duly made in Gandolfo, 1979), it is not surprising that the results obtained by the new approach are different. Given the preliminary nature of our model, it would be out of place to draw general conclusions or policy prescriptions from our results; they, however, certainly confirm that to rely on partial approaches and the like may be misleading.

6.5. Conclusion

The model presented here can be considered as no more than a preliminary attempt to determine the equilibrium exchange rate in a general (dis)equilibrium macroeconomic context (in such a context, of course, this determination represents just one of the many possible applications of the model); for the various caveats the reader is referred to ch. 5, sections 5.1 and 5.2. However, the estimation results are fairly good and stand above the average results so far obtained in the estimation of continuous macrodynamic models; also the analysis and simulation of the model are encouraging.

As usual, the main conclusion is that much remains to be done. Work is under way on a number of issues, both to improve the present model and to test hypotheses in a complete real-monetary macrodynamic framework.

Appendix I. Specification of the approximate discrete analogue

In order to estimate the continuous model presented in ch. 5 it is necessary to put it into a discrete form. In what follows the approximate discrete equivalent model is presented according to formulae (44″) of chapter 3, para. 3.3.3.

Let us first rewrite model (1) – (12) in log-linear form:[10]

$$\begin{aligned} \mathrm{D}\log C = {} & \alpha_1 \log \gamma_1 + \alpha_1\beta_1 \mathrm{D}\log Y + \alpha_1\beta_2 \log P \\ & - \alpha_1\beta_2 \log PMGS + \alpha_1 \log Y - \alpha_1 \log C + \alpha_2 m, \end{aligned} \tag{I.1}$$

[10]Equations (2), (5) and (12) have to be linearized fully or in part. The linearization procedures about sample means are described below in the text.

$$\mathrm{D}k = \alpha_3\alpha'\gamma_2 c_1 \log \tilde{Y} - \alpha_3\alpha'\gamma_2 c_1 \log K - \alpha_3 k + \alpha_3\alpha'\gamma_2 c_2 - \alpha_3\alpha' + \alpha_4 m, \tag{I.2}$$

$$\mathrm{D}\tilde{Y} = \eta(Y - \tilde{Y}), \tag{I.3}$$

$$\begin{aligned}\mathrm{D}\log MGS = {} & \alpha_5 \log\gamma_3 + \alpha_5\beta_3 \log P - \alpha_5\beta_3 \log PMGS \\ & + \alpha_5\beta_4 \log\gamma_2 \\ & + \alpha_5\beta_4 \log Y - \alpha_5\beta_4 \log K + \alpha_5\beta_5 \log C \\ & + \alpha_5\beta_6 c_3 k \\ & + \alpha_5\beta_6 \log K + \alpha_5\beta_6 c_4 + \alpha_5\beta_7 \log XGS \\ & - \alpha_5 \log MGS \\ & + \alpha_6 \log\gamma_4 + \alpha_6 \log\tilde{Y} - \alpha_6 \log V,\end{aligned} \tag{I.4}$$

$$\begin{aligned}\mathrm{D}\log XGS = {} & \alpha_7 \log\gamma_5 - \alpha_7\beta_8 \log PXGS + \alpha_7\beta_8 \log PF \\ & + \alpha_7\beta_9 \log YF \\ & - \alpha_7\beta_{10} \log\gamma_2 - \alpha_7\beta_{10} \log Y + \alpha_7\beta_{10} \log K \\ & - \alpha_7 \log XGS,\end{aligned} \tag{I.5}$$

$$\mathrm{D}\log Y = \alpha_8 \log\tilde{Y} - \alpha_8 \log Y + \alpha_9 \log\gamma_4 + \alpha_9 \log\tilde{Y} - \alpha_9 \log V, \tag{I.6}$$

$$\mathrm{D}\log P = \alpha_{10} \log\gamma_6 + \alpha_{10}\beta_{11} \log PMGS + \alpha_{10}\beta_{12} \log W - \alpha_{10}\beta_{13} \log PROD - \alpha_{10} \log P + \alpha_{11} m, \tag{I.7}$$

$$\begin{aligned}\mathrm{D}\log PXGS = {} & \alpha_{12} \log\gamma_7 + \alpha_{12}\beta_{14} \log P + \alpha_{12}\beta_{15} \log PF \\ & + \alpha_{12}\beta_{16} \log W - \alpha_{12}\beta_{17} \log PROD \\ & - \alpha_{12} \log PXGS,\end{aligned} \tag{I.8}$$

$$\mathrm{D}\log W = \alpha_{13} \log\gamma_8 + \alpha_{13}\beta_{18} \log P + \alpha_{13}\lambda_5 t - \alpha_{13} \log W, \tag{I.9}$$

$$\begin{aligned}\mathrm{D}m = {} & \alpha_{14}\delta_1 \log PXGS + \alpha_{14}\delta_1 \log XGS \\ & - \alpha_{14}\delta_1 \log\gamma_9 - \alpha_{14}\delta_1 \log PMGS \\ & - \alpha_{14}\delta_1 \log MGS + \alpha_{14}\delta_2 \mathrm{D}\log PXGS \\ & + \alpha_{14}\delta_2 \mathrm{D}\log XGS \\ & - \alpha_{14}\delta_2 \mathrm{D}\log PMGS - \alpha_{14}\delta_2 \mathrm{D}\log MGS \\ & - \alpha_{14}\delta_3 \mathrm{D}\log P \\ & + \alpha_{14}\delta_3 \mathrm{D}\log PMGS + \alpha_{14}\delta_4 \lambda_y\end{aligned}$$

$$- \alpha_{14}\delta_4 \, \mathrm{D} \log Y + \alpha_{14}\delta_5 \log N$$

$$+ \alpha_{14}\delta_6 \, \mathrm{D} \log N - \alpha_{14}\delta_5 \log \gamma_{10} - \alpha_{14} m, \qquad \text{(I.10)}$$

$$\mathrm{D} \log K = k, \qquad \text{(I.11)}$$

$$\mathrm{D} \log V = c_5 \log Y + c_6 \log MGS - c_7 \log C$$

$$- c_8 \log XGS - c_9 k$$

$$- c_{10} \log K - c_{11} \log V + c_{12}. \qquad \text{(I.12)}$$

The values of the constants c_i, $i = 1, 2, \cdots, 12$, are as follows (bars over symbols denote sample means):

$$c_1 = \exp[\,\overline{\log \tilde{Y}} - \overline{\log K}\,],$$

$$c_2 = c_1(1 - \overline{\log \tilde{Y}} + \overline{\log K}),$$

$$c_3 = \bar{k}^{-1},$$

$$c_4 = \log \bar{k} - 1,$$

$$c_5 = \exp[\,\overline{\log Y} - \overline{\log V}\,],$$

$$c_6 = \exp[\,\overline{\log MGS} - \overline{\log V}\,],$$

$$c_7 = \exp[\,\overline{\log C} - \overline{\log V}\,],$$

$$c_8 = \exp[\,\overline{\log XGS} - \overline{\log V}\,],$$

$$c_9 = \exp[\,\overline{\log K} - \overline{\log V}\,],$$

$$c_{10} = \bar{k} \exp[\,\overline{\log K} - \overline{\log V}\,],$$

$$c_{11} = c_5 + c_6 - c_7 - c_8 - c_{10},$$

$$c_{12} = c_5(1 - \overline{\log Y} + \overline{\log V}) + c_6(1 - \overline{\log MGS} + \overline{\log V})$$

$$- c_7(1 - \overline{\log C} + \overline{\log V}) - c_8(1 - \overline{\log XGS} + \overline{\log V})$$

$$- c_{10}(1 - \overline{\log K} + \overline{\log V}).$$

Here is an outline of the various linearization procedures.

In eq. (2), $\tilde{Y}/K$ has been linearized according to (I.6), Appendix I to ch. 3:

$$\tilde{Y}/K = \exp[\log \tilde{Y} - \log K] \simeq \exp[\,\overline{\log \tilde{Y}} - \overline{\log K}\,]$$

$$\times (1 + \log \tilde{Y} - \log K - \overline{\log \tilde{Y}} + \overline{\log K}).$$

In eq. (4), $DK \equiv kK$ can be linearized in accordance with several procedures.

The one chosen is the following: since $\log DK \equiv \log kK = \log k + \log K$, we must express $\log k$ in terms of k alone. This in turn can be done in more than one way. For example, by expanding $\log k$ in Taylor's series and neglecting all higher-order terms, we obtain

$$\log k \simeq \log \bar{k} + \frac{1}{\bar{k}}(k - \bar{k}) = (\log \bar{k} - 1) + \bar{k}^{-1}k,$$

where $\bar{k}$ is the sample mean of k and $\log \bar{k}$ is the logarithm of this mean (and *not* the mean of the logarithms). It then follows that:

$$\log DK \simeq \bar{k}^{-1}k + \log K + (\log \bar{k} - 1).$$

As regards eq. (12), if we divide throughout by V, we get:

$$\frac{DV}{V} = D\log V = \frac{Y}{V} + \frac{MGS}{V} - \frac{C}{V} - \frac{XGS}{V} - \frac{DK}{V}. \qquad (I.12.1)$$

The first four terms in the r.h.s. of (I.12.1) are linearized according to (I.6), Appendix I to ch. 3; the linearization of DK/V requires some further explanation. Since $DK \equiv kK$, we obtain $DK/V = kK/V$; then K/V is linearized in the same manner as the other components of (I.12.1). Thus we have:

$$\begin{aligned} k\frac{K}{V} &= k\big[\exp\big[\,\overline{\log K} - \overline{\log V}\,\big] \\ &\qquad \times (1 + \log K - \log V - \overline{\log K} + \overline{\log V})\big] \\ &= k\exp\big[\,\overline{\log K} - \overline{\log V}\,\big]\log K - k\exp\big[\,\overline{\log K} - \overline{\log V}\,\big] \\ &\qquad \times \log V + k\exp\big[\,\overline{\log K} - \overline{\log V}\,\big](1 - \log K + \log V). \end{aligned} \qquad (I.12.2)$$

By expanding (I.12.2) in Taylor's series and neglecting all higher-order terms, we get:

$$\begin{aligned} &\bar{k}\exp\big[\,\overline{\log K} - \overline{\log V}\,\big]\,\overline{\log K} + \exp\big[\,\overline{\log K} - \overline{\log V}\,\big] \\ &\quad \times \overline{\log K}(k - \bar{k}) + \bar{k}\exp\big[\,\overline{\log K} - \overline{\log V}\,\big](\log K - \overline{\log K}) \\ &\quad - \bar{k}\exp\big[\,\overline{\log K} - \overline{\log V}\,\big]\,\overline{\log V} - \exp\big[\,\overline{\log K} - \overline{\log V}\,\big] \\ &\quad \times \overline{\log V}(k - \bar{k}) - \bar{k}\exp\big[\,\overline{\log K} - \overline{\log V}\,\big](\log V - \overline{\log V}) \\ &\quad + \bar{k}\exp\big[\,\overline{\log K} - \overline{\log V}\,\big](1 - \overline{\log K} + \overline{\log V}) \\ &\quad + \exp\big[\,\overline{\log K} - \overline{\log V}\,\big](1 - \overline{\log K} + \overline{\log V})(k - \bar{k}). \end{aligned} \qquad (I.12.3)$$

After suitable cancelling, the above expression reduces to:

$$k\frac{K}{V} \simeq \exp[\,\overline{\log K} - \overline{\log V}\,]k + \bar{k}\exp[\,\overline{\log K} - \overline{\log V}\,]\log K$$
$$- \bar{k}\exp[\,\overline{\log K} - \overline{\log V}\,]\log V$$
$$+ \bar{k}\exp[\,\overline{\log K} - \overline{\log V}\,](1 - \overline{\log K} + \overline{\log V}). \tag{I.12.4}$$

By combining (I.12.4) with the linearization of the remaining components of (I.12.1), we obtain eq. (I.12).

Finally, note that, as pointed out in the text, eq. (3) is not included in the estimated model; it has not, therefore, been linearized in the logarithms.

The continuous linear model (I.1) – (I.12) can be transformed into the approximate discrete analogue according to (44″) of ch. 3, section 3.3.3. The final expression is reported below. We remind that $\Delta x \equiv x_t - x_{t-1}$, $\mathrm{L}x \equiv x_{t-1}$, $\mathrm{M}x \equiv \frac{1}{2}(1 + \mathrm{L})x$. Stock and flow variables have previously been treated according to eqs. (31) and (28) of ch. 3, para. 3.3.1.2, and all variables have been manipulated as shown in eq. (36), same paragraph, in order to eliminate the autocorrelation in the disturbances inherent in a model containing flow data. For estimation purposes eq. (44″) is used; the v's denote the disturbances. Bearing in mind that eq. (I.3) is omitted, we thus have:

$$\left(1 + \tfrac{1}{2}\alpha_1\right)\Delta \log C + \alpha_1 \mathrm{L} \log C - \left(\alpha_1\beta_1 + \tfrac{1}{2}\alpha_1\right)\Delta \log Y$$
$$- \alpha_1 \mathrm{L} \log Y - \tfrac{1}{2}\alpha_1\beta_2 \Delta \log P - \alpha_1\beta_2 \mathrm{L} \log P - \tfrac{1}{2}\alpha_2 \Delta m - \alpha_2 \mathrm{L}m$$
$$+ \alpha_1\beta_2 \mathrm{M} \log PMGS - 0.785\alpha_1 \log \gamma_1 = v_1, \tag{I.1$'$}$$

$$\left(1 + \tfrac{1}{2}\alpha_3\right)\Delta k + \alpha_3 \mathrm{L}k + \tfrac{1}{2}\alpha_3\alpha'\gamma_2 c_1 \Delta \log K + \alpha_3\alpha'\gamma_2 c_1 \mathrm{L} \log K$$
$$- \tfrac{1}{2}\alpha_4 \Delta m - \alpha_4 \mathrm{L}m - \alpha_3\alpha'\gamma_2 c_1 \mathrm{M} \log \tilde{Y}$$
$$- 0.785(\alpha_3\alpha'\gamma_2 c_2 - \alpha_3\alpha') = v_2, \tag{I.2$'$}$$

$$\left(1 + \tfrac{1}{2}\alpha_5\right)\Delta \log MGS + \alpha_5 L \log MGS - \tfrac{1}{2}\alpha_5\beta_3 \Delta \log P$$
$$- \alpha_5\beta_3 L \log P - \tfrac{1}{2}\alpha_5\beta_4 \Delta \log Y - \alpha_5\beta_4 L \log Y$$
$$- \tfrac{1}{2}\alpha_5(\beta_6 - \beta_4)\Delta \log K - \alpha_5(\beta_6 - \beta_4) L \log K - \tfrac{1}{2}\alpha_5\beta_5 \Delta \log C$$
$$- \alpha_5\beta_5 L \log C - \tfrac{1}{2}\alpha_5\beta_6 c_3 \Delta k - \alpha_5\beta_6 c_3 Lk - \tfrac{1}{2}\alpha_5\beta_7 \Delta \log XGS$$

$$
\begin{aligned}
&- \alpha_5\beta_7 L \log XGS + \tfrac{1}{2}\alpha_6 \Delta \log V + \alpha_6 L \log V \\
&+ \alpha_5\beta_3 M \log PMGS - \alpha_6 M \log \tilde{Y} \\
&- 0.785(\alpha_5 \log \gamma_3 + \alpha_5\beta_4 \log \gamma_2 + \alpha_5\beta_6 c_4 + \alpha_6 \log \gamma_4) = v_4,
\end{aligned} \tag{I.4$'$}
$$

$$
\begin{aligned}
&\left(1 + \tfrac{1}{2}\alpha_7\right) \Delta \log XGS + \alpha_7 \mathrm{L} \log XGS + \tfrac{1}{2}\alpha_7\beta_8 \Delta \log PXGS \\
&+ \alpha_7\beta_8 \mathrm{L} \log PXGS + \tfrac{1}{2}\alpha_7\beta_{10} \Delta \log Y + \alpha_7\beta_{10} \mathrm{L} \log Y \\
&- \tfrac{1}{2}\alpha_7\beta_{10} \Delta \log K - \alpha_7\beta_{10} \mathrm{L} \log K - \alpha_7\beta_8 \mathrm{M} \log PF - \alpha_7\beta_9 \log YF \\
&- 0.785(\alpha_7 \log \gamma_5 - \alpha_7\beta_{10} \log \gamma_2) = v_5,
\end{aligned} \tag{I.5$'$}
$$

$$
\begin{aligned}
&\left(1 + \tfrac{1}{2}\alpha_8\right) \Delta \log Y + \tfrac{1}{2}\alpha_9 \Delta \log V + \alpha_9 \mathrm{L} \log V \\
&- (\alpha_8 + \alpha_9) \mathrm{M} \log \tilde{Y} - 0.785\alpha_9 \log \gamma_4 = v_6,
\end{aligned} \tag{I.6$'$}
$$

$$
\begin{aligned}
&\left(1 + \tfrac{1}{2}\alpha_{10}\right) \Delta \log P + \alpha_{10} \mathrm{L} \log P - \tfrac{1}{2}\alpha_{10}\beta_{12} \Delta \log W \\
&- \alpha_{10}\beta_{12} \mathrm{L} \log W - \tfrac{1}{2}\alpha_{11} \Delta m - \alpha_{11} \mathrm{L} m - \alpha_{10}\beta_{11} \mathrm{M} \log PMGS \\
&+ \alpha_{10}\beta_{13} \mathrm{M} \log PROD - 0.785\alpha_{10} \log \gamma_6 = v_7,
\end{aligned} \tag{I.7$'$}
$$

$$
\begin{aligned}
&\left(1 + \tfrac{1}{2}\alpha_{12}\right) \Delta \log PXGS + \alpha_{12} \mathrm{L} \log PXGS - \tfrac{1}{2}\alpha_{12}\beta_{14} \Delta \log P \\
&- \alpha_{12}\beta_{14} \mathrm{L} \log P - \tfrac{1}{2}\alpha_{12}\beta_{16} \Delta \log W \\
&- \alpha_{12}\beta_{16} \mathrm{L} \log W - \alpha_{12}\beta_{15} \mathrm{M} \log PF \\
&+ \alpha_{12}\beta_{17} \mathrm{M} \log PROD - 0.785\alpha_{12} \log \gamma_6 = v_8,
\end{aligned} \tag{I.8$'$}
$$

$$
\begin{aligned}
&\left(1 + \tfrac{1}{2}\alpha_{13}\right) \Delta \log W + \alpha_{13} \mathrm{L} \log W - \tfrac{1}{2}\alpha_{13}\beta_{18} \Delta \log P \\
&- \alpha_{13}\beta_{18} \mathrm{L} \log P - \alpha_{13}\lambda_5 \mathrm{M} t - 0.785\alpha_{13} \log \gamma_8 = v_9,
\end{aligned} \tag{I.9$'$}
$$

$$
\begin{aligned}
&\left(1 + \tfrac{1}{2}\alpha_{14}\right) \Delta m + \alpha_{14} \mathrm{L} m - \alpha_{14}\left(\tfrac{1}{2}\delta_1 + \delta_2\right) \Delta \log PXGS \\
&- \alpha_{14}\delta_1 \mathrm{L} \log PXGS - \alpha_{14}\left(\tfrac{1}{2}\delta_1 + \delta_2\right) \Delta \log XGS \\
&- \alpha_{14}\delta_1 \mathrm{L} \log XGS + \alpha_{14}\left(\tfrac{1}{2}\delta_1 + \delta_2\right) \Delta \log MGS + \alpha_{14}\delta_2 \mathrm{L} \log MGS \\
&+ \alpha_{14}\delta_3 \Delta \log P + \alpha_{14}\delta_4 \Delta \log Y \\
&+ \alpha_{14}\delta_1 \mathrm{M} \log PMGS + \alpha_{14}(\delta_2 - \delta_3) \Delta \log PMGS \\
&- \alpha_{14}\delta_5 \mathrm{M} \log N \\
&- \alpha_{14}\delta_6 \Delta \log N + 0.785\alpha_{14}(\delta_1 \log \gamma_9 + \delta_5 \log \gamma_{10} - \delta_4 \lambda_y) = v_{10},
\end{aligned} \tag{I.10$'$}
$$

$$\Delta \log K - \tfrac{1}{2}\Delta k - \mathrm{L}k = 0, \qquad (\mathrm{I}.11')$$

$$\begin{aligned}
&\left(1 + \tfrac{1}{2}c_{11}\right)\Delta \log V + c_{11}\mathrm{L}\log V - \tfrac{1}{2}c_5 \Delta \log Y - c_5 \mathrm{L}\log Y \\
&\quad - \tfrac{1}{2}c_6 \Delta \log MGS - c_6 \mathrm{L}\log MGS + \tfrac{1}{2}c_7 \Delta \log C + c_7 \mathrm{L}\log C \\
&\quad + \tfrac{1}{2}c_8 \Delta \log XGS + c_8 \mathrm{L}\log XGS + \tfrac{1}{2}c_9 \Delta k + c_9 \mathrm{L}k + \tfrac{1}{2}c_{10} \Delta \log k \\
&\quad + c_{10}\mathrm{L}\log K - 0.785 c_{12} = 0. \qquad (\mathrm{I}.12')
\end{aligned}$$

In the case in which a multiplicative dummy variable is introduced in eq. (10) of the model, as discussed in the text, we have (let Z = the variable):

$$\begin{aligned}
\mathrm{D}m = \alpha_{14}\Bigg[& Z\delta_1 \log \frac{PXGS \cdot XGS}{\gamma_9 PMGS \cdot MGS} + Z\delta_2 \\
& \times \mathrm{D}\log \frac{PXGS \cdot XGS}{\gamma_9 PMGS \cdot MGS} - \delta_3 \mathrm{D}\log \frac{P}{PMGS} \\
& + \delta_4(\lambda_y - \mathrm{D}\log Y) \\
& + Z\delta_5 \log \frac{1}{\gamma_{10}} N + Z\delta_6 \mathrm{D}\log \frac{1}{\gamma_{10}} N - m \Bigg], \qquad (\mathrm{I}.10.1)
\end{aligned}$$

where $Z = 0$ from 1966-II to 1969-II, and otherwise $Z = 1$. Now,

$$\begin{aligned}
\mathrm{D}m = \alpha_{14}\big[& Z\delta_1 \log PXGS + Z\delta_1 \log XGS - Z\delta_1 \log \gamma_9 \\
& - Z\delta_1 \log PMGS - Z\delta_1 \log MGS + Z\delta_2 \mathrm{D}\log PXGS \\
& + Z\delta_2 \mathrm{D}\log XGS - Z\delta_2 \mathrm{D}\log PMGS \\
& - Z\delta_2 \mathrm{D}\log MGS - \delta_3 \mathrm{D}\log P + \delta_3 \mathrm{D}\log PMGS \\
& + \delta_4 \lambda_y - \delta_4 \mathrm{D}\log Y - Z\delta_5 \log \gamma_{10} + Z\delta_5 \log N \\
& + Z\delta_6 \mathrm{D}\log N - m \big], \qquad (\mathrm{I}.10.2)
\end{aligned}$$

and by expanding the relevant products in Taylor's series about sample means and neglecting all higher-order terms, we obtain

$$\begin{aligned}
\mathrm{D}m = \alpha_{14}\big[& \bar{Z}\delta_1 \log PXGS + \bar{Z}\delta_1 \log XGS \\
& - \bar{Z}\delta_1 \log PMGS - \bar{Z}\delta_1 \log MGS \\
& + \bar{Z}\delta_2 \mathrm{D}\log PXGS + \bar{Z}\delta_2 \mathrm{D}\log XGS \\
& - \bar{Z}\delta_2 \mathrm{D}\log PMGS - \bar{Z}\delta_2 \mathrm{D}\log MGS - \delta_3 \mathrm{D}\log P
\end{aligned}$$

$$+ \delta_3 \,\mathrm{D}\log PMGS + \delta_4\lambda_y - \delta_4 \,\mathrm{D}\log Y$$
$$+ \bar{Z}\delta_5 \log N + \bar{Z}\delta_6 \,\mathrm{D}\log N$$
$$+ (-\delta_1 \log\gamma_9 - \delta_5 \log\gamma_{10} + c_{13}\delta_1 + c_{14}\delta_2$$
$$+ (\overline{\log N})\delta_5 + (\overline{\mathrm{D}\log N})\delta_6)Z - m\Big], \qquad \text{(I.10.3)}$$

where

$$c_{13} = \overline{\log PXGS} + \overline{\log XGS} - \overline{\log PMGS} - \overline{\log MGS}\,,$$
$$c_{14} = \overline{\Delta\log PXGS} + \overline{\Delta\log XGS} - \overline{\Delta\log PMGS} - \overline{\Delta\log MGS}\,.$$

Eq. (I.10.3) can be written for estimation purposes as

$$\left(1 + \tfrac{1}{2}\alpha_{14}\right)\Delta m + \alpha_{14}\mathrm{L}m - \alpha_{14}\left(\tfrac{1}{2}\delta_1 + \delta_2\right)\bar{Z}\Delta\log PXGS$$
$$- \alpha_{14}\delta_1\bar{Z}\mathrm{L}\log PXGS - \alpha_{14}\left(\tfrac{1}{2}\delta_1 + \delta_2\right)\bar{Z}\Delta\log XGS$$
$$- \alpha_{14}\delta_1\bar{Z}\mathrm{L}\log XGS + \alpha_{14}\left(\tfrac{1}{2}\delta_1 + \delta_2\right)\bar{Z}\Delta\log MGS$$
$$+ \alpha_{14}\delta_1\bar{Z}\mathrm{L}\log MGS + \alpha_{14}\delta_3\Delta\log P + \alpha_{14}\delta_4\Delta\log Y$$
$$+ \alpha_{14}\delta_1\bar{Z}\mathrm{M}\log PMGS + \alpha_{14}\left(\delta_2\bar{Z} - \delta_3\right)\Delta\log PMGS$$
$$- \alpha_{14}\delta_5\bar{Z}\mathrm{M}\log N - \alpha_{14}\delta_6\bar{Z}\Delta\log N + \alpha_{14}(\delta_1\log\gamma_9 + \delta_5\log\gamma_{10}$$
$$- \delta_1 c_{13} - \delta_2 c_{14} - \delta_5\overline{\log N} - \delta_6\overline{\Delta\log N})\mathrm{M}Z$$
$$- 0.785\alpha_{14}\delta_4\lambda_y = v_{10}. \qquad \text{(I.10'')}$$

Appendix II. Data sources and definitions

Sources of data

BI	Bollettino (Banca d'Italia)
DOT	Direction of Trade (International Monetary Fund)
DSA	Da Empoli, Siesto, Antonello (1979)
IFS	International Financial Statistics
ISTAT	Annuario di Contabilità Nazionale (Istituto Centrale di Statistica)
MAIN	Main Economic Indicators (OECD)
QNA	Quarterly National Accounts (OECD)

Definitions of series (all series are quarterly)

C = real consumption expenditure (1970 prices) of the private and public sector. Source: DSA.

K = total gross fixed investment (1970 prices) *less* interpolated capital consumption (1970 prices) cumulated on a base stock of 124497.1 billion (10^9) lire in 1959-IV. Sources: fixed investment, DSA; capital consumption, author's interpolation of yearly ISTAT data.

$\tilde{Y}$ = author's computation (see text).

MGS = real imports of goods and services (1970 prices), national accounts basis. Source: DSA.

XGS = real exports of goods and services (1970 prices), national accounts basis. Source: DSA.

Y = gross domestic product (1970 prices), *less* interpolated capital consumption (1970 prices). Sources: gross domestic product, DSA; capital consumption, author's interpolation of yearly ISTAT data.

V = change in real inventories (1970 prices) cumulated on a base stock of 1072.9 billion (10^9) lire in 1959-IV. Source: DSA.

P = domestic product implicit price deflator (1970 = 100). Source: domestic product at current and 1970 prices, DSA.

$PXGS$ = implicit price deflator of exports of goods and services (1970 = 100). Source: exports of goods and services at current and 1970 prices, DSA.

W = income from employment at current prices divided by employees in employment. Source: ISTAT

m = $D \log M$ where M is the sum of money plus quasi-money. Source: IFS, lines 34 + 35.

r = period-average market exchange-rate, lire per US dollar. Source: IFS

$PMGS$ = implicit price deflator of imports of goods and services (1970 = 100). Source: imports of goods and services at current and 1970 prices, DSA.

PF = this index was built, following Houthakker and Magee (1969) and further contribution by Drollas (1976), in order to take account of the competition between rival international suppliers to each market. Countries considered both as competitors on third markets and as importing economies were 18 OECD countries (i = Italy)

$$PF = tc \cdot PF^{\$},$$

$$PF^{\$} = \sum_{\substack{j=1 \\ j \neq i}}^{18} w_{ij}^{x} \sum_{\substack{k=1 \\ j \neq k \\ k \neq i}}^{18} w_{jk}^{*} PX_k^{\$}, \qquad \text{where}$$

$$w_{ij}^{x} = XGS_{ij} \Big/ \sum_{\substack{j=1 \\ j \neq i}}^{18} XGS_{ij},$$

$$w_{jk}^{*} = MGS_{jk} \Big/ \sum_{\substack{k=1 \\ k \neq i \\ k \neq j}}^{18} MGS_{jk},$$

$PX_k^{\$}$ = export price index of country k. Source: MAIN.
XGS_{ij} = Italy's exports of goods and services to country j. Source: DOT.
MGS_{jk} = imports of goods and services of country j from country k. Source: DOT.
tc = trade conversion factor. Source: IFS.

YF = weighted sum of OECD countries' incomes, i = Italy (see Houthakker and Magee, 1969; Drollas, 1976):

$$YF = tc \cdot YF^{\$}$$

$$YF^{\$} = \sum_{\substack{j=1 \\ j \neq i}}^{18} w_{ij}^{x} Y_j^{\$}, \qquad \text{where}$$

tc = defined above,
w_{ij}^{x} = defined above,
$Y_j^{\$}$ = real gross national product of country j (1970 prices), 10^9\$. Source: QNA.

$PROD$ = value added of industrial sector (1970 prices) divided by industrial sector employment. Source: ISTAT.

N = autonomous capital inflows divided by autonomous capital outflows. Source: BI.

t = time trend, where the first quarter of 1960 is −30.5, the following quarter is −29.5 ... the fourth quarter of 1975 is 30.5 so that the sample mean is zero.

The sample period covers 1960-I to 1975-IV. We decided not to cover the period after 1975-IV for two reasons. Firstly, at the time of estimation quarterly national accounting data for that period were available only in a provisional version.

Secondly, in 1979 ISTAT carried out extensive revisions of national accounts, but published the revised data series (1960–78) on an annual basis only and not for all variables. Therefore homogeneous series up to 1978 were not available and we were compelled to use the unrevised series.

All stock series were measured at the end of period while prices are period averages. The logarithms of all variables were deseasonalized by removing the mean seasonal variation about the sample mean with trend adjustment according to procedures developed by Durbin (1963). All series measured at the end of period were adjusted in order to be consistent with flow data in accordance with eqs. (30) and (31) of ch. 3, para. 3.3.1.2. The moving average inherent in a model containing flow data was eliminated from data in accordance with eq. (33) of ch. 3.

References

Bailey, R. E., Hall, V. B. and Phillips, P. C. B., 1979, A Model of Output, Employment and Inflation in an Open Economy, paper presented at the Australia and New Zealand Association for the Advancement of Science, 29th Congress, Auckland, 1979.

Bergstrom, A. R. and Wymer, C. R., 1976, A Model of Disequilibrium Neoclassical Growth and its Application to the United Kingdom, in: Bergstrom, A. R., ed., 1976, *Statistical Inference in Continuous Time Economic Models* (North-Holland, Amsterdam), 267–327.

Carter, R. A. L. and Nagar, A. L., 1977, Coefficients of Correlation for Simultaneous Equation Systems, *Journal of Econometrics* **6**, 39–50.

Da Empoli, D., Siesto, V. and Antonello, P., 1979, *Finanza pubblica e contabilità nazionale su base trimestrale* (Cedam, Padova).

Drollas, L. P., 1976, The Foreign Trade Sector in Disequilibrium: A Comparative Study of Sixteen Developed Countries, unpublished Ph.D. Thesis (London School of Economics).

Durbin, J., 1963, Trend Elimination for the Purpose of Estimating Seasonal and Periodic Components in Time Series, in: Rosenblatt, M., ed., 1963, *Time Series Analysis* (Wiley, New York), 3–16.

Gandolfo, G. *et al.*, 1976, *Il tasso di cambio di equilibrio: aspetti teorici e risultati empirici* (Isedi, Milano).

Gandolfo, G. 1979, The Equilibrium Exchange Rate: Theory and Empirical Evidence, in: Sarnat, M. and Szegö, G. P., eds., 1979, *International Finance and Trade* (Ballinger, Cambridge, Mass.), Vol. I, 99–130.

Goldstein, M. and Khan, M. S., 1976, Large versus Small Price Changes and the Demand for Imports, *IMF Staff Papers* **23**, 200–25.

Houthakker, H. S. and Magee, S. P., 1969, Income and Price Elasticities in World Trade, *Review of Economics and Statistics* **51**, 111–25.

Jonson, P. D., 1976, Money and Economic Activity in the Open Economy: The United Kingdom, 1880–1970, *Journal of Political Economy* **84**, 979–1012.

Knight, M., 1976, Output, Prices and the Floating Exchange Rate in Canada: A Monetary Approach, International Monetary Fund Research Department DM/77/1, mimeo.

Knight, M. D. and Mathieson, D. J., 1979, Model of an Industrial Country under Fixed and Flexible Exchange Rates, in: Martin, J. and Smith, A., eds., 1979, *Trade and Payments Adjustment under Flexible Exchange Rates* (Macmillan, London), 86–119.

Knight, M. D. and Wymer, C. R., 1978, A Macroeconomic Model of the United Kingdom, *IMF Staff Papers* **25**, 742–78.

Leamer, E. E. and Stern, R. M., 1970, *Quantitative International Economics* (Allyn and Bacon, Boston).

Reserve Bank of Australia, 1977, *Conference in Applied Economic Research* (Reserve Bank of Australia, Sydney).

Sassanpour, C. and Sheen, J. R., 1976, A Comparison of Money and Economic Activity in France and West Germany, 1959–1973, mimeo (Paper prepared for the SSRC-Ford Foundation Conference on "Macroeconomic Policy and Adjustment in Open Economies" at Fanhams Hall, Ware, England, April 28–May 1, 1976).

Wymer, C. R., various dates, TRANSF, RESIMUL, CONTINEST, PREDIC, APREDIC Computer Programs and relative manuals; Supplement No. 3 (Oct. 1979) on Solution of Non-linear Differential Equation Systems.

Author index*

*Numbers followed by n refer to footnotes, and those followed by r to references.

Subject index*

*Numbers followed by n refer to footnotes.